COMMODORE 16 GAMES BOOK

Edited by
Richard Woolcock
and
Cameron Duffy

MELBOURNE HOUSE
PUBLISHERS

First Published in the United Kingdom by Melbourne House

This Remastered Edition
Published by
Acorn Books
www.acornbooks.co.uk

This book is a page-by-page reproduction of the original 1984 edition as published by Beam Software and Melbourne House. The entirety of the book (apart from a final publisher feedback section) is presented with no changes, corrections nor updates to the original text, images and layout; therefore no guarantee is offered as to the accuracy of the information within.

Contents

Contents (cont.)

Appendices

Preface

The Commodore 16 represents tremendous value and, while intended for the novice, has many surprises in store for the experienced programmer. The improved version of Commodore BASIC has many powerful graphics statements, making it ideal for developing games.

With this book, Melbourne House continues its tradition of producing high quality literature and software in support of personal computers.

Arrangement of Programs

The games programs are graded within the book from easy to difficult. However, because different people have preferences for particular kinds of games, they are listed in the Contents page grouped by type. If you enjoy strategy games, you will find them all by consulting the Contents.

Ease of Use

Like us, you have probably gone crosseyed while trying to type in programs from computer magazines. Counting spaces and trying to distinguish Commodore graphics characters are the two most frustrating experiences of program typing.

Be of good cheer! In this book programs have been formatted for greater clarity. Graphics characters have been redefined to resemble keyboard pictographs, and spaces within strings are indicated by small black pyramids.

To speed program debugging, the ChexSum utility program enables you to identify incorrectly-typed lines immediately. (This aid is unique to Melbourne House games books.)

But — and this is an important but — read the chapter 'Program Accuracy' first if you want to get the maximum benefit from all the aids to accurate transcription.

Programming Projects

We hope that as you read and use our book, you will absorb the principles of programming the Commodore 16 by osmosis. Lists of variables have been provided and subroutine names inserted in listings to help you discover how programs work.

We have also suggested improvements you may make to the games as a challenge to your programming skills.

Suggestions

Melbourne House is always interested in feedback from readers, whether it be suggestions, praise or complaints — see Appendix E, 'Reader Feedback'.

Happy computer gaming!

Richard Woolcock
Cameron Duffy
September 1984

Program Accuracy

Programs take a long time to type in and debug. To help make programs easier to read and debug, printouts have been specially formatted, and utilities have been provided to help you get programs running. Read the rest of this chapter, and enter the Merge and ChexSum programs before you enter any games programs.

FORMATTED LISTINGS

The program listings in this book have been processed through a formatting program to improve their appearance and readability. The formatter:

- Aligns statements at the left, avoiding the margin stepping that occurs as line numbers increase,
- Inserts spaces between keywords,
- Transforms SPACE characters occurring in strings, i.e. between quote marks ("), into a small black pyramid (▲),
- Makes the colon easier to see by redefining it as two small opposed triangles (⬍), and
- Redefines graphics characters to resemble the keyboard pictographs and inserts spaces between them so that they are readily distinguished.

Because the redefined alphanumeric and graphics characters do not exactly resemble the screen display, you may make typing errors until you become familiar with them. To assist you in determining which symbol corresponds to a particular key, tables of colour and control characters, and keyboard pictographs are illustrated overleaf.

These tables are also reproduced in Appendix D, 'Printout Symbols'. We suggest you photocopy or cut out Appendix D and keep it with you for ready reference.

KEYBOARD CHARACTERS*

Symbol in book	Key	Symbol in book	Key
┴	C= E		C= ↑
┤	C= W	┬	C= R
	C= D	├	C= Q
	C= C		C= F
	C= B		C= V
	C= T		C= +
	C= U		C= Y
	C= O		C= I
	C= @		C= P
	C= G		C= –
	C= J		C= H
	C= L		C= K
	C= M		C= N
	C= S		C= £
	C= A		C= X
◥	C= *		C= Z
└	SHIFT L	┘	SHIFT @
┌	SHIFT O	┐	SHIFT P
	SHIFT I		SHIFT U
	SHIFT K		SHIFT J
○	SHIFT W	●	SHIFT Q
┼	SHIFT +	╳	SHIFT V
╲	SHIFT M	╱	SHIFT N
♦	SHIFT Z	♥	SHIFT S
♣	SHIFT X	♠	SHIFT A
	SHIFT E		SHIFT D
	SHIFT *		SHIFT C
	SHIFT F		SHIFT R
	SHIFT T		SHIFT G
	SHIFT B		SHIFT –
	SHIFT H		SHIFT Y
◤	SHIFT £	←	SHIFT =
↑	SHIFT ZERO		

* These characters are designed to emulate the pictographs which appear on the front of the keys. The C= symbol is the special shift key located to the left of the left hand shift key.

Unfortunately different keyboard characters can produce identical symbols on the screen and printout. If a program doesn't work, these symbols may have been interchanged in a string:

‖	CTRL ,	CURSOR LEFT
	SHIFT *	SHIFT C
	SHIFT B	SHIFT –

COLOUR AND CONTROL CHARACTERS*

Symbol in book	Key
	CLR
	HOME
	CURSOR DOWN
	CURSOR UP
	CURSOR RIGHT
	CURSOR LEFT
	CTRL 1
	CTRL 2
	CTRL 3
	CTRL 4
	CTRL 5
	CTRL 6
	CTRL 7
	CTRL 8
	CTRL 9
	CTRL 0
	C= 1
	C= 2
	C= 3
	C= 4
	C= 5
	C= 6
	C= 7
	C= 8
	CTRL ,
	CTRL .

* These characters are designed to emulate the characters which appear on the screen.

TYPING RULES

In the program listings spaces have only been used as an aid to readability. For example, the line

```
100    POKE 54273, I : PRINT "▲ S T R I N G ▲ "
```

would be entered into your computer as

```
100POKE54273,I:PRINT"▲STRING▲"
```

Spaces are often used in strings but only enter a space when you see a (▲) symbol. This character does not appear on the keyboard but is used to tell you when to press the SPACE bar.

Character Confusion

In the printouts certain similar characters may be confused and entered incorrectly, and cause your program to crash: they are the letter I and the figure 1, and the letter O and the figure 0. In the text, figure zero (0) is shown cancelled (Ø). In listings these confusing characters are soon recognised:

CHARACTER	PRINTOUT
Letter I	I
Figure 1	1
Letter O	O
Figure Ø	0

If you are modifying programs and entering code from your own notes, a number of handwritten characters are easily confused unless clearly distinguished. We offer you this guide:

CONFUSED CHARACTERS	RECOMMENDED FORM
Letter Z, figure 2	Ƶ, 2
Letter O, figure Ø	O, Ø
Letter S, figure 5	S, 5
Letter I, figures 1 and 7	I, 1, 7

Punctuation may also be a trap:

- Commas (,) and full stops or periods (.) are not interchangeable.
- Colons (:) and semi-colons (;) are not interchangeable.
- Apostrophes (') and double quotes (") are not interchangeable.
- Use parentheses () and not brackets []. Always ensure that parentheses are correctly paired: a quick check is to make sure that you have as many righthand as lefthand parentheses in a mathematical expression.
- The SHIFT key must be pressed when some characters (such as ! " # $ %, etc.) are entered.

SAVE Before RUNning

Do you remember the old proverb?

> Programs typed and SAVEd today, live to RUN another day.

Be sure to progressively SAVE the programs onto cassette or disk as you enter the listings. From time to time the keyboard may lock up, especially if you try to RUN a program that contains an error. We strongly recommend that you keep SAVEing copies of the program as you enter it into the computer and debug any typing errors.

Note Some programs contain loaders to place machine language routines in high memory and which may alter certain system pointers. If such a program is RUN and crashes, the machine language program and the pointers will remain as they were even when the NEW command has been entered. When debugging programs, SAVE your work before RUNning and always reset the computer after a crash to avoid crashing a program subsequently entered or loaded.

CHEXSUM PROGRAM VERIFICATION

When games programs such as these are keyed in, invariably reading and typing mistakes creep in. You then spend ages trying to sort out where and what is causing the error. Even experienced programmers often cannot easily identify an error and need to do the tedious job of double-checking with the book, especially with DATA statements.

To avoid this major cause of frustration when entering the programs, there are two short routines in this book which you should enter and save before you enter other programs:

- Merge and
- ChexSum.

The program ChexSum calculates a unique check-sum number for each line of a games program, then prints out a table of program line-numbers and their corresponding line check-sums, plus a grand total for the whole program.

When you have entered a game program, run ChexSum and compare the check-sum table with that in the book. Any discrepancies immediately identify a mistyped line.

Other versions of BASIC have a MERGE command which enables you to construct new programs by combining pre-written subroutines or sections of existing programs. To use ChexSum it must be appended to the end of the games program it is to check. The Merge utility program performs this job and overcomes the lack of a MERGE command in Commodore BASIC. (Merge may also be used to join other programs — see Appendix C, 'Merging Programs'.)

Saving Merge and ChexSum

Follow these instructions to enter Merge and ChexSum, and save them to tape or disc. If saving to tape, do not put games programs on the same tape or you will spend considerable time winding and rewinding the tape to, first, load your program and, second, to load and use ChexSum.

1 Type in the Merge and ChexSum listings below and SAVE them before you do anything else.
  Note Hand check Merge character by character after you have saved it. Merge is the only program in the book which cannot be verified by ChexSum. Why? Because you need Merge to load ChexSum to verify Merge and, if Merge is incorrect, this won't happen.

2 Load ChexSum and RUN it. It will first of all process itself, generating a table of line sums and a grand total for the whole program.

3 At this point you may or may not have had a crash. If a table was successfully generated, compare your table with that given below. If the grand totals differ, check the line sums to find the incorrect line.

4 Repeat steps 2 and 3 until ChexSum is debugged.

5 In line 62020, alter the value of E = 62194 to E = 61999. Save a copy to tape or disk.

Note This is your working copy used to check all the other programs in the book. Make sure you don't confuse it with your initial version, which is used only to verify ChexSum itself.

MERGE PROGRAM

```
5     POKE 55,202:POKE 56,63:CLR
10    FOR I=16331 TO 16331+34:READA:POKE I,A:C=C+A:NEXT
20    IF C<>4094THEN PRINT "C H E C K S U M ▲ E R R O R "
      :STOP
100   DATA165,43,141,238,63,165,44,141,239,63,56,165,45,2
      33,2,133,43,165
110   DATA46,233,0,133,44,96,173,238,63,133,43,173,239,63
      ,133,44,96
120   NEW
```

CHEXSUM PROGRAM

```
62000 T=PEEK(62)*256+PEEK(61)+1
62005 INPUT  "F R O M ▲ L I N E ▲ ";FROM
62010 INPUT "T O ▲ P R I N T E R ▲ ( Y / N ) ";Q$
62011 IF  Q$<>"Y "THEN 62020
62015 CLOSE4:OPEN4,4:CMD4:PRINT CHR$(1);CHR$(129)
62020 LINK=PEEK(44)*256+PEEK(43):E=62194
62120 T=LINK
62130 LINK=PEEK(T+1)*256+PEEK(T)
62135 LN=PEEK(T+3)*256+PEEK(T+2):IF LN<FROMTHEN 62120
62136 IF LN>ETHEN PRINT :PRINT "T O T A L = ";CH:CLOSE4:
      END
62137 S$=STR$(LN):L=LEN(S$)-1:S$=MID$(S$,2,L)+MID$("▲ ▲ ▲
      ▲ ▲ ▲ ",1,6-L)
```

```
62138 PRINT S$;
62140 CS=0:N=0:C=0
62150 FOR P=T+4 TO LINK-2:PK=PEEK(P)
62160 IF PK=143THEN P=LINK-2:GOTO 62190
62165 IF PK=34THEN C=(C=0)
62170 IF C=0ANDPK=32THEN 62190
62180 IF PK=137THEN N=N+1:CS=CS+(203ORN):PK=164
62185 N=N+1:CS=CS+(PKORN)
62190 NEXT:CH=CH+CS
62192 H$=STR$(CS):Y=LEN(H$):H$=MID$(H$,2,Y):H$=MID$("▲ ▲
      ▲ ▲ ▲ ",1,5-(Y-1))+H$
62194 PRINT "= ▲ ";H$:GOTO 62120
62196 REM
```

ChexSum Tables

```
62000 =  1848      62130 =  2067      62160 =  2373
62005 =  1332      62135 =  3540      62165 =  1431
62010 =  1618      62136 =  2407      62170 =  1554
62011 =  1281      62137 =  4234      62180 =  3320
62015 =  2020      62138 =   338      62185 =  1862
62020 =  2502      62140 =  1142      62190 =  1001
62120 =   577      62150 =  2251      62192 =  4892
                                      62194 =  1247
                                      TOTAL = 44837
```

Using ChexSum

The greatest problem encountered when typing in programs from a book is errors made by the user. Most of these are picked up when the computer responds to the RUN command with the 'Syntax Error' message. The user then has only to LIST the line and compare it with the line in the book. Unfortunately, some errors are more subtle and not fatal to program operation. These types of errors will cause the program to run, but incorrectly, and the computer will not be able to detect them as such.

Checksum is a special program which generates a unique sum for each line in a program and a grand total of all line sums. After each program listing is a table of check sums. You need only compare the numbers in the ChexSum table for each program with those generated by ChexSum. If two numbers differ, check that particular line.

1 Load and run the Merge program by typing LOAD "MERGE" (for tape) or LOAD "MERGE",8 (for disk), and then entering RUN.
2 From your games tape or disk, load the program you want to verify.

Note Always SAVE your program to tape before running ChexSum.

For the first program, enter LOAD "BLOCKADE" for tape or LOAD "BLOCKADE", 8 for disk. Do not RUN the program at this point.

3 Enter SYS16331 to protect the first game program, i.e. BLOCKADE.
4 Load ChexSum by entering LOAD "CHEXSUM" for tape or LOAD "CHEXSUM", 8 for disk.
5 Enter SYS16355 to merge the game program BLOCKADE with ChexSum.
6 Enter RUN 62ØØØ to activate ChexSum.
7 The program will respond with the prompt:

LINE NUMBER: ?

Pressing the RETURN key at this point will cause ChexSum to start with the first line of your program. Entering a line number will start ChexSum at that line.

8 ChexSum next prompts with:

PRINTER (Y/N) ?

A 'Y' will send the ChexSum table to the printer or an 'N' will send it to the screen.

9 Check your grand total with that in the book. If they differ, a line has been typed incorrectly. Compare line numbers until you locate the bad lines and then edit them.
10 Repeat steps 6 to 8 until the games program is debugged. In step 6, enter the number of the first bad line to avoid ChexSum verifying the games program from the first line.

DEBUGGING HINTS

Limitations of ChexSum

ChexSum is not entirely foolproof and cannot detect two errors which give a (seemingly) correct output:

1. If your grand total is correct but the program crashes, two lines have been typed in incorrectly and, although their individual line sums are incorrect, they cancel. Please check that all line sums are correct.
2. At certain column positions in a statement line, a full point (.) and a comma (,) may be interchanged and yet still give a correct line sum. When occurring in a DATA statement a (.) for (,) substitution will cause two adjacent integer numbers to be read as a single real number and will usually generate an 'Out of Data' message. When either possible substitution occurs in a program statement, a 'Syntax Error' message will be generated.

It is impossible for ChexSum to completely eliminate typing errors — it merely reduces the probability of them occurring to a very low level.

Pointer Corruption

Sometimes a program will run incorrectly even when thoroughly debugged by ChexSum and by hand. In this case there are two possibilities:

- The program is wrong — please write and tell us (see Appendix E, 'Reader Feedback').
- A previous run has left system pointers corrupted and they continue to crash the program despite the use of the NEW command. Always reset the computer after a crash to avoid this problem.

Blockade

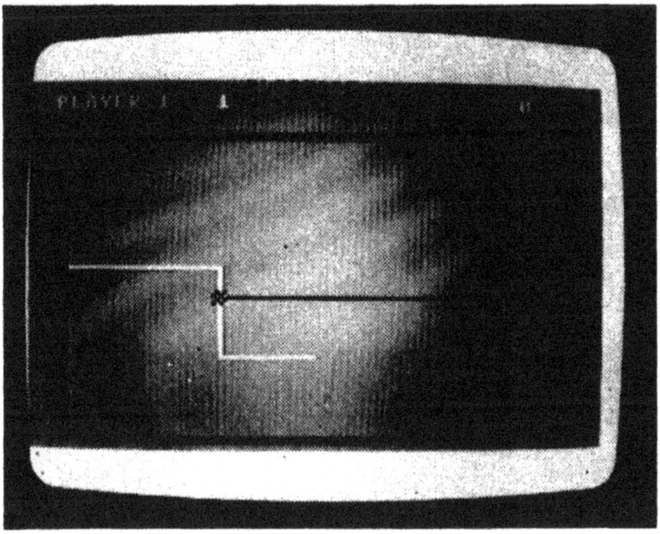

CLASSIFICATION: Evasion

In this fast-paced game, your goal is to build a wall in front of your opponent so that he crashes into it. Only by quick maneouvres, either left or right, can you avoid the walls. May you outlast your opponent.

The controls are:

Player 1, Q move left, Z move right; player 2, I move left, P move right.

PROGRAMMING SUGGESTIONS

Add a computer opponent. Give the computer limited (or perhaps random!) intelligence when making a decision to turn left or right at each step.

Add obstacles to the board. Set up a routine in the board so that non-blank characters on the field will act as obstacles.

PROGRAM
Variables

CH	Wall characters
CX, CY	Corner characters
X1, Y1	Player 1 co-ordinates
X2, Y2	Player 2 co-ordinates
P1, P2	Scores, player 1 and player 2
D1, D2	Direction of players 1 and 2
A1, B1	Player 1 step value
A2, B2	Player 2 step value
W	Winner

Listing

Initialisation

```
10    COLOR0,2,5:COLOR4,15:VOL 8:P1=0:P2=0
20    X$="█ █ █ █ █ █ █ █ █ █ █ █ ":DIMCH(1,1):CH(1,0)=64:C
      H(0,1)=93:DIMCX(3):DIMCY(3)
30    CX(0)=109:CX(1)=125:CX(2)=110:CX(3)=112
40    CY(0)=112:CY(1)=109:CY(2)=125:CY(3)=110
50    B$="▄ ▄ ▄ ▄ ▄ ▄ ▄ ▄ ▄ ▄ ▄ ▄ ▄ ▄ ▄ ▄ ▄ ▄ ▄ ▄ ▄ ▄ ▄ ▄ ▄ ▄ ▄
       ▄ ▄ ▄ ▄ ▄ ▄ ▄ ▄ ▄ ▄ ▄ "
60    L$="▲ ▲ █ █ ■ ▲ ▲ ▲ ▲ ▲ ▲ ▲ ▲ ▲ ▲ ▲ ▲ ▲ ▲ ▲ ▲ ▲ ▲ ▲ ▲ ▲ ▲ ▲
       ▲ ▲ ▲ ▲ ▲ ▲ ▲ ▲ ▲ ▲ ▲ ▲ ▲ ▲ ▲ ▲ ▲ █ ▲ ▲ ▲ "
70    COLOR1,16,4:PRINT "█ █ █ █ █ ▲ ▲ ▲ T = ▲ T ▲ ▲ ▲
      ▲ ▲ = ▲ ▲ ▲ = ▲ ▲ T ▲ T ▲ ▲ ▲ = ▲ ▲ T = ▲ ▲ ▲ = ▲ ▲ ▲
       █ "
80    PRINT "▲ ▲ ▲ ├ = ┤ ▲ █ ▲ ▲ ▲ █ ▲ █ ▲ █ ▲ ▲ ▲ ├ = ▲
      ▲ ▲ ├ = ┤ ▲ █ ▲ █ ▲ ├ = ▲ ▲ ▲ █ "
90    PRINT "▲ ▲ ▲ ┴ = ▲ ▲ ▲ = ▲ ▲ ▲ = ▲ ▲ ▲ = ▲ ▲ ┴ ▲ ▲
      ▲ ▲ ┴ ▲ ┴ ▲ ┴ = ▲ ▲ ▲ = ▲ ▲ ▲ ● "
100   COLOR1,9,4:PRINT :PRINT :PRINT "▲ ▲ ▲ ▲ ▲ ▲ ▲ ▲ ▲ ▲ ▲ ▲
       ▲ ▲ ▲ ▲ C O N T R O L S "
110   PRINT :PRINT "▲ ▲ ▲ ▲ ▲ ▲ ▲ ▲ ▲ ▲ ▲ P L A Y E R 1 ▲ ▲ ▲
       ▲ ▲ P L A Y E R ▲ 2 "
120   PRINT :PRINT "▲ L E F T ▲ ▲ : ▲ ▲ ▲ < Q > ▲ ▲ ▲ ▲ ▲ ▲
       ▲ ▲ ▲ ▲ < + > "
130   PRINT :PRINT "▲ R I G H T ▲ : ▲ ▲ ▲ < Z > ▲ ▲ ▲ ▲ ▲ ▲
       ▲ ▲ ▲ ▲ < / > "
140   COLOR1,7,4:PRINT :PRINT :PRINT :PRINT "▲ ▲ ▲ ▲ ▲ ▲ H
      I T ▲ < R E T U R N > ▲ T O ▲ C O N T I N U E . . .
       "
150   PRINT :PRINT "▲ ▲ ▲ ▲ ▲ ▲ ▲ ▲ ▲ ▲ ▲ ▲ < E > ▲ T O ▲ E X I
       T . "
160   GETA$:IF A$=""THEN 160
170   IF A$="E "THEN PRINT "█ █ █ █ █ T H E ▲ E N D . . .
       ":END
180   IF ASC(A$)<>13THEN 160
190   COLOR1,3,3:PRINT "█ ▲ ▲ ▲ ▲ ▲ ▲ ▲ ▲ ▲ ▲ ▲ ▲ ▲ ▲ ▲ ▲ ▲ ▲ ▲ ▲ B
       L O C K A D E ":PRINT :PRINT :PRINT "▲ ▲ █ ";B$;"█
       "
200   COLOR1,3,3:FOR I=1 TO 20:PRINT L$:NEXT:PRINT "▲ ▲ █
       █ ";B$;"■ █ ";
210   COLOR1,8:PRINT "█ █ ▲ ▲ P L A Y E R ▲ 1 "
220   COLOR1,15,2:PRINT "█ █ █ █ █ █ █ █ █ █ █ █ █ █ █ █ █ █
      █ █ █ █ █ █ █ █ █ █ █ █ P L A Y E R ▲ 2 "
230   X1=2:X2=37:Y1=12:Y2=14:A1=1:A2=-1:B1=0:B2=0:D1=0:D2
      =2:S=0
```

```
240   COLOR1,2:PRINT "█ █ █ ";X$;"▲ ▲ ▲ ▲ ▲ █ █ █ █ █ ";P
      1;X$;"█ █ █ █ █ █ ▲ ▲ ▲ ▲ ▲ █ █ █ █ ";P2
```

Get Player Input

```
250   GETA$:C1=CH(ABS(A1),ABS(B1)):C2=CH(ABS(A2),ABS(B2))
      :S=S+1:IF S=2THEN S=0
260   X1=X1+A1:X2=X2+A2:Y1=Y1+B1:Y2=Y2+B2
270   IF A$="Q "THEN C=B1:B1=-A1:A1=C:D1=INT(((D1+1)/4-
      INT((D1+1)/4))*4):C1=CX(D1)
280   IF A$="+ "THEN C=B2:B2=-A2:A2=C:D2=INT(((D2+1)/4-
      INT((D2+1)/4))*4):C2=CX(D2)
290   IF A$="Z "THEN C=-B1:B1=A1:A1=C:D1=INT((ABS((D1+3)
      /4)-INT(ABS((D1+3)/4)))*4):C1=CY(D1)
300   IF A$="/ "THEN C=-B2:B2=A2:A2=C:D2=INT((ABS((D2+3)
      /4)-INT(ABS((D2+3)/4)))*4):C2=CY(D2)
```

Collision Detection

```
310   IF PEEK(3072+40*Y1+X1)<>32THEN A1=0:B1=0:P2=P2+1:W
      =2:X=X1:Y=Y1:GOSUB 400:GOTO 160
320   IF PEEK(3072+40*Y2+X2)<>32THEN A2=0:B2=0:P1=P1+1:W
      =1:X=X2:Y=Y2:GOSUB 400:GOTO 160
330   GOSUB 350
340   GOTO 250
```

Draw New Bricks In Each Player's Wall

```
350   POKE 3072+40*Y1+X1,C1:POKE 2048+40*Y1+X1,119
360   POKE 3072+40*Y2+X2,C2:POKE 2048+40*Y2+X2,46
370   IF S=0THEN SOUND 1,400+20*D1,5
380   IF S=1THEN SOUND 1,320+20*D2,5
390   RETURN
400   SOUND 3,850,20:SOUND 3,800,100
410   FOR I=1 TO 10:POKE 3072+40*Y+X,102:POKE 2048+40*Y
      +X,96:FOR J=1 TO 20:NEXTJ
420   POKE 3072+40*Y+X,230:POKE 2048+40*Y+X,44:FOR J=1
       TO 20:NEXTJ
430   NEXTI
```

Determine Winner

```
440   IF W=1THEN COLOR1,8:PRINT "█ █ █ ▲ ▲ P L A Y E R ▲
      1 ▬ "
```

```
450    IF W=2THEN COLOR1,15,2:PRINT "█ █ █ █ █ █ █ █ █ █ █ █ █
       █ █ █ █ █ █ █ █ █ █ █ █ █ █ █ █ █ █ █ █ P L A Y E R ▴ 2 ▀
       "
460    COLOR1,2:PRINT "█ █ █ ";X$;"▴ ▴ ▴ ▴ ▴ █ █ █ █ █ ";P
       1;X$;"█ █ █ █ █ █ ▴ ▴ ▴ ▴ ▴ █ █ █ █ ";P2
470    RETURN
```

ChexSum Tables

Line	Sum	Line	Sum	Line	Sum
10	= 2228	170	= 2259	330	= 299
20	= 4384	180	= 1378	340	= 526
30	= 2904	190	= 4121	350	= 3105
40	= 2916	200	= 3324	360	= 3055
50	= 6342	210	= 1453	370	= 1843
60	= 2670	220	= 2559	380	= 1844
70	= 6651	230	= 5263	390	= 143
80	= 4821	240	= 4358	400	= 1419
90	= 5645	250	= 5280	410	= 4997
100	= 2784	260	= 3367	420	= 4047
110	= 2292	270	= 6413	430	= 206
120	= 1992	280	= 6374	440	= 2432
130	= 2051	290	= 7025	450	= 3738
140	= 4049	300	= 6980	460	= 4358
150	= 1745	310	= 6585	470	= 143
160	= 1214	320	= 6593	TOTAL	= 160175

Zapp

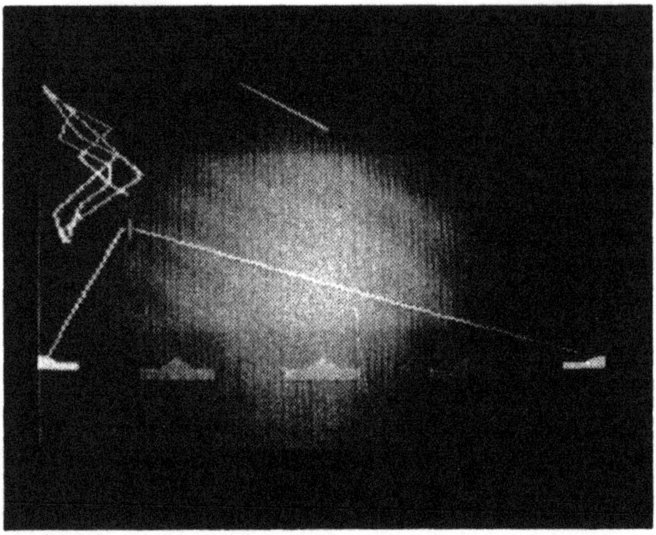

CLASSIFICATION: Shoot Up

Control your gunsights to target the attacking pods: fire either 1 or 2 zaps to destroy them and to protect your cities and weapon emplacements. You have only limited energy reserves, so zap sparingly. You receive bonus points for remaining energy. Be prepared to zap heavily when later waves of high-tech pods swarm in. The game is over when all cities are destroyed.

Controls are:

Q up, Z down, I left, P right, SPACE fire.

PROGRAMMING SUGGESTIONS

Create a new type of pod — one that must take more zaps to be destroyed, or perhaps one that can split open to drop more pods. Increase the speed of the game with each level. Give some special pods more intelligence — have them either home in on the gun emplacements or on the cities. Give bonus cities for surviving each wave.

PROGRAM
Variables

NM	Pod co-ordinates
E	Energy
LX, LY	Co-ordinates of sights
G%	Gun damage
C%	City damage
LV	Level
SC	Score
T	Speed of pods
MV	Gunsight step distance

Listing

Select Graphics Mode and Initialise

```
10    DIMNM%(3,2):C%=7:T=0:G%=3:SC%=0:LV=1:LX=79:LY=79:
      GRAPHIC4,1
20    COLOR0,2,2:COLOR4,1:COLOR1,8:COLOR2,3,4:COLOR3,15,5
      :VOL 8
30    GOSUB 400
```

Get Player's Input, Fire Remaining Zappers
Draw Gunsight

```
40    GETA$:T=T+1:GOSUB 190:IF T=6-LVTHEN GOSUB 220
50    IF A$="I "THEN GOSUB 200:LX=LX-7:IF LX<4THEN LX=4
60    IF A$="P "THEN GOSUB 200:LX=LX+7:IF LX>155THEN LX
      =155
70    IF A$="Q "THEN GOSUB 200:LY=LY-9:IF LY<5THEN LY=5
80    IF A$="Z "THEN GOSUB 200:LY=LY+9:IF LY>147THEN LY
      =147
90    IF A$<>"▲ "ORG%=0THEN GOTO 40
100   IF (G%AND2)=2THEN DRAW1,3,148 TO LX-2,LY
110   IF (G%AND1)=1THEN DRAW1,156,148 TO LX+2,LY
120   DRAW0,3,148 TO LX-2,LY:DRAW0,156,148 TO LX+2,LY:
      SOUND 3,1000,15
130   FOR I=0 TO 3:IF NM%(I,0)<=0THEN 160
140   IF NM%(I,0)<LX-3ORNM%(I,0)>LX+3ORNM%(I,1)<LY-5ORNM%
      (I,1)>LY+5THEN 160
150   SOUND 3,900,25:SC%=SC%+LV*5:NM%(I,0)=-1:CIRCLE2,LX,
      LY,2,4:K%=K%+1
160   NEXTI
170   IF K%=LV*4THEN LV=LV+1:SCNCLR:K%=0:PRINT "▙ ◙ ◙ ◙ ◙
       ◙ ◙ ◙ ◙ ◙ ◙ ◙ ◙ ◙ ◙ ◙ ◙ ◙ ◙ ◙ ◙ ◙ S C O R E ";SC%:
      GOSUB 400
```

Move Pods, Check If Pods Hit Cities or Zappers. End Game

```
180   GOTO 40
190   B%=2:GOTO 210
200   B%=0
210   DRAWB%,LX,LY-5 TO LX,LY+5:DRAWB%,LX-3,LY TO LX+3,LY
      :RETURN
220   FOR I=0 TO 3
230   IF NM%(I,0)>0THEN 260
240   IF RND(1)>.08*LVTHEN 390
250   NM%(I,0)=INT(RND(1)*140+5):NM%(I,1)=0
```

```
260   IF RND(1)<.3THEN NM%(I,2)=INT(RND(1)*11-5)
270   IF NM%(I,0)+NM%(I,2)<5THEN NM%(I,2)=INT(RND(1)*6)
280   IF NM%(I,0)+NM%(I,2)>154THEN NM%(I,2)=-INT(RND(1)
      *6)
290   NM%(I,0)=NM%(I,0)+NM%(I,2):NM%(I,1)=NM%(I,1)+5
300   DRAW3,NM%(I,0),NM%(I,1) TO NM%(I,0)-NM%(I,2),NM%(I,
      1)-5
310   IF NM%(I,1)<154THEN 380
320   IF (C%AND1)>0ANDNM%(I,0)>24ANDNM%(I,0)<56THEN C%=C%
      -1:D%=0:GOSUB 510
330   IF (C%AND2)>0ANDNM%(I,0)>64ANDNM%(I,0)<96THEN C%=C%
      -2:D%=1:GOSUB 510
340   IF (C%AND4)>0ANDNM%(I,0)>104ANDNM%(I,0)<136THEN C%
      =C%-4:D%=2:GOSUB 510
350   IF NM%(I,0)<13THEN G%=(G%AND1):CHAR1,1,19,"* "
360   IF NM%(I,0)>147THEN G%=(G%AND2):CHAR1,38,19,"* "
370   IF C%=0THEN CHAR1,12,12,"G A M E   O V E R ":END
380   IF NM%(I,1)>159THEN NM%(I,0)=-1
390   NEXTI:T=0:RETURN
400   IF (G%AND2)=0THEN 430
```

Draw Screen

```
410   DRAW3,0,148 TO 3,148 TO 6,151 TO 12,151 TO 12,154
       TO 0,154 TO 0,148:PAINT3,3,151
420   DRAW3,159,148 TO 156,148 TO 153,151 TO 147,151
       TO 147,154 TO 159,154 TO 159,148:PAINT3,156,150
430   IF (G%AND1)=0THEN 450
440   DRAW3,159,148 TO 156,148 TO 153,151 TO 147,151
       TO 147,154 TO 159,154 TO 159,148:PAINT3,156,150
450   FOR I=0 TO 2:IF (C%AND(2↑I))=0THEN 500
460   DRAW2,25+I*40,154 TO 25+I*40,159 TO 55+I*40,159
       TO 55+I*40,154 TO 53+I*40,154
470   FOR J=0 TO 3:DRAW2 TO 53+I*40-J*7,146 TO 48+I*40-J
      *7,146 TO 48+I*40-J*7,154
480   DRAW2 TO 46+I*40-J*7,154:NEXT
490   PAINT2,38+I*40,157
500   NEXTI:RETURN
510   CHAR1,7+D%*10,19,"# # # # # # ":SOUND 3,600,20:
      RETURN
```

ChexSum Tables

Line	ChexSum	Line	ChexSum	Line	ChexSum
10	= 4555	180	= 476	350	= 2742
20	= 3054	190	= 949	360	= 2857
30	= 298	200	= 337	370	= 2404
40	= 2717	210	= 4134	380	= 2122
50	= 3199	220	= 655	390	= 791
60	= 3413	230	= 1210	400	= 1170
70	= 3216	240	= 1506	410	= 4163
80	= 3430	250	= 2754	420	= 5367
90	= 1955	260	= 2819	430	= 1169
100	= 2458	270	= 3286	440	= 5367
110	= 2601	280	= 3568	450	= 2261
120	= 3916	290	= 3479	460	= 5613
130	= 2102	300	= 3705	470	= 5875
140	= 5785	310	= 1313	480	= 1994
150	= 4962	320	= 4561	490	= 1212
160	= 206	330	= 4567	500	= 407
170	= 5460	340	= 4672	510	= 2571
				TOTAL	= 145403

Unscramble

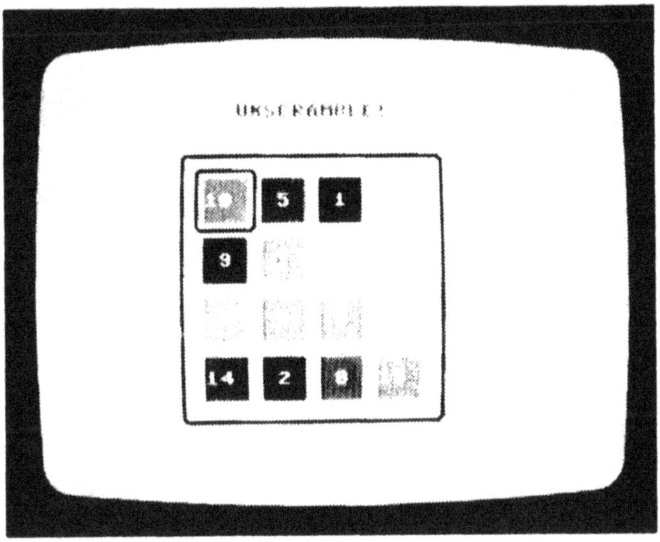

CLASSIFICATION: Logic COLOUR ILLUSTRATION OBC

A four-by-four matrix of numbers ranging from 1 to 15; 1 is blank and 15 are scrambled. You have to re-organise them into sequence from 1 in the top left to 15 in the bottom right. Use I and P to move the blinking cursor, then hit the SPACE bar to shift the pieces.

PROGRAMMING SUGGESTIONS

Increase the size of the matrix for a more challenging game.

PROGRAM
Variables

N	Board array
NZ$	Tile patterns
X, Y	Cursor co-ordinates
X1, Y1	Empty square co-ordinates

Listing

Initialise Game; Display Title and Define Tiles

```
10    COLOR0,2:COLOR4,2:VOL 8
20    DIMN(3,3):DIMNZ$(15)
30    X=0:Y=0:C2$="":C3$=""
40    TP$="[illegible]":S$="[illegible]"
50    CX$="▲ ▲ ▲ ▲ ▲ [illegible] ▲ "
60    CD$="[illegible]":CR$="[illegible]":CS$="[illegible]"
70    BD$="[illegible]":BR$="[illegible]"
80    COLOR1,3,3:PRINT "[illegible]"
90    PRINT "[illegible]"
100   PRINT "[illegible]"
110   COLOR1,9,4:PRINT "[illegible]I N S T R U C T I O N S"
120   PRINT "[illegible]' I ' ▲ ▲ ▲ ▲ C U R S O R ▲ L E F T "
130   PRINT "[illegible]' P ' ▲ ▲ ▲ ▲ C U R S O R ▲ R I G H T "
140   PRINT "[illegible]' Q ' ▲ ▲ ▲ ▲ C U R S O R ▲ U P "
150   PRINT "[illegible]' Z ' ▲ ▲ ▲ ▲ C U R S O R ▲ D O W N "
160   PRINT "[illegible]S P A C E ▲ ▲ ▲ S H I F T ▲ P I E C E S "
170   PRINT "[illegible]( H I T ▲ R E T U R N ▲ T O ▲ S T A R T ) "
180   GETA$:IF ASC(A$)<>13THEN 180
190   NZ$(0)="[illegible] ▲ ▲ ▲ [illegible] ▲ ▲ ▲ [illegible] ▲ ▲ ▲ "
200   NZ$(1)="[illegible] ▲ ▲ ▲ [illegible] ▲ 1 ▲ [illegible] ▲ ▲ ▲ "
210   NZ$(2)="[illegible] ▲ ▲ ▲ [illegible] ▲ 2 ▲ [illegible] ▲ ▲ ▲ "
220   NZ$(3)="[illegible] ▲ ▲ ▲ [illegible] ▲ 3 ▲ [illegible] ▲ ▲ ▲ "
230   NZ$(4)="[illegible] ▲ ▲ ▲ [illegible] ▲ 4 ▲ [illegible] ▲ ▲ ▲ "
240   NZ$(5)="[illegible] ▲ ▲ ▲ [illegible] ▲ 5 ▲ [illegible] ▲ ▲ ▲ "
250   NZ$(6)="[illegible] ▲ ▲ ▲ [illegible] ▲ 6 ▲ [illegible] ▲ ▲ ▲ "
260   NZ$(7)="[illegible] ▲ ▲ ▲ [illegible] ▲ 7 ▲ [illegible] ▲ ▲ ▲ "
270   NZ$(8)="[illegible] ▲ ▲ ▲ [illegible] ▲ 8 ▲ [illegible] ▲ ▲ ▲ "
280   NZ$(9)="[illegible] ▲ ▲ ▲ [illegible] ▲ 9 ▲ [illegible] ▲ ▲ ▲ "
```

```
290   NZ$(10)="▪ ▪ ▴ ▴ ▴ ▪ ▪ ▪ ▪ 1 0 ▴ ▪ ▪ ▪ ▪ ▴ ▴ ▴ "
300   NZ$(11)="▪ ▪ ▴ ▴ ▴ ▪ ▪ ▪ ▪ 1 1 ▴ ▪ ▪ ▪ ▪ ▴ ▴ ▴ "
310   NZ$(12)="▪ ▪ ▴ ▴ ▴ ▪ ▪ ▪ ▪ 1 2 ▴ ▪ ▪ ▪ ▪ ▴ ▴ ▴ "
320   NZ$(13)="▪ ▪ ▴ ▴ ▴ ▪ ▪ ▪ ▪ 1 3 ▴ ▪ ▪ ▪ ▪ ▴ ▴ ▴ "
330   NZ$(14)="▪ ▪ ▴ ▴ ▴ ▪ ▪ ▪ ▪ 1 4 ▴ ▪ ▪ ▪ ▪ ▴ ▴ ▴ "
340   NZ$(15)="▪ ▪ ▴ ▴ ▴ ▪ ▪ ▪ ▪ 1 5 ▴ ▪ ▪ ▪ ▪ ▴ ▴ ▴ "
350   FOR I=0 TO 3:FOR J=0 TO 3:N(I,J)=I*4+J:NEXTJ,I
360   PRINT "▪ ▪ ▪ ▪ ▪ ▪ ▪ ▪ ▪ ▪ ▪ ▪ ▪ ▪ ▪ ▪ ▪ U N S C R A
      M B L E ! ":GOSUB 550
```

Shuffle Tiles Randomly; Draw Cursor

```
370   X1=0:Y1=0:X=0:Y=0:Z=20+INT(RND(0)*25)
380   FOR J=1 TO Z:X=INT(RND(0)*4):GOSUB 620:Y=INT(RND(0)
      *4):GOSUB 620:NEXT
390   COLOR1,3,3:PRINT CD$;CR$;"▪ ▪ ";C2$;C3$;CS$;"▪ ":X
      =0:Y=0
```

Get Input; Move and Draw Cursor

```
400   GETA$:IF A$<>"▴ "ANDA$<>"P "ANDA$<>"I "ANDA$<>"Q "
      ANDA$<>"Z "THEN 400
410   IF A$="▴ "AND(X1=XORY1=Y)THEN GOSUB 620:GOTO 400
420   PRINT CD$;CR$;"▪ ▪ ";C2$;C3$;CX$
430   IF A$<>"▴ "THEN SOUND 1,400,7
440   IF A$="P "THEN X=X+1:C2$=C2$+"▪ ▪ ▪ ▪ ":IF X>3
      THEN X=0:C2$=""
450   IF A$<>"I "THEN 480
460   X=X-1:IF X>=0THEN C2$=LEFT$(C2$,X*4):GOTO 520
470   X=3:C2$="▪ ▪ ▪ ▪ ▪ ▪ ▪ ▪ ▪ ▪ ▪ ▪ ":GOTO 520
480   IF A$<>"Q "THEN 510
490   Y=Y-1:IF Y>=0THEN C3$=LEFT$(C3$,Y*4):GOTO 520
500   Y=3:C3$="▪ ▪ ▪ ▪ ▪ ▪ ▪ ▪ ▪ ▪ ▪ ▪ "
510   IF A$="Z "THEN Y=Y+1:C3$=C3$+"▪ ▪ ▪ ▪ ":IF Y>3
      THEN Y=0:C3$=""
520   COLOR1,3,3:PRINT CD$;CR$;"▪ ▪ ";C2$;C3$;CS$
530   GOTO 400
540   END
```

Draw Board and Tiles On Screen

```
550   COLOR1,1:PRINT CD$;CR$;"▪ ";TP$;"▪ ▪ ▪ ";S$;
560   PRINT CD$;CR$;"▪ ";S$;"▪ ";TP$;"▪ ";
570   PRINT CD$;"▪ ▪ ▪ ▪ ";
580   FOR I=0 TO 3:PRINT CR$;"▪ ▪ ";:FOR J=0 TO 3
590   PRINT "□ □ ";NZ$(I*4+J);"▬ ▴ ";:N(I,J)=I*4+J
600   NEXTJ:PRINT :PRINT :PRINT :PRINT :NEXTI
610   RETURN
```

Shuffle Tiles

```
620   IF X1=XANDY1=YTHEN RETURN
630   IF Y<Y1THEN FOR I=Y1-1 TO Y STEP -1:N(I+1,X)=N(I,X)
      :GOSUB 680:Y1=Y:NEXT
640   IF Y>Y1THEN FOR I=Y1+1 TO Y:N(I-1,X)=N(I,X):
      GOSUB 690:NEXT:Y1=Y:RETURN
650   IF X<X1THEN FOR I=X1-1 TO X STEP -1:N(Y,I+1)=N(Y,I)
      :GOSUB 710:NEXT:X1=X:RETURN
660   IF X>X1THEN FOR I=X1+1 TO X:N(Y,I-1)=N(Y,I):
      GOSUB 720:NEXT:X1=X:RETURN
670   PRINT BD$;BR$;NZ$(0):COLOR1,1:RETURN
```

Shuffle Down

```
680   Z$=BD$:BD$=LEFT$(BD$,I*4+7):GOTO 700
```

Shuffle Up

```
690   Z$=BD$:BD$=BD$+"▙ ▙ ▙ ▙ "
700   SOUND 1,1000-5*I,2:GOSUB 670:PRINT Z$;BR$;NZ$(N(I,X
      )):RETURN
```

Shuffle Right

```
710   Z$=BR$:BR$=LEFT$(BR$,I*4+12):GOTO 730
```

Shuffle Left

```
720   Z$=BR$:BR$=BR$+"▟ ▟ ▟ ▟ "
730   SOUND 1,970+5*I,2:GOSUB 670:PRINT BD$;Z$;NZ$(N(Y,I)
      ):RETURN
```

ChexSum Tables

Line		ChexSum
10	=	1171
20	=	1100
30	=	1770
40	=	12924
50	=	4369
60	=	9603
70	=	1522
80	=	6927
90	=	5657
100	=	6244
110	=	2443
120	=	1883
130	=	1952
140	=	1701
150	=	1892
160	=	2194
170	=	2257
180	=	1709
190	=	2137
200	=	2277
210	=	2155
220	=	2285
230	=	2285
240	=	2159
250	=	2161
260	=	2285
270	=	2277
280	=	2297
290	=	2351
300	=	2354
310	=	2349
320	=	2352
330	=	2347
340	=	2350
350	=	3185
360	=	2195
370	=	3202
380	=	4131
390	=	3259
400	=	4985
410	=	3011
420	=	1590
430	=	1525
440	=	4019
450	=	1124
460	=	3425
470	=	1840
480	=	1133
490	=	3428
500	=	1116
510	=	4014
520	=	2220
530	=	529
540	=	129
550	=	2587
560	=	2098
570	=	634
580	=	2142
590	=	3195
600	=	1351
610	=	143
620	=	1477
630	=	4803
640	=	4594
650	=	5030
660	=	4582
670	=	1709
680	=	2745
690	=	1489
700	=	3286
710	=	2848
720	=	1583
730	=	3212
TOTAL	=	203307

SAM

CLASSIFICATION: Shoot Up

You are the commander of a ground-based guided-missile launcher. You launch surface-to-air missiles at attacking enemy craft flying overhead, and try to intercept and destroy them. The smaller and faster the target, the more points you earn.

Use Q to move the missile up, Z down, I left and P right. The SPACE bar will launch a new missile and abort one currently zooming about.

PROGRAMMING SUGGESTIONS

Have the enemy shoot their own anti-missile missiles — you must evade them. Have the enemy drop paratroopers who will try to overrun your emplacement.

PROGRAM
Variables

DR%	Direction table
D	Current direction
SC	Screen memory
CL	Colour memory
MX, MY	Missile's (X, Y) co-ordinates
X, Y	Step values for missile
TG	Missile collision
EX, EY	Enemy (X, Y) co-ordinates
SX, SY	Enemy missile (X, Y) co-ordinates
S	Score

Listing

Draw Title Page and Initialise Game
Draw Screen and Start Game

```
10    VOL 8:COLOR0,14,6:COLOR4,6:SC=3072:CL=2048
20    DIMDR%(7,1):DIMMC%(7):EX=-1:LV=1
30    FOR I=0 TO 7:READDR%(I,0):READDR%(I,1):NEXT:FOR I
      =0 TO 7:READMC%(I):NEXT
40    DATA1,0,1,-1,0,-1,-1,-1,-1,0,-1,1,0,1,1,1,62,78,30,
      77,60,78,33,77
50    PRINT "▣ ▣ ▣ ▣ ▣ ▣ "
60    PRINT "▲ ▲ ▲ ▲ ▲ ▲ ▲ ▲ ▲ ▲ ╔ ═ ═ ╗ ▲ ▲ ▲ ╔ ═ ═ ╗ ▲ ▲ ▲
      ╔ ═ ╗ ╔ ═ ╗ "
70    PRINT "▲ ▲ ▲ ▲ ▲ ▲ ▲ ▲ ▲ ▲ ║ ▲ ▲ ┴ ▲ ▲ ▲ ║ ▲ ▲ ║ ▲ ▲ ▲
      ║ ▲ ║ ║ ▲ ║ "
80    PRINT "▲ ▲ ▲ ▲ ▲ ▲ ▲ ▲ ▲ ▲ ╚ ═ ═ ╗ ▲ ▲ ▲ ├ ═ ═ ┤ ▲ ▲ ▲
      ║ ▲ ╚ ╝ ▲ ║ "
90    PRINT "▲ ▲ ▲ ▲ ▲ ▲ ▲ ▲ ▲ ▲ ┬ ▲ ▲ ║ ▲ ▲ ▲ ║ ▲ ▲ ║ ▲ ▲ ▲
      ║ ▲ ▲ ▲ ▲ ║ "
100   PRINT "▲ ▲ ▲ ▲ ▲ ▲ ▲ ▲ ▲ ▲ ╚ ═ ═ ╝ ▲ ● ▲ ┴ ▲ ▲ ┴ ▲ ● ▲
      ┴ ▲ ▲ ▲ ▲ ┴ ▲ ● "
110   PRINT "■ ▣ ▣ ▲ ▲ ▲ ▲ ▲ ▲ ▲ ▲ ▲ ▲ ▲ ▲ ▲ ▲ ▲ ▲ C O N T R O
      L S "
120   PRINT "▣ ▣ ▣ ▲ ▲ ▲ ▲ ▲ ▲ ▲ ▲ ' I ' ▲ ▲ T U R N ▲ M I S
      S I L E ▲ L E F T "
130   PRINT "▣ ▲ ▲ ▲ ▲ ▲ ▲ ▲ ▲ ' P ' ▲ ▲ T U R N ▲ M I S S I
      L E ▲ R I G H T "
140   PRINT "▣ ▲ ▲ ▲ ▲ ▲ ▲ ▲ ▲ S P A C E B A R ▲ F I R E S
      ▲ M I S S I L E "
150   PRINT "▣ ▣ ▲ ▲ ▲ ▲ ▲ ▲ ▲ ▲ ▲ ▲ ▲ ▲ ▲ R E T U R N ▲ T O ▲
      S T A R T "
160   GETA$:IF A$=""THEN 160
170   IF ASC(A$)<>13THEN 160
180   PRINT "▣ ▣ ▲ ▲ ▲ ▲ ▲ ▲ ▲ ▲ ▲ ▲ ▲ ▲ ▲ ▲ ▲ ▲ ▲ S . A . M . "
190   GOSUB 670:K=0:N=LV*5:PC=0
200   FOR I=0 TO 39:POKE 4032+I,104:POKE 3008+I,57:NEXT
210   POKE 4050,85:POKE 4051,66:POKE 4052,73
220   MX=2:MY=22:D=2:F$=""
```

Get Player's Command, Move and Fire Missile
Generate and Move Enemy

```
230   GETA$:TN=TN+1
240   IF A$<>"▲ "THEN 280
250   SOUND 3,750,5:SOUND 3,765,5:SOUND 3,780,5:SOUND 3,7
      95,10
260   PT=PT-1:PC=PC-1:GOSUB 670
```

```
270   POKE SC+40*MY+MX,32:MY=22:MX=19:D=2:POKE SC+40*MY
      +MX,MC%(D):F$="F "
280   IF F$=""THEN 380
290   POKE SC+40*MY+MX,32:POKE CL+40*MY+MX,0
300   MX=MX+DR%(D,0):MY=MY+DR%(D,1)
310   IF MX<0ORMX>39ORMY<2ORMY>23THEN 220
320   TG=PEEK(SC+40*MY+MX)
330   IF TG<>32THEN GOSUB 560:GOTO 230
340   POKE SC+40*MY+MX,MC%(D):POKE CL+40*MY+MX,0
350   IF A$="I "THEN D=D+1:IF D>7THEN D=0
360   IF A$="P "THEN D=D-1:IF D<0THEN D=7
370   SOUND 1,1000-ABS(EX-MX)-ABS(EY-MY),3
380   IF TN<6-LVTHEN 230
390   TN=0:IF EX>=0ANDEX<=39THEN 430
400   FOR I=1 TO 10:SOUND 2,900-5*I,4:FOR J=1 TO 4:NEXTJ:
      NEXTI
410   EX=0:ED=1:IF RND(0)>.5THEN EX=39:ED=5
420   EY=INT(RND(0)*8+RND(0)*8+2)
430   POKE SC+40*EY+EX,32
440   IF EY+DR%(ED,1)<3THEN EY=3:ED=INT(RND(0)*5+4):
      GOTO 510
450   IF EY+DR%(ED,1)>23THEN EY=23:ED=INT(RND(0)*5):
      GOTO 530
460   EX=EX+DR%(ED,0):EY=EY+DR%(ED,1)
470   ED=ED+INT(RND(0)*3)-1
480   IF EX<0THEN EX=1:ED=INT(RND(0)*4+6)
490   IF EX>39THEN EX=38:ED=INT(RND(0)*5+2)
500   IF ED<0THEN ED=ED+7
510   IF ED>7THEN ED=ED-7
520   EG=PEEK(SC+40*EY+EX)
530   POKE SC+40*EY+EX,65:POKE CL+40*EY+EX,49
540   IF EG<>32THEN GOSUB 560
550   GOTO 230
```

Collision Detection and Scoring

```
560   POKE SC+40*MY+MX,42:PT=PT+5*LV+1:PC=PC+5*LV+1
570   FOR I=1 TO 25:SOUND 3,1000-5*I,5:NEXT
580   FOR I=60 TO 127:POKE CL+40*MY+MX,I:NEXT
590   F$="":POKE SC+40*MY+MX,32:X=19:MY=22:EX=-1:K=K+1
600   IF K<>NTHEN 670
610   FOR I=1 TO 20+2*LV:SOUND 1,600+I*5,5:SOUND 2,900-4
      *I,5:FOR J=1 TO 5:NEXTJ:NEXTI
620   PRINT "■ ⍗ ⍗ ⍗ ⍗ ⍗ ◨ ◨ ◨ ◨ L E V E L ▲ ";LV;"▲ C O
      M P L E T E D . "
630   PRINT "⍗ ▲ ▲ ▲ ▲ K I L L ▲ R A T I O ▲ = ▲ ";100*PC
      /(N*5*LV);"% "
640   PRINT "⍗ ⍗ ◨ ▲ ▲ ▲ ▲ R E T U R N ▲ T O ▲ C O N T I
      N U E "
```

```
650    LV=LV+1:IF LV>5THEN LV=5
660    PRINT "■ ■ ▲ ▲ ■ S C O R E ▲ ■ ";PT:GOTO 160
670    PRINT "■ ■ ▲ ▲ ■ S C O R E ▲ ■ ▲ ▲ ▲ ▲ ▲ ▲ ▮▮▮▮
       ▮▮ ";PT:RETURN
```

ChexSum Tables

Line		Sum	Line		Sum	Line		Sum
10	=	2655	240	=	1080	470	=	1705
20	=	2292	250	=	2687	480	=	2669
30	=	4029	260	=	1939	490	=	2795
40	=	3521	270	=	5684	500	=	1413
50	=	471	280	=	848	510	=	1414
60	=	3899	290	=	2988	520	=	1752
70	=	2879	300	=	2541	530	=	3050
80	=	3489	310	=	2810	540	=	1257
90	=	2556	320	=	1768	550	=	528
100	=	3365	330	=	1868	560	=	4370
110	=	1732	340	=	3299	570	=	2187
120	=	2443	350	=	2361	580	=	2607
130	=	2345	360	=	2367	590	=	4326
140	=	2395	370	=	2672	600	=	935
150	=	1986	380	=	1242	610	=	5218
160	=	1214	390	=	2358	620	=	2482
170	=	1378	400	=	3350	630	=	3194
180	=	1434	410	=	2830	640	=	2149
190	=	1868	420	=	2213	650	=	1928
200	=	2771	430	=	1435	660	=	1851
210	=	1759	440	=	4053	670	=	2740
220	=	1813	450	=	3927	TOTAL	=	163007
230	=	1075	460	=	2682			

Tank Ambush

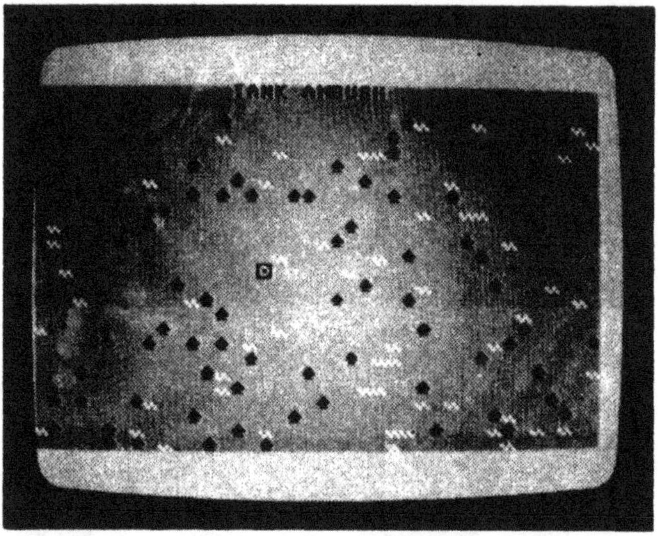

CLASSIFICATION: Shoot Up

The hunter against the hunted: hiding within the woods or lying behind hedges are devious infantrymen with dangerous heat-seeking missiles.

These missiles will always home in on your tank. You can shoot them with keys 1 to 8, or manoeuvre by pressing Q for up, Z for down, I for left and Z for right.

PROGRAMMING SUGGESTIONS

Have an enemy helicopter that fires heat-seeking missiles at your tank — shoot them or avoid them by manoeuvring. Introduce limited ammunition in the tank and ammunition dumps (where the tank must wait until it is reloaded). Give the killer tank hit points so it can suffer up to five hits before being destroyed. Also, create a repair station to fix up damages, and create the fuel for the killer tank and fuel dumps where it can refuel.

PROGRAM
Variables

SC	Screen memory
CC	Colour memory
BR	Background brightness level
LV	Level of difficulty
TB, TC	Character and colour beneath tank
F$	Fired flag
X, Y	Co-ordinates of tank
E	Delay for moving misSile
EX, EY	Co-ordinates of enemy missile
EB, EC	Character and colour behind missile
SX, SY	Howitzer shell co-ordinates
GB, GC	Character and colour behind shell
D	Firing direction
PT	Score

Listing

Title Screen and Instructions; Initialise game

```
10    VOL 8:SC=3072:CL=2048:BR=7:COLOR0,2,BR:Y=12:X=0
20    PRINT ""
30    PRINT ""
40    PRINT ""
50    PRINT "INSTRUCTIONS"
60    PRINT "YOUR TANK":PRINT "ENEMY MISSILE (SHOOT)"
70    PRINT "LAND MINE (AVOID)":PRINT "TREE/HEDGE"
80    PRINT "FIRING MOVEMENT"
90    PRINT "8 1 2 Q"
100   PRINT "\ / RETURN"
110   PRINT "7 3 TO I P"
120   PRINT "/ \ BEGIN."
130   PRINT "6 5 4 Z"
140   GETA$:IF ASC(A$)<>13THEN 140
150   GOSUB 710:GOSUB 660
160   TB=PEEK(SC+40*Y+X):TC=PEEK(CL+40*Y+X)
170   POKE SC+40*Y+X,215:POKE CL+40*Y+X,0
```

Get Input; Move Missile In; Move and Fire Tank

```
180   GETA$
190   IF F$="F "THEN GOSUB 450
200   E=E+1:IF E<8-LVTHEN 340
210   E=0
```

```
220   POKE SC+40*EY+EX,EB:POKE CL+40*EY+EX,EC:SOUND 1,100
      0-ABS(EX-X)-ABS(EY-Y),2
230   IF EY=YANDABS(EX-X)>1THEN EY=EY+INT(RND(0)*3-1):
      GOTO 260
240   IF EY<YTHEN EY=EY+1
250   IF EY>YTHEN EY=EY-1
260   IF EX=XANDABS(EY-Y)>1THEN EX=EX+INT(RND(0)*3-1):
      GOTO 290
270   IF EX<XTHEN EX=EX+1
280   IF EX>XTHEN EX=EX-1
290   IF EY<2THEN EY=3:
300   IF EY>24THEN EY=24
310   IF EX<0THEN EX=1
320   IF EX>39THEN EX=38
330   GOSUB 670
340   IF A$=""THEN 180
350   POKE SC+40*Y+X,TB:POKE CL+40*Y+X,TC
360   IF A$="Q "THEN Y=Y-1:SOUND 3,400,10:IF Y<2THEN Y=2
370   IF A$="Z "THEN Y=Y+1:SOUND 3,380,10:IF Y>24THEN Y
      =24
380   IF A$="I "THEN X=X-1:SOUND 3,420,10:IF X<0THEN X=0
390   IF A$="P "THEN X=X+1:SOUND 3,440,10:IF X>39THEN X
      =39
400   IF VAL(A$)>0ANDF$=""THEN F$="F ":SX=X:SY=Y:D=VAL(A$
      ):TS=0:GB=215:GC=0:SOUND 3,800,20
410   TB=PEEK(SC+40*Y+X):TC=PEEK(CL+40*Y+X):IF TB=42
      THEN 780
420   IF TB=43THEN TB=GB:TC=GC
430   POKE SC+40*Y+X,215:POKE CL+40*Y+X,0
440   GOTO 180
450   POKE SC+40*SY+SX,GB:POKE CL+40*SY+SX,GC
460   IF D=8ORD=1ORD=2THEN SY=SY-1:IF SY<2THEN SY=2:
      GOTO 640
470   IF D=2ORD=3ORD=4THEN SX=SX+1:IF SX>39THEN SX=39:
      GOTO 640
480   IF D=4ORD=5ORD=6THEN SY=SY+1:IF SY>24THEN SY=24:
      GOTO 640
490   IF D=6ORD=7ORD=8THEN SX=SX-1:IF SX<0THEN SX=0:
      GOTO 640
500   GB=PEEK(SC+40*SY+SX):GC=PEEK(CL+40*SY+SX)
```

Shell Collision With Missile; Increase Level

```
510   IF GB=215THEN GB=TB:GC=TC
520   IF GB<>81ANDEB<>43THEN 610
530   PRINT "■ ":IF BR=7THEN PRINT "■ "
540   SOUND 3,1000,15:PT=PT+1:PRINT "■ ■ ■ ■ S C O R E ";
      PT:GB=42:GC=0:GOSUB 660
```

```
550  PU=PU+1:IF PU=LV+1THEN BR=BR-1:PU=0
560  IF BR>=0THEN 600
570  IF BR=-1THEN COLOR0,1:GOTO 640
580  BR=7:COLOR0,2,BR:LV=LV+1:IF LV>8THEN LV=8
590  FOR I=1 TO 500:NEXT:PRINT "▘▣▣▣▣▣▣▣▪ L E V E
     L ";LV;"▴ C O M P L E T E D ":FOR I=1 TO 1000:
     NEXT:GOTO 150
600  COLOR0,2,BR:GOTO 640
610  POKE SC+40*SY+SX,43:POKE CL+40*SY+SX,0
620  TS=TS+1:IF TS>10THEN 640
630  RETURN
640  POKE SC+40*SY+SX,GB:POKE CL+40*SY+SX,GC
650  F$="":RETURN
```

Initialise Enemy Missile Location

```
660  EX=INT(RND(0)*40):EY=INT(RND(0)*22+2)
670  EB=PEEK(SC+40*EY+EX):EC=PEEK(CL+40*EY+EX)
680  IF EX=XANDEY=YTHEN 780
690  POKE SC+40*EY+EX,81:POKE CL+40*EY+EX,0
700  RETURN
```

Display Score and Generate Background; End Game

```
710  PRINT "▘▪▴▴▴▴▴▴▴▴▴▴▴▴▴▴▴▴▴▴T A N K ▴ A
     M B U S H "
720  PRINT "▣▣▴▴ S C O R E ";PT;"/ ";LV+1
730  A=INT(RND(0)*50+50-6*LV)
740  FOR I=1 TO A:B=INT(RND(0)*920+80):POKE SC+B,65:
     POKE CL+B,53:NEXT
750  A=INT(RND(0)*30+30-3*LV)
760  FOR I=1 TO A:B=INT(RND(0)*920+80):POKE SC+B,104:
     POKE CL+B,88:NEXT
770  RETURN
780  POKE SC+40*Y+X,102:FOR I=1 TO 15:COLOR0,I:SOUND 3,8
     00+10*I,9:FOR J=1 TO 50:NEXTJ:NEXTI
790  COLOR0,2,7:PRINT "▘▣▣▣▣▣▣▣▣▣▣▣▣▣▣▣▣
     ▣G ▴ A ▴ M ▴ E ▴▴▴ O ▴ V ▴ E ▴ R▪"
800  PRINT "▣▣▣▣▣▣▣▣▣▣▣▣▣▣▣▣▣▣▣▪ S C O R
     E ";PT;"/ ";LV+1:END
```

ChexSum Tables

Line		ChexSum	Line		ChexSum	Line		ChexSum
10	=	3640	280	=	1494	550	=	3158
20	=	6091	290	=	1171	560	=	1050
30	=	4916	300	=	1229	570	=	1875
40	=	4620	310	=	1109	580	=	3168
50	=	1932	320	=	1238	590	=	5518
60	=	6531	330	=	302	600	=	1203
70	=	5860	340	=	843	610	=	3007
80	=	2724	350	=	2824	620	=	1773
90	=	3249	360	=	3174	630	=	143
100	=	3413	370	=	3288	640	=	3168
110	=	3391	380	=	3160	650	=	570
120	=	2854	390	=	3284	660	=	2876
130	=	3121	400	=	6547	670	=	3747
140	=	1705	410	=	4483	680	=	1550
150	=	679	420	=	1843	690	=	2987
160	=	3403	430	=	2704	700	=	143
170	=	2704	440	=	533	710	=	2125
180	=	267	450	=	3168	720	=	1724
190	=	1079	460	=	4302	730	=	2055
200	=	1753	470	=	4401	740	=	4273
210	=	298	480	=	4404	750	=	2050
220	=	5929	490	=	4298	760	=	4321
230	=	4367	500	=	3797	770	=	143
240	=	1496	510	=	1882	780	=	5514
250	=	1495	520	=	1912	790	=	3027
260	=	4377	530	=	1585	800	=	2529
270	=	1495	540	=	4226	TOTAL	=	220287

Alien Overrun

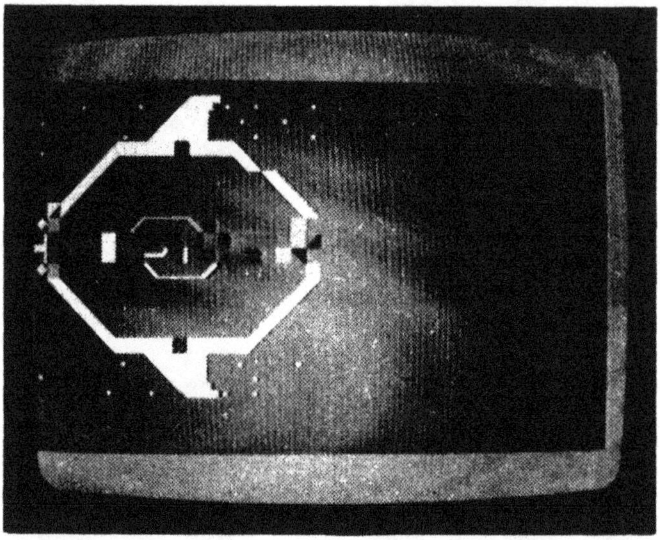

CLASSIFICATION: Defender

Your spaceship has been invaded by hordes of menacing aliens and they are multiplying prodigiously. You must move around your spaceship for as long as possible without being destroyed. Wipe the aliens out by moving onto the green chequered squares. Don't stand still as you don't score when you're still.

PROGRAMMING SUGGESTIONS

Make your ship a multi-level vehicle and arm your man with more than one weapon.

PROGRAM
Variables

X1, Y1	Next position of player
X, Y	Current position of player
Z	Level of difficulty
SC	Score
X( ), Y( )	Array of locations of each alien
A, B	Location of a particular alien
A1, B1	Next location of a particular alien
N	Number of aliens

Listing

```
10      REM ALIEN OVERUN
20      COLOR4,5,5:COLOR0,7,4
```

> **Input Difficulty Level, Define Variables and Draw the Spaceship**

```
30      INPUT "▙ D I F F I C U L T Y ▲ 1 - 5 ";Z:Z=Z*10
40      IF Z>50ORZ<10THEN 30
50      C=2048:S=3072:SC=0:DIMX(Z),Y(Z):X=6:Y=10:N=1
60      PRINT "▙ ▣ ▣ ▲ ▲ ▲ · ▲ ▲ ▲ · ▲ ▲ ▣ ◤ ▲ ⁙ ■ · ▲ · ▲
        ▲ ▲ · "
70      PRINT ". ▲ ▲ ▲ ▲ ▲ ▲ ▲ ▲ ▲ ▲ ▣ ◤ ▲ ▲ ■ ⁙ ▲ · ▲ ▲ · "
80      PRINT "▲ ▲ ▲ ▲ ▲ ▲ ▲ · ▲ ▣ ◤ ▲ ▲ ▲ ■ ⁙ ▲ ▲ · ▲ ▲ ▲ ·
        "
90      PRINT ". ▲ ▲ ▲ ▲ ▲ ▣ ◤ ▲ ▲ ▲ ▲ ▲ ▣ ■ ✲ ▣ ▣ ▲ ▲ ▣ ▲ ◥ "
100     PRINT "▲ ▲ ▲ ▲ ▣ ◤ ■ ◤ ▲ ▲ ▣ ▲ ▲ ▲ ▲ ▲ ▲ ▲ ▲ ◥ ▣ ◥ "
110     PRINT "▲ ▲ ▲ ▣ ◤ ■ ◤ ▲ ▲ ▲ ▲ ▲ ▲ ▲ ▲ ▲ ▲ ▲ ▲ ▲ ◥ ▣ ◥ "
120     PRINT "▲ ▲ ▣ ◤ ■ ◤ ▲ ▲ ▲ ▲ ▲ ▲ ▲ ▲ ▲ ▲ ▲ ▲ ▲ ▲ ▲ ◥ ▣ ◥
        "
130     PRINT "▲ ▣ ◤ ■ ◤ ▲ ▲ ▲ ▲ ▲ ▲ ▲ ▲ ▲ ▲ ▲ ▲ ▲ ▲ ▲ ▲ ▲ ◥ ▣
        ◥ "
140     PRINT "▣ ◆ ◣ ▣ ▲ ■ ▲ ▲ ▲ ▲ ▲ ▣ ▲ ▣ ╱ ⁙ ⁙ ⁙ ╲ ▲ ▲ ▲ ▲
        ▲ ▲ ◣ ▣ ▲ "
150     PRINT "▣ ┘ ▣ ✲ ▲ ▲ ▲ ▣ ▣ ▲ ■ ▲ ▲ ▣ ✲ ▣ ▣ ≡ ⁙ ⁙ ▲ ▲
        ▣ ◆ ▣ ▲ ▲ ■ ▲ ◣ ▣ ▲ ▣ ◤ "
160     PRINT "▣ ┐ ▣ ✲ ▲ ▲ ▲ ▣ ▣ ▲ ■ ▲ ▣ ▣ ▣ ≡ ⁙ ⁙ ▲ ▲ ▣ ◆
        ▣ ▲ ■ ▣ ✲ ▲ ◣ ◣ ▣ ▲ ■ ▣ ◥ "
170     PRINT "▣ ◆ ◣ ▣ ▲ ■ ▲ ▲ ▲ ▲ ▲ ▲ ▲ ▣ ╲ ⁙ ⁙ ⁙ ╱ ▲ ▲ ▲ ▲
        ▲ ▲ ◣ ▣ ▲ "
180     PRINT "▣ ▲ ◥ ■ ▣ ◥ ■ ▲ ▲ ▲ ▲ ▲ ▲ ▲ ▲ ▲ ▲ ▲ ▲ ▲ ▲ ▲ ▲
        ▣ ◤ ■ ◤ "
190     PRINT "▣ ▲ ▲ ◥ ■ ▣ ◥ ■ ▲ ▲ ▲ ▲ ▲ ▲ ▲ ▲ ▲ ▲ ▲ ▲ ▲ ▲ ▣
        ◤ ■ ◤ "
200     PRINT "▣ ▲ ▲ ▲ ◥ ■ ▣ ◥ ■ ▲ ▲ ▲ ▲ ▲ ▲ ▲ ▲ ▲ ▲ ▲ ▲ ▣ ◤
        ■ ◤ "
210     PRINT "▣ ▲ ▲ ▲ ▲ ◥ ■ ▣ ◥ ■ ▲ ▲ ▲ ▲ ▲ ▲ ▲ ▲ ▲ ▲ ▣ ◤ ■
        ◤ "
220     PRINT "▲ ▲ ▲ ▲ ▲ ◥ ▣ ▲ ▲ ▲ ▲ ▣ ✲ ▣ ▲ ▲ ▲ ▲ ▲ ■ ◤ "
230     PRINT "▲ ▲ ▲ ▲ ▲ ▲ ▲ · ▲ ◥ ▣ ▲ ▲ ▲ ■ ⁙ ▲ · ▲ ▲ ▲ · "
240     PRINT ". ▲ ▲ ▲ ▲ ▲ ▲ ▲ ▲ ▲ ◥ ▣ ▲ ▲ ■ ⁙ ▲ ▲ · "
250     PRINT "▲ ▲ ▲ ▲ ▲ ▲ · ▲ ▲ ▲ · ▲ ◥ ▣ ▲ ⁙ ■ · ▲ · "
260     A=14:B=10:FOR I=0 TO N
270     X(I)=A:Y(I)=B:POKE C+B*40+A,2:POKE S+B*40+A,81
280     A1=A+INT(RND(1)*3-1):B1=B+INT(RND(1)*3-1)
290     IF PEEK(S+B1*40+A1)<>32THEN 280
300     B=B1:A=A1:NEXT
```

```
310   FOR I=0 TO N:PRINT "█ ■ ▲ S C O R E : ";SC;:IF SC
      <10THEN PRINT "█ ▲ "
320   C1=1:A=X(I):B=Y(I)
330   IF RND(1)>.7THEN 350
340   A1=A+(A>X)-(A<X):B1=B+(B>Y)-(B<Y):GOTO 360
350   B1=B+INT(RND(1)*3-1):A1=A+INT(RND(1)*3-1)
360   IF PEEK(S+B1*40+A1)=32ORPEEK(S+B1*40+A1)=81ORPEEK(S
      +B1*40+A1)=88THEN 400
370   C1=C1+1:IF C1<10THEN 350
380   IF I<NTHEN A=X(I+1):B=Y(I+1)
390   GOTO 410
400   POKE S+B*40+A,32
410   A=A1:B=B1:IF A=XANDB=YTHEN 580
420   X(I)=A:Y(I)=B:POKE C+B*40+A,2:POKE S+B*40+A,81
```

Scan Keyboard; Move Player in Response; Multiply and Move Aliens

```
430   GETA$:IF A$<>"A "ANDA$<>"D "ANDA$<>"W "ANDA$<>"X "
      THEN 530
440   X1=X+(A$="A ")-(A$="D "):Y1=Y+(A$="W ")-(A$="X ")
450   P=PEEK(S+Y1*40+X1)
460   IF P=81THEN 580
470   IF P<>32ANDP<>102ANDP<>230THEN 530
480   SC=SC+1
490   POKE C+Y1*40+X1,7:POKE S+Y1*40+X1,88:POKE S+Y*40+X,
      32:Y=Y1:X=X1
500   IF P<>102ANDP<>230THEN 530
510   FOR J=0 TO N:POKE S+Y(J)*40+X(J),32:NEXT:SC=SC-30:
      IF SC<0THEN SC=0
520   N=1:GOTO 260
530   IF N<ZANDRND(1)>.8THEN N=N+1:X(N)=X(N-1):Y(N)=Y(N
      -1)
540   IF N=ZTHEN FOR J=1 TO Z:POKE S+Y(J)*40+X(J),32:
      NEXT:N=1
550   NEXTI:GOTO 310
560   POKE S+Y(0)*40+X(0),32:IF C1=10THEN 430
570   GOTO 310
580   REM
590   FOR I=1 TO 500:NEXT
```

Print the Score and Ask Player If He Wants Another Game

```
600   FOR I=1 TO 1000:NEXT:PRINT "█ ■ T H E ▲ █ █ A L I E
       N S █ ■ ▲ G O T ▲ Y O U ! ! ":PRINT :PRINT "■ █ █
      █ █ S C O R E "SC
610   PRINT :PRINT "■ A N O T H E R ▲ G A M E ? "
620   GETA$:IF A$<>"Y "ANDA$<>"N "THEN 620
```

```
630    IF A$="N "THEN PRINT :PRINT "■ B Y E ▲ B Y E ▲ T H
       E N . ":END
640    PRINT :PRINT :PRINT "■ * * * S T A N D ▲ B Y * * *
       "
650    FOR I=1 TO 1500:NEXT
660    RUN
```

ChexSum Tables

Line		Sum
10	=	0
20	=	1058
30	=	2270
40	=	1392
50	=	3678
60	=	1863
70	=	1508
80	=	1612
90	=	1624
100	=	1768
110	=	1858
120	=	1915
130	=	1961
140	=	2813
150	=	3311
160	=	3668
170	=	2852
180	=	2360
190	=	2295
200	=	2235
210	=	2180
220	=	1621
230	=	1612
240	=	1442
250	=	1457
260	=	1572
270	=	3668
280	=	3417
290	=	2231
300	=	1009
310	=	3376
320	=	1544
330	=	1117
340	=	4067
350	=	3419
360	=	5833
370	=	1624
380	=	2236
390	=	530
400	=	1167
410	=	2247
420	=	3668
430	=	4118
440	=	4047
450	=	1582
460	=	848
470	=	2637
480	=	716
490	=	5141
500	=	1897
510	=	4892
520	=	917
530	=	4296
540	=	3756
550	=	803
560	=	2548
570	=	526
580	=	0
590	=	964
600	=	5627
610	=	1617
620	=	2337
630	=	2654
640	=	1778
650	=	1021
660	=	139
TOTAL	=	147939

Micro Minotaur

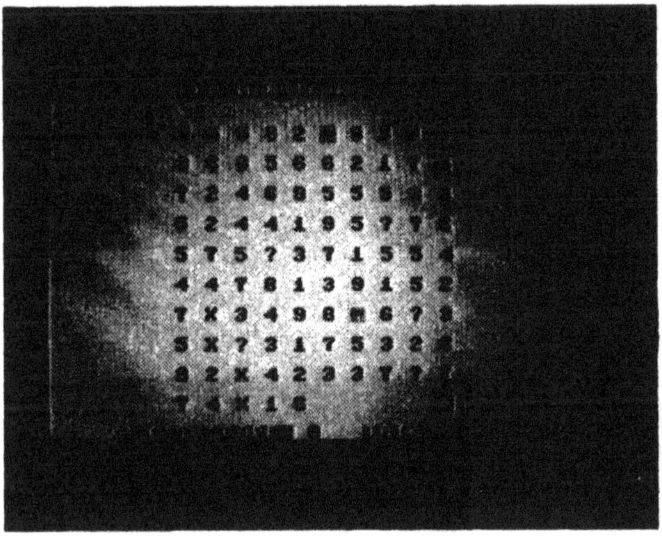

CLASSIFICATION: Educational

This is a smaller version of the number guessing game Minotaur. The objective is to guess a number in the range of 0 to 99. You do it by moving a piece around a board of numbers. As you pass over a number, it is removed from the board and added to your score. If you pass over an X, a clue appears at the top of the board for a short time. If you pass over a question mark, a random number is added to your Score.

If you pass over a number greater than five as you move around the board, you are pursued by a minotaur. If he captures you, you're dead. Remember, once you pass over a number it is removed from the board and you cannot pass over spaces. If you become encircled by spaces, press T to escape. Move your piece around using I for left, P for right, Q for up and Z for down. When you have guessed the number, move your piece to the white cursor.

PROGRAMMING SUGGESTIONS

Add different pieces to the board, such as bombs and mines. Place temporary barriers in the path of both the player and the minotaur.

PROGRAM

Variables

SC	Screen memory
CO	Colour memory
H$	Characters to place on screen
R	Row co-ordinate of player's piece
C	Column co-ordinate of player's piece
PO	Player's pieces position
PE	Player's pieces previous position
BE	Start of matrix on screen
C1	Column position of minotaur
R1	Row position of minotaur
MA	Minotaur's screen position

Listing

```
10      REM MICRO MINOTAUR
20      CLR
```

Draw Border, Rows of Numbers; Generate Number to Guess

```
30      SCNCLR:VOL 8:COLOR1,1,3
40      SC=3072:CO=2048:COLOR0,7,4:COLOR4,6,4:C=0:R=0:PO=SC
        +(R*40)+C:BE=SC+130
50      PRINT "▣ ";
60      FOR I=1 TO 24:RR$=RR$+"▣ ":NEXT
70      FOR I=1 TO 40:CC$=CC$+"▣ ":NEXT
80      FOR I=1 TO 34:CL$=CL$+"▲ ":NEXT
90      H$="1 2 3 4 5 6 7 8 9 ? "+CHR$(24):DIMCL$(10)
100     FOR I=SC TO SC+39:POKE I,160:NEXT
110     FOR I=SC+(24*40) TO SC+(24*40)+39:POKE I,160:NEXT
120     FOR I=SC TO SC+(24*40) STEP 40:POKE I,160:NEXT
130     FOR I=SC+39 TO SC+(24*40)+39 STEP 40:POKE I,160:
        NEXT
140     PRINT "▣ ▣ ▲ ▲ ▲ ▲ ▲ ▲ ▲ ▲ ▲ ▲ M I C R O ▲ M I N O T
        A U R ";"▣ ▲ ▲ ▲ ▲ ▲ P L A Y E R "
150     FOR I=SC+130 TO SC+850 STEP 80
160     FOR J=I TO I+18 STEP 2
170     Q=INT(RND(1)*12):IF Q=0THEN 170
180     A=ASC(MID$(H$,Q,1))
190     POKE J,A:NEXT:NEXT
200     NU=INT(RND(1)*100):IF NU=0THEN 200
210     NU$=STR$(NU):RA=INT(RND(1)*3):IF RA=0THEN GOTO 210
220     IF NU<10THEN NU$="0 "+NU$
```

Make up Clues About Random Number

```
230     IF RA=1THEN CL$(1)="F I R S T ▲ D I G I T ▲ E Q U A
         L S ▲ "+MID$(NU$,2,1)
240     IF RA=2THEN CL$(1)="S E C O N D ▲ D I G I T ▲ E Q U
         A L S ▲ "+MID$(NU$,3,1)
250     CN=2:FOR I=2 TO NU-1
260     A=NU/I:B=INT(A):IF A<>BTHEN 290
270     IF CN=7THEN 300
280     CL$(CN)="A ▲ F A C T O R ▲ O F ▲ T H E ▲ N U M B E
        R ▲ I S ▲ "+STR$(A):CN=CN+1
290     NEXT
300     IF NU/2=INT(NU/2)THEN CL$(CN)="T H E ▲ N U M B E R
        ▲ I S ▲ E V E N "
```

```
310   IF NU/2<>INT(NU/2)THEN CL$(CN)="T H E ▴ N U M B E R
      ▴ I S ▴ O D D "
320   GB=VAL(MID$(NU$,3,1)):FOR I=2 TO 9:A=GB/I:IF A=
      INT(GB/I)THEN GOSUB 1060:GOTO 340
330   NEXT
340   GB=VAL(MID$(NU$,2,1)):FOR I=2 TO 9:A=GB/I:IF A=
      INT(GB/I)THEN GOSUB 1070:GOTO 360
350   NEXT
360   SD=VAL(MID$(NU$,2,1)):IF SD/2=INT(SD/2)THEN CL$(7)
      ="F I R S T ▴ D I G I T ▴ I S ▴ E V E N "
370   IF SD/2<>INT(SD/2)THEN CL$(7)="F I R S T ▴ D I G I
      T ▴ I S ▴ O D D "
380   SD=VAL(MID$(NU$,3,1)):IF SD/2=INT(SD/2)THEN CL$(8)
      ="S E C O N D ▴ D I G I T ▴ I S ▴ E V E N "
390   IF SD/2<>INT(SD/2)THEN CL$(8)="S E C O N D ▴ D I G
      I T ▴ I S ▴ O D D "
400   FOR I=1 TO 9:IF I*I=NUTHEN CL$(9)="N U M B E R ▴ I
      S ▴ T H E ▴ P R O D U C T ▴ O F ▴ A ▴ S Q U A R E "
```

Place Minotaur and Player On Board; Move Them Around

```
410   NEXT
420   HO=BE+10:POKE HO,160
430   C1=6:R1=6:MA=BE+(R1*40)+C1:VE=PEEK(MA):POKE MA,13
440   C=10:R=18:PO=BE+(R*40)+C:VA=PEEK(PO):POKE PO,209
450   A=PEEK(198):POKE MA,13:IF A=64THEN 550
460   IF A=62THEN GOSUB 560
470   IF A=12THEN GOSUB 620
480   IF A=33THEN GOSUB 680
490   IF A=41THEN GOSUB 740
500   IF A=22THEN GOTO 1040
510   GOSUB 850:SOUND 2,15,12:SOUND 1,23,23
520   PRINT "▣ ";LEFT$(RR$,2);LEFT$(CC$,2);CL$;
530   TT=TT+CU
540   PRINT "▣ ";LEFT$(RR$,23);LEFT$(CC$,7);"▣ L A S T ▴
      S C O R E : ■ ";CU;"▴ ▴ ▣ T O T A L ▴ S C O R E : ■
      ";TT;
550   CU=0:POKE MA,141:GOTO 450
560   IF R=0THEN RETURN
570   R=R-2:PE=PO:PO=BE+(R*40)+C:DA=PEEK(PO):IF DA=32
      THEN R=R+2:PO=BE+(R*40)+C:RETURN
580   IF DA=13THEN GOTO 920
590   GOSUB 800
600   POKE PE,VA:FL=PEEK(PE):CU=VAL(CHR$(FL)):POKE PE,32:
      VA=PEEK(PO)
610   POKE PO,203:RETURN
620   IF R=18THEN RETURN
630   R=R+2:PE=PO:PO=BE+(R*40)+C:DA=PEEK(PO):IF DA=32
      THEN R=R-2:PO=BE+(R*40)+C:RETURN
```

```
640   IF DA=13THEN GOTO 920
650   GOSUB 800
660   POKE PE,VA:FL=PEEK(PE):CU=VAL(CHR$(FL)):POKE PE,32
670   VA=PEEK(PO):POKE PO,209:RETURN
680   IF C=0THEN RETURN
690   C=C-2:PE=PO:PO=BE+(R*40)+C:DA=PEEK(PO):IF DA=32
      THEN C=C+2:PO=BE+(R*40)+C:RETURN
700   IF DA=13THEN GOTO 920
710   GOSUB 800
720   POKE PE,VA:FL=PEEK(PE):CU=VAL(CHR$(FL)):POKE PE,32
730   VA=PEEK(PO):POKE PO,209:RETURN
740   IF C=18THEN RETURN
750   C=C+2:PE=PO:PO=BE+(R*40)+C:DA=PEEK(PO):IF DA=32
      THEN C=C-2:PO=BE+(R*40)+C:RETURN
760   IF DA=13THEN GOTO 920
770   GOSUB 800
780   POKE PE,VA:FL=PEEK(PE):CU=VAL(CHR$(FL)):POKE PE,32
790   VA=PEEK(PO):POKE PO,209:RETURN
800   IF DA=63THEN CU=INT(RND(1)*10)
810   FU=INT(RND(1)*10):DI=(40-LEN(CL$(FU)))/2
820   IF DA=24THEN PRINT "▣ ";LEFT$(CC$,DI);LEFT$(RR$,2);
      CL$(FU);:GOSUB 1050
830   IF DA=160THEN GOSUB 1000
840   RETURN
```

Work Out Minotaur's Position and Move Him Closer To You

```
850   IF CU<5THEN RETURN
860   IF C1>CTHEN C1=C1-2
870   IF C1<CTHEN C1=C1+2
880   IF R1>RTHEN R1=R1-2
890   IF R1<RTHEN R1=R1+2
900   POKE MA,VE:MA=BE+(R1*40)+C1:IF PEEK(MA)=209THEN
      GOSUB 920:STOP
910   VE=PEEK(MA):POKE MA,13:RETURN
920   PRINT "◣ ";LEFT$(RR$,10);"T H E ▲ M I N O T A U R ▲
       H A S ▲ E A T E N ▲ Y O U "
930   PRINT "▣ ";LEFT$(RR$,13);"T H E ▲ N U M B E R ▲ W A
       S ";NU;
940   PRINT :PRINT :PRINT
950   PRINT "D O ▲ Y O U ▲ W A N T ▲ A N O T H E R ▲ G A
      M E ( Y / N ) : ";
960   GETA$:IF A$=""THEN 960
970   IF A$="Y "THEN GOTO 20
980   IF A$="N "THEN END
990   GOTO 960
1000  PRINT "◣ ";LEFT$(RR$,2);LEFT$(RR$,3);"W H A T ▲ I S
       ▲ T H E ▲ N U M B E R ";:INPUT VT
```

```
1010  IF VT<>NUTHEN PRINT "W R O N G , ▲ T H E ▲ N U M B
      E R ▲ W A S ▲ ";NU:GOTO 940
1020  PRINT "C O N G R A T U L A T I O N S ▲ Y O U ▲ H A
      V E ▲ B E A T E N ▲ M I N O T A U R "
1030  GOTO 940
1040  PRINT "▙ ";:GOTO 930
1050  FOR I=1 TO 1200:NEXT:RETURN
1060  CL$(6)="A ▲ F A C T O R ▲ O F ▲ S E C O N D ▲ D I G
       I T ▲ I S "+STR$(I):RETURN
1070  CL$(5)="A ▲ F A C T O R ▲ O F ▲ F I R S T ▲ D I G I
       T ▲ I S "+STR$(I):RETURN
```

ChexSum Tables

Line		Sum	Line		Sum	Line		Sum
10	=	0	370	=	4090	730	=	1614
20	=	157	380	=	5953	740	=	809
30	=	1125	390	=	4216	750	=	7311
40	=	5999	400	=	5668	760	=	1287
50	=	295	410	=	131	770	=	302
60	=	1942	420	=	1346	780	=	3195
70	=	1892	430	=	4005	790	=	1614
80	=	1914	440	=	3984	800	=	2033
90	=	2293	450	=	2185	810	=	3162
100	=	1868	460	=	986	820	=	3756
110	=	3341	470	=	982	830	=	1175
120	=	2612	480	=	982	840	=	143
130	=	3242	490	=	982	850	=	839
140	=	2922	500	=	1278	860	=	1363
150	=	1872	510	=	1647	870	=	1364
160	=	1222	520	=	2034	880	=	1425
170	=	2025	530	=	857	890	=	1426
180	=	1198	540	=	5677	900	=	3944
190	=	739	550	=	1579	910	=	1533
200	=	2287	560	=	761	920	=	3677
210	=	3559	570	=	7374	930	=	2735
220	=	1726	580	=	1287	940	=	585
230	=	3881	590	=	302	950	=	2628
240	=	4040	600	=	4201	960	=	1214
250	=	1484	610	=	729	970	=	1271
260	=	2422	620	=	824	980	=	895
270	=	857	630	=	7373	990	=	535
280	=	4306	640	=	1287	1000	=	4192
290	=	131	650	=	302	1010	=	3955
300	=	4034	660	=	3195	1020	=	3802
310	=	4141	670	=	1614	1030	=	533
320	=	5441	680	=	746	1040	=	1051
330	=	131	690	=	7312	1050	=	1226
340	=	5443	700	=	1287	1060	=	3662
350	=	131	710	=	302	1070	=	3546
360	=	5832	720	=	3195	TOTAL	=	250979

Dumper

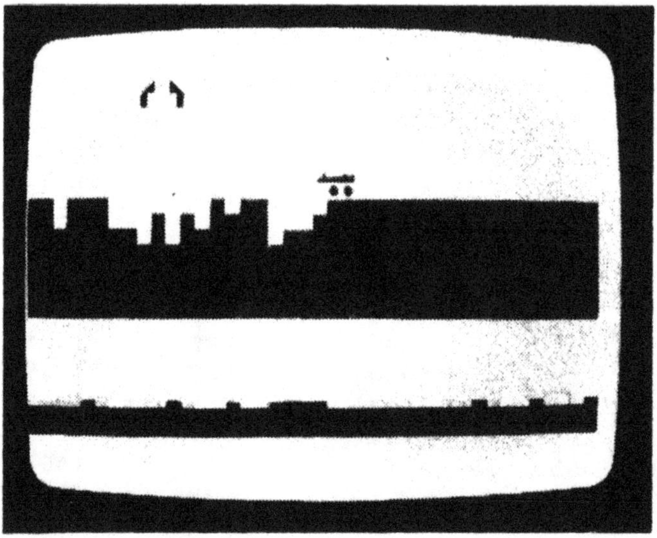

CLASSIFICATION: Defender COLOUR ILLUSTRATION OBC

An alien spacecraft is dropping bombs on your city's shield and gradually eating it away. You have three dumper trucks with which to drop bricks onto the shield and rebuild it. (Be careful, the trucks can be destroyed by the UFO's bombs.) Use the I key to move left, the P key to move right, and the SPACE bar to drop bricks on the shield.

PROGRAMMING SUGGESTIONS

Change or vary the effect of the alien's bombs so that one bomb may take one piece of the shield and another several pieces. Also give bonus points each time the UFO's bombs break the shield if you reseal it before the city is destroyed.

PROGRAM
Variables

HS	Highest score
S	Score
B	Position of bomb
G$	INKEY$
AL	Alien
P	Position of dumper
DI	Holes
DU	Number of dumpers

Listing

```
10    REM DUMPER
20    HS=0:VOL 8
30    COLOR0,4,5:COLOR4,2,5
40    PRINT "◘ ◘ ◘ ◘ ◘ ◘ ◘ ◘ ◘ ◘ ◘ ◘ ◘ ◘ ";
```

Set the Colors; Draw the Sky, Shield and City; Define the Alien

```
50    FOR I=1 TO 8:PRINT "▲ ▲ ▲ ▲ ▲ ▲ ▲ ▲ ▲ ▲ ▲ ▲ ▲ ▲ ▲ ▲ ▲ ▲ ▲ ▲ ▲ ▲ ▲ ▲ ▲ ▲ ▲ ▲ ▲ ▲ ▲ ▲ ▲ ▲ ▲ ▲ ▲ ▲ ▲ ▲ ";
      :NEXT
60    PRINT "▀ ◘ ◘ "TAB(8)"◘ ▒ ◘ ▌ + ◘ ▌ ▒ ◘ ▌ ◘ ▲ "
70    PRINT "◘ ◘ ▄ ▄ ▄ ◘ ▲ ▀ ◘ ▀ ▲ ▌ ◘ ◘ ■ ▄ ◘ ▄ ◘ / \ ◘
      ▄ ◘ ┌ ┐ ▲ ■ ▄ ▄ ▄ ";
80    PRINT "◘ ▄ ▄ ▄ ◘ ▲ ▀ ◘ ▀ ▲ ▌ ◘ ◘ ■ ▄ ◘ ▄ ◘ / \ ◘ ▄
      ◘ ┌ ┐ ▲ ■ ▄ ";
90    PRINT "◘ ▲ ▲ ▲ ▲ ▲ ▲ ▲ ▲ ▲ ▲ ▲ ▲ ▲ ▲ ▲ ▲ ▲ ▲ ▲ ▲ ▲ ▲ ▲ ▲ ▲ ▲ ▲ ▲ ▲ ▲ ▲ ▲ ▲ ▲ ▲ ▲ ▲ ";
100   PRINT "◘ ▲ ▲ ▲ ▲ ▲ ▲ ▲ ▲ ▲ ▲ ▲ ▲ ▲ ▲ ▲ ▲ ▲ ▲ ▲ ▲ ▲ ▲ ▲ ▲ ▲ ▲ ▲ ▲ ▲ ▲ ▲ ▲ ▲ ▲ ▲ ▲ ▲ ";
110   PRINT "◘ ◘ ◘ ▌ ▌ ▌ ▌ ▀ ◘ ▄ ▌ ▌ ▌ ▌ ▌ ▌ ▌ ▌ ▌ ▌ ▌
      ▄ "
120   DU=3:S=0
130   AL=1:A$="▲ ◘ ◘ ◤ ◘ ▀ ● ◘ ◘ ◥ ▀ ▲ ◘ ▌ ▌ ▌ ▌ ▌ ▲ ▌ ◘
      ▀ ◘ ◘ ▌ ▀ ▲ "
140   P=3387
150   B=0
160   K=64:GOTO 220
170   GETG$
180   IF G$=""THEN K=64
190   IF G$="I "THEN K=12
200   IF G$="P "THEN K=20
210   IF G$="▲ "THEN 450
220   D=(K=12)-(K=20)*2+P:IF D<3351THEN 310
230   IF PEEK(D)=160THEN D=D-40
240   IF D>PTHEN D=D-1
250   POKE P,32:POKE P-41,32:POKE P-39,32:POKE P+1,32:
      POKE P-40,32
260   POKE P-81,32:POKE P-80,32:POKE P-79,32:POKE P-121,3
      2:POKE P-119,32:P=D
270   POKE P,81:POKE P+1,81:POKE P-41,233:POKE P-40,98:
      POKE P-39,248
280   IF PEEK(P+40)<>32ANDPEEK(P+40)<>160THEN 520
290   IF PEEK(P+40)=160THEN 310
300   D=P+40:GOTO 250
310   AL=AL+INT(RND(1)*3-1):IF AL<0THEN AL=0
320   IF AL>18THEN AL=18
```

Move the Alien Invader Along the Top of the Screen and the Dumper

```
330    PRINT "▣ "TAB(AL)A$
340    IF B>0THEN 370
350    IF RND(1)<.8THEN 440
360    B=3154+AL
370    POKE B,32:B=B+40:IF PEEK(B)=32THEN 430
380    IF PEEK(B)<>160THEN 410
390    POKE B,32
400    B=0:GOTO 440
410    IF B>3711THEN 520
420    GOTO 540
430    POKE B,46
440    GOTO 170
450    DI=P-1:IF PEEK(DI+40)<>160THEN S=S+5
460    POKE P-41,95
470    POKE P-41,233:GOTO 500
480    S=S+1:POKE DI,160
490    FOR I=1 TO 10:NEXT
500    IF PEEK(DI+40)=160ORDI>3671THEN 310
510    POKE DI,32:DI=DI+40:GOTO 480
520    GOTO 530
530    GOTO 610
```

Generate Sound, Print the Score and Prompt for Another Game

```
540    REM SOUND
550    SOUND 2,55,5:POKE B-1,77:POKE B,121:POKE B+1,78
560    IF DU=1THEN 610
570    POKE B,32:POKE B-1,32:POKE B+1,32
580    POKE P,32:POKE P+1,32:POKE P-41,32:POKE P-40,32:
       POKE P-39,32
590    PRINT "▣ "TAB(AL+1)"▲ ▲ ▲ ▲ ▣ ▮▮ ▮▮ ▮▮ ▲ ▲ ▲ "
600    DU=DU-1:GOTO 140
610    FOR I=1 TO 1000:NEXT:PRINT "▣ ▣ ▣ ■ S C O R E "S
620    IF S>HSTHEN HS=S
630    PRINT "▣ H I ▲ ▲ ▲ "HS
640    PRINT "▣ A N O T H E R ▲ G A M E ? ":POKE 198,0
650    GETA$:IF A$="Y "THEN 40
660    IF A$<>"N "THEN 650
670    PRINT :PRINT "▣ ▣ ▣ ▣ T O O ▲ T O U G H ▲ F O R ▲ Y
        O U , ▲ E H ▲ ? "
680    END
```

ChexSum Tables

Line		ChexSum
10	=	0
20	=	736
30	=	1053
40	=	720
50	=	3160
60	=	2018
70	=	5020
80	=	4551
90	=	2151
100	=	2151
110	=	1716
120	=	779
130	=	3865
140	=	481
150	=	296
160	=	972
170	=	271
180	=	1062
190	=	1145
200	=	1150
210	=	905
220	=	2971
230	=	1652
240	=	1198
250	=	3449
260	=	4378
270	=	3580
280	=	3058
290	=	1503
300	=	1231
310	=	2965
320	=	1203
330	=	721
340	=	769
350	=	1113
360	=	781
370	=	2315
380	=	1393
390	=	374
400	=	903
410	=	957
420	=	529
430	=	371
440	=	528
450	=	2909
460	=	679
470	=	1347
480	=	1161
490	=	908
500	=	2316
510	=	1930
520	=	532
530	=	530
540	=	0
550	=	2477
560	=	867
570	=	1778
580	=	3465
590	=	1762
600	=	1333
610	=	2084
620	=	1179
630	=	696
640	=	1746
650	=	1243
660	=	1128
670	=	2640
680	=	129
TOTAL	=	106983

Scrambler

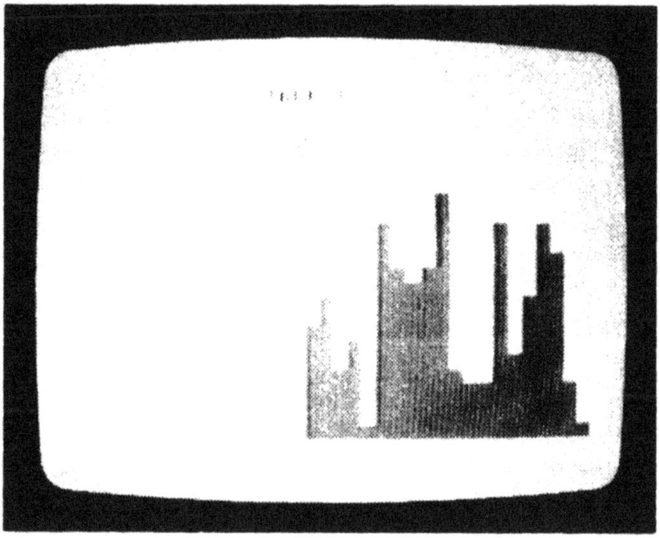

CLASSIFICATION: Evasion

You are the commander of a spaceship which must fly through an obstacle course of mountains, corridors and meteors. To move your space vehicle, use the Q key for up, the Z key for down. The program uses a small machine-language routine to scroll the screen, so the program should be saved before running in case you make a 'typo' and crash the program.

PROGRAMMING SUGGESTIONS

Give the player more landscapes to travel through. Cause a missile or a rocket to drift up from the ground occasionally. Give the player a fuel limit or a time limit to complete a given piece of scenery, otherwise he is destroyed.

PROGRAM
Variables

SA	Start of screen memory
PO	Position of spaceship
SL	Start of colour memory
R	Row position of spaceship
C	Column position of spaceship
P	Keyscan location
I$	Vertical bar
CC$	Column positioning variable
RR$	Row positioning variable
S1	Score

Listing

```
10      REM SCRAMBLER
20      POKE 55,16:POKE 56,39:CLR
30      GOSUB 450
40      T$="▣ ▲ ▀ ▌▌□ ▌▌□ ▌▌□ ▌▌□ ▌▌□ ▌▌□ ▌▌▣ ▲ ▀ "
50      COLOR0,7,5:COLOR4,7,5
60      K$="▣ ▲ ▀ □ ▌▌ ":FOR I=1 TO 19:I$=I$+K$:NEXT
70      SA$="▲ ▲ ▲ ▲ ▲ ▣ ▌▌▌▌▌▌▌▌▌▌▲ / □ \ ▲ ▣ ▌▌▌▌▌▌▌▌▌▌▲
        \ □ / ▲ ▣ ▌▌▌▌▌▌▌▌▌▌▲ ▲ ▲ ▲ "
80      RR$="▣ ":FOR I=1 TO 24:RR$=RR$+"▣ ":NEXT:FOR I=1
         TO 39:CC$=CC$+"▣ ":NEXT
90      W$="▣ "+LEFT$(RR$,22)+LEFT$(CC$,38)
```

Define Variables; Read Machine Program Into Memory

```
100     FOR I=11000 TO 11071:READA:POKE I,A:NEXT
110     PRINT "▣ ";:K1=11000
120     P=198:R=12:C=20:SA=3072:SL=2048:LM=300
130     PO=SA+(R*40)+C
140     PRINT "▣ ";TAB(16);"S T A G E ▲ O N E ▲ ▲ ";
```

Stage One: Fly Ship Over Mountains With Lowest Possible Altitude

```
150     FOR SC=1 TO 300:SYS K1:PRINT W$;LEFT$(I$,RND(1)*70)
        ;
160     IF PEEK(PO+83)=160ORPEEK(PO+82)=160THEN GOSUB 560:
        GOTO 140
170     A=PEEK(P):IF A=62THEN GOSUB 320
180     IF A=12THEN GOSUB 340
190     S1=S1+R-6:PRINT "▣ ▣ ";:PRINT USING"# # # ";S1;:
        PRINT "▀ ▲ ▲ ";
200     PRINT LEFT$(RR$,R);LEFT$(CC$,C);SA$;:NEXT
210     PRINT "▣ ";TAB(16);"S T A G E ▲ T W O ▲ ▲ ▲ ";
```

Stage Two: Fly Ship Through Meteor Storm and Keep Dodging Them

```
220     FOR SC=1 TO 300:SYS K1
230     IF SW=0THEN SW=1:GOTO 270
240     SW=0
250     HK=INT(RND(1)*22):IF HK<5THEN 250
260     FK=3072+(HK*40)+39:POKE FK,81
270     IF PEEK(PO+83)=81ORPEEK(PO+3)=160ORPEEK(PO+43)=81
        ORPEEK(PO+4)=81THEN GOSUB 560
280     A=PEEK(P):IF A=62THEN GOSUB 320
290     IF A=12THEN GOSUB 340
```

```
300   S1=S1+1:PRINT "▣▣ ";:PRINT USING"# # # ";S1;:
      PRINT "▀ ▲ ";
310   PRINT LEFT$(RR$,R);LEFT$(CC$,C);SA$;:NEXT:PRINT "▙
      Y O U R ▲ S C O R E ▲ W A S : ▲ ";SC:STOP
320   IF R=5THEN RETURN
330   R=R-1:PO=SA+(R*40)+C:RETURN
340   IF R=22THEN RETURN
350   R=R+1:PO=SA+(R*40)+C:RETURN
360   REM DATA FOR BLOCK MOVE
370   REM ==================
380   DATA173,11,255,201,204,208,249,160,0,162,199,185,20
      1,12,153,200,12,185
390   DATA145,13,153,144,13,185,89,14,153,88,14,185
400   DATA33,15,153,32,15,200,202,208,228,160,0,162
410   DATA5,142,238,46,169,32,153,239,12
420   DATA153,183,13,153,127,14,153,71,15,152,24,105,40,1
      68,174,238,46,202
430   DATA208,228,96
440   NEXT
450   PRINT "▙ ";TAB(14);"▣ S C R A M B L E R ▀ ";
460   PRINT :PRINT :PRINT "G U I D E ▲ T H E ▲ S H I P ▲
      A C R O S S ▲ T H E ▲ M O U N T A I N S . T H E ":
      PRINT
470   PRINT "L O W E R ▲ Y O U ▲ S T A Y ▲ T H E ▲ M O R
      E ▲ P O I N T S ▲ Y O U ▲ G A I N . ":PRINT
480   PRINT "I F ▲ Y O U ▲ L I F T ▲ Y O U R ▲ S H I P ▲
      T O ▲ I T S ▲ M A X I M U M ":PRINT
490   PRINT "H E I G H T ▲ Y O U ▲ W I L L ▲ B E G I N ▲
      L O S I N G ▲ P O I N T S . ":PRINT
500   PRINT "B E ▲ C A R E F U L ▲ N O T ▲ T O ▲ C R A S
      H ▲ I N T O ▲ M O U N T A I N S . ":PRINT
510   PRINT "O N C E ▲ Y O U ▲ H A V E ▲ P A S S E D ▲ T
      H E ▲ M O U N T A I N S ▲ Y O U ":PRINT
520   PRINT "W I L L ▲ H A V E ▲ T O ▲ S U R V I V E ▲ A
      ▲ M E T E O R ▲ S T O R M ":PRINT
530   PRINT TAB(10);"P R E S S ▲ A N Y ▲ K E Y ▲ T O ▲ S
      T A R T ";
540   GETA$:IF A$=""THEN 540
550   RETURN
560   FOR I=1 TO 15:FOR J=1 TO 99:NEXT:COLOR4,I,3:NEXT:
      RETURN
```

ChexSum Tables

Line		ChexSum
10	=	0
20	=	1149
30	=	302
40	=	2859
50	=	1060
60	=	2816
70	=	4857
80	=	4718
90	=	2201
100	=	2093
110	=	1121
120	=	3254
130	=	1399
140	=	1838
150	=	2911
160	=	3748
170	=	1680
180	=	981
190	=	3016
200	=	2061
210	=	1761
220	=	1205
230	=	1751
240	=	401
250	=	2195
260	=	2109
270	=	5547
280	=	1680
290	=	981
300	=	2697
310	=	4581
320	=	762
330	=	2296
340	=	819
350	=	2295
360	=	0
370	=	0
380	=	4072
390	=	2422
400	=	2393
410	=	1828
420	=	3852
430	=	669
440	=	131
450	=	1946
460	=	4372
470	=	3855
480	=	3518
490	=	3538
500	=	3769
510	=	3716
520	=	3385
530	=	2500
540	=	1212
550	=	143
560	=	2797
TOTAL	=	125262

Siege

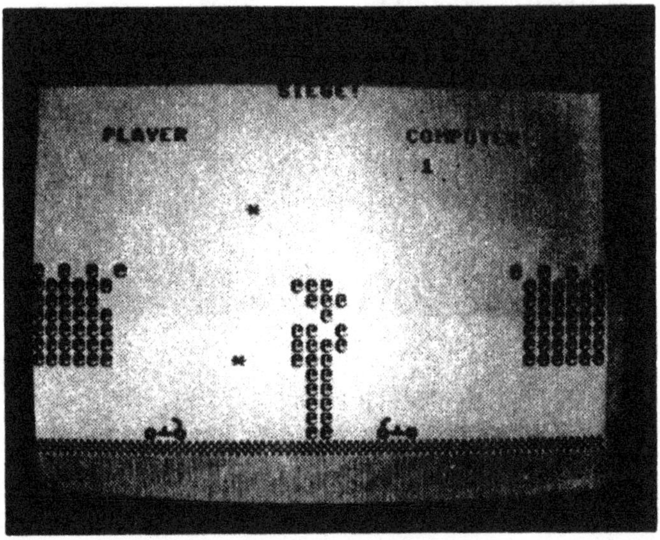

CLASSIFICATION: Shoot Up

It's you versus the Commodore 16. Use your ballista to lob huge rocks at the castle, trying to demolish it before it destroys your castle. You can raise and lower your ballista with Q and Z, and trundle it closer to or further away with P or I. Hitting the SPACE bar will fling your boulder.

PROGRAMMING SUGGESTIONS

Put flags on towers for extra points if hit. Have limited ammunition or reloading times. Have a different type of ammunition which starts fires which you must put out. You cannot shoot while extinguishing fires. Adapt the game for two players..

PROGRAM
Variables

CX	Computer position
PX	Player position
EV	Elevation of player's ballista
BY	Height of player's rock
VY	Velocity of player's rock
B%	Horizontal position of player's rock
CY	Height of computer's rock
FY	Velocity of computer's rock
C%	Horizontal position of computer's rock
PB	Bricks remaining in player's castle
CB	Bricks remaining in computer's castle
CH	Character beneath player's rock
C2	Character beneath computer's rock
F$	Player fired flag
F2$	Computer fired flag
M	Computer move distance

Listing

Title Screen

```
10    COLOR0,14:COLOR4,11:VOL 8:PRINT "  ":COLOR1,6,6
20    PRINT "              ┌─┐ ┌─┐ ┬ ┌─┐ ┌─┐"
30    PRINT "              │   │   │ │   │ o "
40    PRINT "              └─┐ ├─  │ │   ├─ "
50    PRINT "              │ │ │   │ │ ┬ │   o "
60    PRINT "              └─┘ └─┘ ┴ └─┘ └─┘"
70    PRINT :PRINT :PRINT "                    CONTROLS: "
80    PRINT :PRINT "        'Q'     INCREASE RANGE"
90    PRINT :PRINT "        'Z'     DECREASE RANGE"
100   PRINT :PRINT "        'P'     MOVE BALLISTA RIGHT"
110   PRINT :PRINT "        'I'     MOVE BALLISTA LEFT"
120   PRINT :PRINT "        SPACE   FIRES BALLISTA"
130   PRINT :PRINT :PRINT :PRINT "           (HIT RETURN TO BEGIN)"
```

Initialise Game and Draw Game Screen

```
140   GETA$:IF A$=""THEN 140
150   IF ASC(A$)<>13THEN 140
160   PRINT "  ":CD$="                        "
170   CR$="":CC$="                                  "
180   CX=4:PX=1:EV=1.9:B%=0:BY=0:VY=0:CH=32:C%=0:CY=0:FY=0:C2=32:PB=40:CB=40
190   B$=" o + o  "
200   B1$="  * ┐      ":C1$=" ┌ *        "
210   B2$="   │      ":C2$=" │      "
220   B3$="   ┐       ":C3$=" ┌        "
```

```
230   CT$="e ▲ e ▲ e ▲ e ":CW$="e e e e e ":SP$="▲ ▲ ▲
      ▲ ▲ ▲ ▲ ▲ ▲ ▲ ▲ ▲ "
240   COLOR1,9,5:PRINT "▣ ▲ ▲ ▲ ▲ ▲ ▲ ▲ ▲ ▲ ▲ ▲ ▲ ▲ ▲ ▲ ▲ ▲ ▲
      ▲ S I E G E ! ":PRINT "▣ ▣ ▣ ▣ ▣ ▣ ▣ ▣ ▣ P L A Y E
      R ";
250   COLOR1,15,5:PRINT "▲ ▲ ▲ ▲ ▲ ▲ ▲ ▲ ▲ ▲ ▲ ▲ ▲ ▲ ▲ ▲ ▲ ▲ ▲ C
      O M P U T E R ":COLOR1,2,3
260   PRINT "▣ ▣ ▣ ▣ ▣ ▣ ▣ ▣ ▣ ▣ ▣ ▣ ▣ ▣ ";CT$;SP$;"▲ ▲ ";S
      P$;CT$;
270   FOR I=1 TO 6:PRINT CW$;SP$;"e e e e ";SP$;CW$;:
      PRINT :NEXT
280   PRINT ,"▲ ▲ ▲ ▲ ▲ ▲ ▲ ▲ ▲ ▲ ▲ e e ▣ ‖ ‖ e e ▣ ‖ ‖ e e ▣
      ‖ ‖ e e ▣ ‖ ‖ e e ":COLOR1,10,2
290   PRINT "※ ※ ※ ※ ※ ※ ※ ※ ※ ※ ※ ※ ※ ※ ※ ※ ※ ※ ※ ※ ※ ※ ※
      ※ ※ ※ ※ ※ ※ ※ ※ ※ ※ ※ ※ ※ ※ ※ ※ ※ ※ ";:POKE 4071,102:
      POKE 3047,31
300   F$="":F2$="":BX$=B1$:CX$=C1$
```

Get Input

```
310   GETA$
320   COLOR1,10,4:PRINT CD$;CR$;BX$;B$;CD$;CC$;CX$;B$
330   IF A$="I "THEN PX=PX-1:SOUND 2,100,2:CR$=LEFT$(CR$,
      PX):IF PX<1THEN PX=1
340   IF A$="P "THEN PX=PX+1:SOUND 2,100,2:CR$=CR$+"▣ ":
      IF PX>14THEN PX=14:CR$=LEFT$(CR$,14)
350   IF A$="Q "THEN EV=EV+.01:SOUND 2,1000,1:IF EV>2.4
      THEN EV=2.4
360   IF A$="Z "THEN EV=EV-.01:SOUND 2,1000,1:IF EV<1.5
      THEN EV=1.5
370   IF RND(0)<.5THEN 430
380   M=INT(RND(0)*3)-1
390   CX=CX+M:IF CX>15THEN CX=15:M=0
400   IF CX<4THEN CX=4:M=0
410   IF M=1THEN CC$=LEFT$(CC$,36-CX)
420   IF M=-1THEN CC$=CC$+"▣ "
430   IF F$="F I R E D "THEN GOSUB 510
440   IF F2$="F I R E D "THEN GOSUB 610:GOTO 470
```

Fire Computer's Ballista

```
450   F2$="F I R E D ":PRINT CD$;CC$;C2$;B$;CD$;CD$;CC$;C
      3$;B$;:FY=1.5+RND(0)*.24:Y=1
460   SOUND 2,850,1:CX$=C3$:F2=37-CX:GOSUB 620
```

Fire Player's Ballista

```
470   IF A$<>"▲ "ORF$="F I R E D "THEN 310
480   PRINT CD$;CR$;B2$;B$;CD$;CD$;CD$;CR$;B3$;B$;
490   VY=EV*.7071:BY=1:SOUND 3,200,10
500   BX$=B3$:FS=PX+2:F$="F I R E D ":GOSUB 520:GOTO 310
```

Move Player's Rock and Check For Collision

```
510   POKE 3992+FS-INT(BY)*40+B%,CH
520   B%=B%+1:BY=BY+VY:VY=VY-.1
530   CH=PEEK(3992+FS-INT(BY)*40+B%):IF CH=32THEN 590
540   SOUND 1,0,0:SOUND 3,800,10
550   IF CH=42THEN POKE 3992+FS-INT(BY)*40+B%,32:F$="":B%
      =0:BY=0:VY=0:BX$=B1$:GOTO 700
560   IF B%>16ANDCH<>32ANDCH<>102THEN P1=P1+1:COLOR1,3,4:
      PRINT "■ ■ ■ ■ ■ ■ ■ ■ ■ ■ ■ ■ ■ ";P1
570   POKE 3992+FS-INT(BY)*40+B%,32:IF B%>16ANDCH=0
      THEN CB=CB-1
580   IF CB=0THEN SOUND 1,1000,9:PRINT "■ ■ ▲ ▲ ▲ ▲ ▲ ▲ ▲ ▲
       ▲ ▲ ▲ ▲ ▲ ▲ ▲ ▲ ▲ ▲ Y O U ▲ W O N ! ! ! ":GOTO 710
590   IF CH=32ANDB%+FS<40ANDINT(BY)>0THEN POKE 3992+FS-
      INT(BY)*40+B%,42:RETURN
600   F$="":B%=0:BY=0:VY=0:BX$=B1$:RETURN
```

Move Computer's Rock and Check For Collision

```
610   POKE 3992+F2-INT(CY)*40-C%,C2
620   C%=C%+1:CY=CY+FY:FY=FY-.1
630   C2=PEEK(3992+F2-INT(CY)*40-C%):IF C2=32THEN 690
640   SOUND 1,0,0:SOUND 3,900,20
650   IF C2=42THEN POKE 3992+FS-INT(BY)*40+B%,32:F$="":B%
      =0:BY=0:VY=0:BX$=B1$:GOTO 700
660   IF C%>17ANDC2<>32ANDC2<>102THEN P2=P2+1:PRINT "■ ■
      ■ ■ ■ ■ ■ ■ ■ ■ ■ ■ ■ ■ ■ ■ ■ ■ ■ ■ ■ ■ ■ ■ ■ ■ ■
       ■ ■ ■ ■ ■ ";P2
670   POKE 3992+F2-INT(CY)*40-C%,32:IF C%>17ANDC2=0
      THEN PB=PB-1
680   IF PB=0THEN PRINT "■ ■ ▲ ▲ ▲ ▲ ▲ ▲ ▲ ▲ ▲ ▲ ▲ ▲ T H E
      ▲ ■ C O M P U T E R ■ ▲ W O N . . . ":GOTO 710
690   IF C2=32ANDC%-F2<0ANDINT(CY)>0THEN POKE 3992+F2-
      INT(CY)*40-C%,42:RETURN
700   F2$="":C%=0:CY=0:FY=0:CX$=C1$:RETURN
```

End Game

```
710   PRINT "■■■■■■■■      ANOTHER GA
      ME ? "
720   GETA$:IF A$=""THEN 720
730   IF A$="Y "THEN RUN160
740   PRINT "■ ":END
```

ChexSum Tables

Line	Sum	Line	Sum	Line	Sum
10	= 2374	260	= 2126	510	= 2177
20	= 3574	270	= 3028	520	= 2471
30	= 2694	280	= 3522	530	= 3512
40	= 2946	290	= 8556	540	= 1191
50	= 2824	300	= 2230	550	= 6534
60	= 3571	310	= 267	560	= 5001
70	= 2244	320	= 2868	570	= 4406
80	= 2784	330	= 4963	580	= 4037
90	= 2590	340	= 6143	590	= 5127
100	= 3098	350	= 3827	600	= 2659
110	= 2957	360	= 3835	610	= 2106
120	= 2752	370	= 1113	620	= 2457
130	= 3162	380	= 1326	630	= 3426
140	= 1212	390	= 2455	640	= 1191
150	= 1376	400	= 1497	650	= 6510
160	= 1513	410	= 2015	660	= 5810
170	= 2362	420	= 1669	670	= 4350
180	= 6916	430	= 1396	680	= 4119
190	= 1063	440	= 2055	690	= 4913
200	= 3213	450	= 5624	700	= 2711
210	= 2774	460	= 2504	710	= 1784
220	= 3206	470	= 2084	720	= 1216
230	= 3005	480	= 2727	730	= 1096
240	= 3853	490	= 2179	740	= 569
250	= 2898	500	= 3343	TOTAL	= 223686

Hunter

CLASSIFICATION: Evasion COLOUR ILLUSTRATION OBC

You are a wild animal in a maze being pursued by a hunter. You can move yourself around the maze by pressing the keys I, P, Q and Z. No matter where you go in the maze, the hunter will know where you are and seek you out. As you move through the maze you eat munchies. When you have eaten all the munchies, you win. There are four levels.

PROGRAMMING SUGGESTIONS

Add a facility at the hardest level of the game so that the player can 'teleport' to another part of the board. He can't, however, control his destination, so he might land on top of the hunter.

PROGRAM
Variables

F$	Barriers of maze
D$	Munchies
SC	Screen start in memory
CC$	Horizontal position string
RR$	Vertical position string
R	Row position of animal
C	Column position of animal
PO	Current position of animal
T1	Previous position of animal
C1	Column position of hunter
R1	Row position of hunter
PC	Hunter's previous position
P1	Hunter's current position

Listing

```
10    REM HUNTER
20    CLR:COLOR0,8,3:COLOR4,7,3:COLOR1,2,7
30    GOSUB 710
40    GOSUB 850
```

Draw the Border, Maze, Power Pills and Define Variables

```
50    SCNCLR
60    SC=3072:CO=2048:BE=3072+207
70    A$="▣ ▲ ▲ ■ ":B$="▲ ":C$=A$+B$
80    E$="▲ ▲ ● "
90    FOR I=1 TO 40:CC$=CC$+"▣ ":NEXT
100   FOR I=1 TO 25:RR$=RR$+"▣ ":NEXT
110   FOR I=SC TO SC+39:POKE I,160:POKE I+960,160:NEXT
120   FOR I=SC TO SC+999 STEP 40:POKE I,160:POKE I+39,160
      :NEXT
130   PRINT "▣ ";TAB(18);"▣ H U N T E R ";
140   FOR I=1 TO 8:F$=F$+E$:NEXT
150   FOR I=1 TO 10:D$=D$+C$:NEXT:PRINT :PRINT :PRINT :
      PRINT :PRINT
160   FOR I=1 TO 5:PRINT TAB(7);D$:PRINT TAB(7);D$:
      PRINT TAB(7);F$:NEXT
170   PRINT TAB(7);D$:PRINT TAB(7);D$
180   R=2:C=0
190   PO=BE+(R*40)+C:POKE PO,102
200   C1=26:R1=16:P1=BE+(R1*40)+C1:VE=PEEK(P1):POKE P1,86
```

Move Your Piece Up, Down, Left and Right; Move the Hunter

```
210   A=PEEK(198):IF A=62THEN GOSUB 370
220   IF A=12THEN GOSUB 420
230   IF A=33THEN GOSUB 470
240   IF A=41THEN GOSUB 520
250   GOSUB 290
260   IF CN=40THEN GOSUB 640:GOTO 10
270   PRINT "▣ ";LEFT$(RR$,3);LEFT$(CC$,16);"▣ S C O R E
      ▲ ";S1;"■ ";
280   GOTO 210
290   IF SW<>AWTHEN SW=SW+1:RETURN
300   SW=0
310   PC=P1:IF C1<CTHEN C2=C1:C1=C1+1:P1=BE+(R1*40)+C1:
      IF PEEK(P1)=160THEN C1=C2:P1=PC
320   IF C1>CTHEN C2=C1:C1=C1-1:P1=BE+(R1*40)+C1:IF
      PEEK(P1)=160THEN C1=C2:P1=PC
```

```
330   IF R1<RTHEN R2=R1:R1=R1+1:P1=BE+(R1*40)+C1:IF
      PEEK(P1)=160THEN R1=R2:P1=PC
340   IF R1>RTHEN R2=R1:R1=R1-1:P1=BE+(R1*40)+C1:IF
      PEEK(P1)=160THEN R1=R2:P1=PC
350   POKE PC,VE:VE=PEEK(P1):IF VE=102THEN GOSUB 600:
      GOTO 10
360   POKE P1,86:RETURN
370   IF R=0THEN RETURN
380   T1=PO:R=R-1:PO=BE+(R*40)+C:IF PEEK(PO)=160THEN PO
      =T1:R=R+1:RETURN
390   IF PEEK(PO)=13THEN GOSUB 570
400   IF PEEK(PO)=81THEN S1=S1+1:CN=CN+1
410   POKE T1,32:POKE PO,102:RETURN
420   IF R=16THEN RETURN
430   T1=PO:R=R+1:PO=BE+(R*40)+C:IF PEEK(PO)=160THEN PO
      =T1:R=R-1:RETURN
440   IF PEEK(PO)=81THEN S1=S1+1:CN=CN+1
450   IF PEEK(PO)=86THEN GOSUB 570
460   POKE T1,32:POKE PO,102:RETURN
470   IF C=0THEN RETURN
480   T1=PO:C=C-1:PO=BE+(R*40)+C:IF PEEK(PO)=160THEN C=C
      +1:PO=T1:RETURN
490   IF PEEK(PO)=81THEN CN=CN+1:S1=S1+1
500   IF PEEK(PO)=86THEN GOSUB 570
510   POKE T1,32:POKE PO,102:RETURN
520   IF C=28THEN RETURN
530   T1=PO:C=C+1:PO=BE+(R*40)+C:IF PEEK(PO)=160THEN C=C
      -1:PO=T1:RETURN
540   IF PEEK(PO)=81THEN CN=CN+1:S1=S1+1
550   IF PEEK(PO)=86THEN GOSUB 570
560   POKE T1,32:POKE PO,102:RETURN
```

You Ran Into the Hunter; You Won the Game; Print Instructions

```
570   SCNCLR:PRINT "Y O U ▲ R A N ▲ S T R A I G H T ▲ I N
       T O ▲ T H E ▲ H U N T E R ! ! ! ! "
580   PRINT :PRINT :PRINT TAB(13);"Y O U   ▲ A T E ▲ ";CN
      ;"P O W E R ▲ P I L L S "
590   PRINT :PRINT :GOSUB 680:GOTO 10
600   SCNCLR:PRINT "▲ ▲ ▲ Y O U ▲ W E R E ▲ C A P T U R E
       D ▲ B Y ▲ T H E ▲ H U N T E R ! ! ! ! ! ! ":
      PRINT :PRINT
610   PRINT TAB(10);"Y O U ▲ A T E ▲ ";CN;"▲ P O W E R ▲
      P I L L S ":PRINT :PRINT
620   GOSUB 680
630   RETURN
640   SCNCLR
650   PRINT "▙ ";TAB(13)"C O N G R A T U L A T I O N S "
```

```
660   PRINT :PRINT :PRINT :PRINT TAB(5);"Y O U ▲ H A V E
      ▲ C O M P L E T E D ▲ L E V E L : ";TY
670   PRINT :PRINT :GOSUB 680:RETURN
680   PRINT TAB(8);"P R E S S ▲ A N Y ▲ K E Y ▲ T O ▲ C O
       N T I N U E ";:FOR I=1 TO 20:GETA$:NEXT
690   GETA$:IF A$=""THEN 690
700   RETURN
710   SCNCLR:PRINT TAB(16);"▣ H U N T E R "
720   PRINT :PRINT :PRINT "M O V E ▲ A R U N D ▲ T H E ▲
      S C R E E N ▲ F O R ▲ A S ▲ L O N G ▲ A S ":
      PRINT
730   PRINT "P O S S I B L E ▲ W I T H O U T ▲ B E I N G
      ▲ D E S T R O Y E D ▲ B Y ▲ T H E ":PRINT
740   PRINT "H U N T E R . ▲ Y O U ▲ G E T ▲ P O I N T S
      ▲ F O R ▲ E A T I N G ▲ T H E ":PRINT
750   PRINT "P O W E R ▲ P I L L S . W H E N ▲ A L L ▲ A
      R E ▲ G O N E ▲ Y O U ▲ G E T ":PRINT
760   PRINT "A N O T H E R ▲ G A M E , M O V E ▲ Y O U R
      ▲ M A N ▲ W I T H ▲ T H E S E ":PRINT
770   PRINT "K E Y ▲ C O M B I N A T I O N S - ":PRINT
780   PRINT :PRINT
790   PRINT TAB(15);"I ▲ - ▲ L E F T "
800   PRINT TAB(15);"P ▲ - ▲ R I G H T "
810   PRINT TAB(15);"Q ▲ - ▲ U P "
820   PRINT TAB(15);"Z ▲ - ▲ D O W N ":PRINT :PRINT
830   GOSUB 680:COLOR1,2,7
840   RETURN
850   SCNCLR:PRINT "D I F F I C U L T Y ▲ L E V E L ▲ ( 1
       - 4 ) ";
860   GETA$:IF A$<"1 "THEN 860ORA$>"4 "THEN 860
870   TY=VAL(A$):AW=4-TY:RETURN
880   FOR I=1  TO 255:GETKEYA$:POKE 3072,I:NEXT
```

ChexSum Tables

Line		Checksum
10	=	0
20	=	1877
30	=	299
40	=	306
50	=	233
60	=	2185
70	=	1988
80	=	656
90	=	1892
100	=	1942
110	=	2799
120	=	3115
130	=	1374
140	=	1664
150	=	2794
160	=	3016
170	=	1266
180	=	682
190	=	1995
200	=	4078
210	=	1779
220	=	980
230	=	986
240	=	978
250	=	302
260	=	1620
270	=	3012
280	=	526
290	=	2023
300	=	401
310	=	6496
320	=	6003
330	=	6080
340	=	6079
350	=	3206
360	=	648
370	=	761
380	=	5535
390	=	1389
400	=	2636
410	=	1283
420	=	818
430	=	5535
440	=	2636
450	=	1392
460	=	1283
470	=	746
480	=	5439
490	=	2556
500	=	1392
510	=	1283
520	=	810
530	=	5439
540	=	2556
550	=	1392
560	=	1283
570	=	3479
580	=	3170
590	=	1301
600	=	4057
610	=	3192
620	=	306
630	=	143
640	=	233
650	=	2157
660	=	3740
670	=	943
680	=	4171
690	=	1213
700	=	143
710	=	1437
720	=	3957
730	=	3862
740	=	3592
750	=	3579
760	=	3604
770	=	1778
780	=	366
790	=	1147
800	=	1250
810	=	1019
820	=	1597
830	=	867
840	=	143
850	=	2250
860	=	2286
870	=	1804
880	=	2167
TOTAL	=	231234

Chess

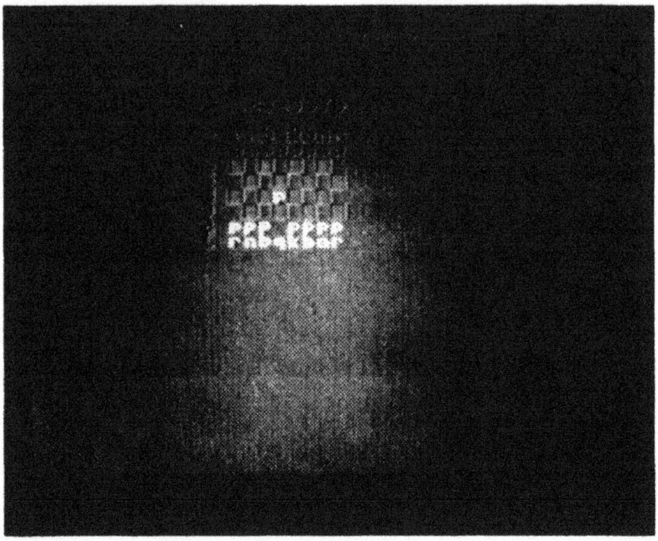

CLASSIFICATION: Logic

This game plays a subset of the standard chess game against you. You move around the screen by entering the starting position and then the destination position in the format (X, Y). The pieces are represented on the screen by the following symbols:

King	K	or	k
Queen	Q	or	q
Rook	R	or	r
Knight	N	or	n
Pawn	P	or	p

You play red from the bottom. When your pawn reaches the top, you must enter the initial of the piece you want to exchange it with, using the same system as above. The computer will tell you when you are in checkmate. If this happens, type 999999 when it is your move. You always go first and the game does not permit castling nor *en passant* moves.

PROGRAMMING SUGGESTIONS

Increase the game's central logic so that it can handle castling and *en passant* moves. Add to the number of pieces that can be fielded by both sides and replace symbols with user-defined characters.

PROGRAM

Variables

B% ( )	Numerical representation of the chess board
D% ( )	Chess board
A$ ( )	Chess in character format
XB, YB	Position of player's next move
X, Y	Position variable
KX, KY	Starting position for Commodore 16
F$	Flag for checkmate

Listing

```
10     REM CHESS
20     COLOR4,10,5:COLOR0,10,5
30     PRINT "♥▮  P L E A S E  W A I T "
40     KX=5:KY=8:DIMB%(8,8),D%(6,8,2),P%(6),A$(6):FOR Y=1
        TO 8:FOR X=1 TO 8
```

Read in Data for Pieces Representation on Board

```
50     B%(X,Y)=0:IF  Y=1 THEN  READ B%(X,Y)
60     IF Y=8THEN B%(X,Y)=-B%(X,1)
70     IF Y=2THEN B%(X,Y)=-1
80     IF Y=7THEN B%(X,Y)=1
90     NEXTX,Y
100    DATA-4,-2,-3,-5,-6,-3,-2,-4
110    FOR X=1 TO 6:P%(X)=2:FOR Y=1 TO 8:IF Y<3ORY=8
       THEN D%(X,Y,2)=1
120    IF Y>1ANDY<5THEN D%(X,Y,1)=1
130    IF Y>5THEN D%(X,Y,1)=-1
140    IF Y>3ANDY<7THEN D%(X,Y,2)=-1
150    NEXTY:IF X<>2THEN 190
160    FOR Y=1 TO 4:READD%(X,Y,1),D%(X,Y,2):D%(X,Y+4,1)=
       -D%(X,Y,1):D%(X,Y+4,2)=D%(X,Y,2)
170    NEXT
180    DATA -2,1,-1,2,1,2,2,1
190    IF X=1THEN P%(X)=8
200    IF X>4THEN P%(X)=1
210    NEXT:FOR  X=1 TO 6:READA$(X):NEXT
220    DATAP,N,B,R,Q,K
230    PRINT "♥ ":GOTO 620
```

Clear All the Variables to Zero and Work Out Next Move

```
240    XB=0:YB=XB:DB=XB:CL=1:BP=XB:X=9:AX=KX:AY=KY:F1$="":
       GOSUB 750:F1$=F$
250    FOR Y=1 TO 8:FOR X=1 TO 8:TB=0:C=1:TY=0:TX=0:D=0
260    IF  B%(X,Y)<1 THEN 600
270    P=B%(X,Y):FOR I=1 TO 8:DY=D%(P,I,2):DX=D%(P,I,1):AX
       =KX:AY=KY:C1=1:PO=0
280    IF X+DX<1ORX+DX>8ORY+DY<1ORY+DY>8THEN 530
290    IF P>2ANDP<6THEN 440
300    IF DY>-1ANDP=1THEN 530
310    IF Y>1ORP>1THEN 360
320    FOR I1=5 TO 1 STEP -1
330    IF P%(I1)<2THEN P%(I1)=P%(I1)+1:B%(X,Y)=I1:I1=1
340    NEXTI1
```

```
350    GOTO 530
360    IF DX<>0ANDB%(X+DX,Y+DY)>-1THEN 530
370    IF P=6THEN KX=X:KY=Y:AX=X+DX:AY=Y+DY:GOSUB 740:
       IF F$="1 "THEN 530
380    IF DX=0ANDB%(X,Y+DY)<>0THEN 530
390    PO=8-P-B%(X+DX,Y+DY)*3
400    IF Y<>7ORDX<>0ORB%(X,5)<>0ORP>1THEN 530
410    IF  F1$="1 " THEN  GOSUB  740:IF F$="" THEN  530
420    IF  F1$="1 " OR RND(1)>.3 THEN  C1=2
430    GOTO 530
440    X1=X:Y1=Y
450    IF P=3ANDINT(I/2)*2<ITHEN 530
460    IF P=4ANDINT(I/2)*2=ITHEN 530
470    IF X1+DX<1ORX1+DX>8ORY1+DY<1ORY1+DY>8THEN C1=C1-1:
       GOTO 530
480    IF B%(X1+DX,Y1+DY)>0THEN C1=C1-1:GOTO 530
490    PO=8-P+INT(RND(1)*3)-B%(X1+DX,Y1+DY)*3
500    IF F1$="1 "THEN GOSUB 740:IF F$=""THEN PO=PO+50:
       GOTO 570
510    IF B%(X1+DX,Y1+DY)<>0THEN 530
520    C1=C1+1:X1=X1+DX:Y1=Y1+DY:GOTO 470
530    IF PO=0THEN 570
540    IF F1$="1 "THEN GOSUB 740:IF F$=""THEN PO=PO+50:
       GOTO 570
550    IF F1$=""THEN GOSUB 740:IF F$="1 "THEN PO=0:GOTO 57
       0
560    IF PO=>TBTHEN AX=X+DX*C1:AY=Y+DY*C1:GOSUB 740:IF F$
       ="1 "THEN PO=PO-P*2
570    IF PO>TBTHEN TB=PO:TX=X:TY=Y:D=I:C=C1
580    NEXTI
590    IF TB>BPORTB=BPAND(RND(1)>.9OR(TY<YBANDRND(1)>.5))
       THEN BP=TB:XB=TX:YB=TY:CL=C:DB=D
600    NEXTX,Y:P=B%(XB,YB):X1=XB+D%(P,DB,1)*CL:Y1=YB+D%(P,
       DB,2)*CL:IF P=6THEN KX=X1:KY=Y1
610    AX=KX:AY=KY:B%(X1,Y1)=B%(XB,YB):B%(XB,YB)=0:Q=1:
       GOSUB 750:Q=0
620    GOSUB 840
```

Check If a Checkmate; If Yes Then Finish Game

```
630    IF  F$="1 " THEN  PRINT "▮C H E C K M A T E ":
       END
640    PRINT "▮▮▮Y O U R ▴ M O V E ":INPUT  "▮F R O M
       ";X,Y:IF  X=999 THEN  END
650    INPUT "▴ ▴ T O ";XB,YB
660    IF B%(XB,YB)>0THEN P%(B%(XB,YB))=P%(B%(XB,YB))-1
670    B%(XB,YB)=B%(X,Y)
680    B%(X,Y)=0
690    IF B%(XB,YB)<-1ORYB<8THEN 720
```

```
700   INPUT "P I E C E S ▴ ";A$:FOR I1=1 TO 5:IF A$(I1)
      =A$ THEN B%(XB,YB)=-I1
710   NEXT
720   GOSUB 840
730   GOTO 240
740   PC=B%(X+DX*C1,Y+DY*C1):B%(X+DX*C1,Y+DY*C1)=B%(X,Y):
      B%(X,Y)=0
750   F$="":FOR P1=1 TO 6:FOR I1=1 TO 8:D1=D%(P1,I1,1):D2
      =D%(P1,I1,2):L=1
760   IF AX+D1*L<1ORAX+D1*L>8ORAY+D2*L<1OR AY+D2*L>8
      THEN 800
770   IF P1=1ANDD2<1ANDQ=0THEN 800
780   IF B%(AX+D1*L,AY+D2*L)=-P1THEN F$="1 ":GOTO 810
790   IF P1>2ANDP1<6ANDB%(AX+D1*L,AY+D2*L)=0THEN L=L+1:
      GOTO 760
800   NEXTI1,P1
810   IF X>8THEN 830
820   B%(X,Y)=B%(X+DX*C1,Y+DY*C1):B%(X+DX*C1,Y+DY*C1)=PC
830   RETURN
```

Print Out Chessboard and the Cartesian Co-ordinates

```
840   PRINT :PRINT :PRINT  :PRINT :PRINT :PRINT :PRINT
850   PRINT "▙ ▣ ▜ ▛ ▴ ▴ ▴ ▴ ▴ ▴ ▴ ▴ ▴ ▴ ▴ ▴ ▴ ▴ ▴ ▴ 1 2 3 4 5
      6 7 8 ▣ ":FOR Y=8 TO 1 STEP -1:PRINT "▴ ▴ ▴ ▴ ▴ ▴ ▴
      ▴ ▴ ▴ ▛ ▜ "Y;
860   FOR X=1 TO 8:IF B%(X,Y)<>0THEN 890
870   IF INT((X+Y)/2)*2=X+YTHENPRINT"▙ ▣ ▴ ▀";:GOTO 920
880   PRINT"▴";:GOTO 920
890   IF B%(X,Y)<0THEN PRINT "▄ ";:GOTO 910
900   PRINT "▚ ";
910   PRINT A$(ABS(B%(X,Y)));
920   NEXT:PRINT :NEXT:RETURN
```

ChexSum Tables

Line	ChexSum	Line	ChexSum	Line	ChexSum
10	= 0	320	= 1110	630	= 1981
20	= 1172	330	= 3514	640	= 3043
30	= 1365	340	= 257	650	= 882
40	= 4458	350	= 532	660	= 3448
50	= 2049	360	= 2848	670	= 1206
60	= 1878	370	= 4816	680	= 671
70	= 1479	380	= 2257	690	= 2079
80	= 1305	390	= 2237	700	= 4088
90	= 361	400	= 3353	710	= 131
100	= 1372	410	= 2092	720	= 306
110	= 4203	420	= 1978	730	= 525
120	= 1954	430	= 532	740	= 5817
130	= 1583	440	= 899	750	= 4715
140	= 2151	450	= 2050	760	= 5120
150	= 1294	460	= 2046	770	= 1908
160	= 6204	470	= 5216	780	= 3753
170	= 131	480	= 3146	790	= 4804
180	= 1003	490	= 3458	800	= 441
190	= 1172	500	= 3394	810	= 808
200	= 1172	510	= 2134	820	= 4966
210	= 1591	520	= 3092	830	= 143
220	= 852	530	= 877	840	= 1449
230	= 988	540	= 3394	850	= 3878
240	= 6086	550	= 2988	860	= 2088
250	= 3667	560	= 5816	870	= [illegible]
260	= 1169	570	= 3297	880	= [illegible]
270	= 6096	580	= 206	890	= 1937
280	= 3803	590	= 7368	900	= 319
290	= 1320	600	= 7424	910	= 1117
300	= 1581	610	= 4899	920	= 746
310	= 1326	620	= 306	TOTAL	= 213926

Mind Quiz

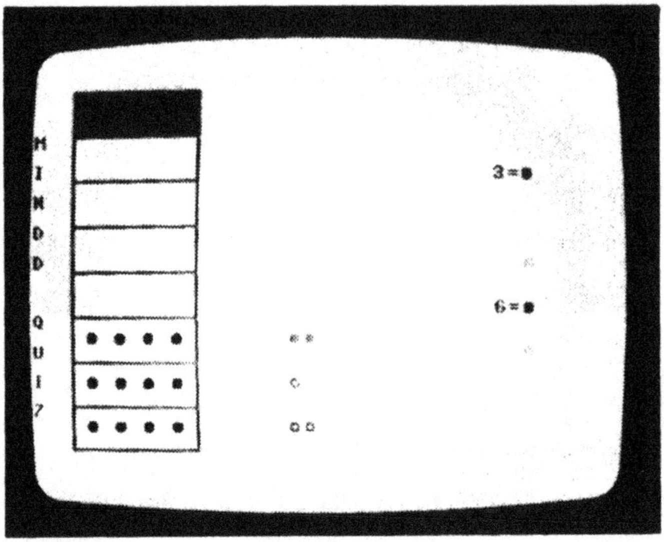

CLASSIFICATION: Logic

The computer or an opponent will generate a sequence of four random numbers in the range of three to eight, represented by the six number keys. You have to guess what the four numbers are by pressing the right sequence of keys. You will get seven chances to guess the numbers. After each guess, the computer will respond by printing a **O** for the right colour in the wrong spot or a ● for the right colour in the right spot.

PROGRAMMING SUGGESTIONS

Add another digit to the number of colours which the player has to guess, giving an extra dimension of complexity.

PROGRAM
Variables

D$	Message 'Instructions Y/N'
A$	Response to input
Y	Flag for end of game and screen position of beads
X	General purpose variable
G$	Response to colour bead input
D%	Array containing random numbers
B%	Array containing input numbers

Listing

```
10    REM MIND QUIZ
20    COLOR4,2,5:COLOR0,2,5:VOL 8:COLOR2,5,6
30    PRINT CHR$(8)CHR$(142):PRINT "■ "
```

Put Border On Screen; Instructions or Play Computer?

```
40    FOR X=3073 TO 3110:POKE X,64:NEXT
50    FOR X=3112 TO 3992 STEP 40:POKE X,93:NEXT
60    FOR X=3151 TO 4031 STEP 40:POKE X,93:NEXT
70    FOR X=4033 TO 4070:POKE X,64:NEXT
80    POKE 3072,85
90    POKE 3111,73:POKE 4032,74:POKE 4071,75
100   PRINT "■ ■ ■ ■ ■ ▲ ▲ ▲ ▲ ▲ ▲ M ▲ ▲ I ▲ ▲ N ▲ ▲ D ▲ ▲
      ▲ ▲ ▲ Q ▲ ▲ U ▲ ▲ I ▲ ▲ Z ▲ ▲ ▲ "
110   DIMA%(4):DIMB%(4):DIMD%(4)
120   D$="▲ ▲ ▲ ▲ ▲ ▲ ▲ ▲ ▲ ▲ ▲ I N S T R U C T I O N S ▲ Y
       / N ▲ ? ▲ ▲ ▲ ▲ ▲ ▲ ▲ ▲ ▲ "
130   PRINT "■ ■ "
140   PRINT "■ ■ ■ ■ ";D$:FOR X=1 TO 79:NEXT
150   D$=D$+LEFT$(D$,1):D$=MID$(D$,2,36)
160   GETA$:IF A$<>"N "ANDA$<>"Y "THEN 140
170   GOSUB  600
180   PRINT "■ ■ "SPC(18)"M ) ▲ P L A Y ▲ M E "CHR$(13)
      SPC(18)"■ S ) ▲ P L A Y ▲ S O M E O N E ▲ E L S E "
190   GETA$:IF A$<>"M "ANDA$<>"S "THEN 190
200   PRINT "■ ■ "SPC(18)"▲ ▲ ▲ ▲ ▲ ▲ ▲ ▲ ▲ ▲ ▲ ▲ "CHR$(13)
      SPC(18)"■ ▲ ▲ ▲ ▲ ▲ ▲ ▲ ▲ ▲ ▲ ▲ ▲ ▲ ▲ ▲ ▲ ▲ ▲ ▲ ▲ ▲ ▲ ▲ ▲ "
210   IF A$="M "THEN GOSUB 790:GOTO 280
220   R=1
230   FOR X=1 TO 4
240   GETA$:IF A$=CHR$(20)ANDX>1THEN X=X-1:R=R-2:POKE 311
      5+R,160
250   IF VAL(A$)<3ORVAL(A$)>8THEN 240
260   A%(X)=VAL(A$):POKE 3115+R,81
270   R=R+2:NEXT
280   GOSUB 770
290   PRINT "■ "SPC(32)"■ ■ ■ ■ ■ ■ 3 = ● ■ ■ ■ ▌ ▌ ▌ ◣ 4
       = ● ■ ■ ■ ▌ ▌ ▌ ■ 5 = ● ■ ■ ■ ▌ ▌ ▌ ■ 6 = ● ■ ■ ■
      ▌ ▌ ▌ ■ 7 = ● ■ ■ ■ ▌ ▌ ▌ ■ 8 = ● ■ "
300   Y=840:R=1
```

Print Your Guess; Make Sound; Input Player's Colour

```
310   PRINT "■ "SPC(25)"Y O U R ▲ G U E S S "
320   SOUND 2,19,19
```

```
330    FOR X=1 TO 350:NEXT
340    PRINT "■ "SPC(25)"▲ ▲ ▲ ▲ ▲ ▲ ▲ ▲ ▲ ▲ ▲ ▲ ▲ ▲ ▲ ▲ ▲ ▲ ▲ "
350    FOR X=1 TO 4:D%(X)=A%(X):NEXT
360    FOR X=1 TO 4
370    GETA$:IF A$=CHR$(20)ANDX>1THEN X=X-1:R=R-2:POKE 311
       5+R+Y,32
380    IF VAL(A$)<3ORVAL(A$)>8THEN 370
390    B%(X)=VAL(A$):POKE 3115+R+Y,81:POKE 2091+R+Y,B%(X)
       -1
400    R=R+2:NEXT
410    FOR X=1 TO 4:IF B%(X)=D%(X)THEN G$=G$+"● ":D%(X)=25
       5:B%(X)=254
420    NEXT
430    IF D%(1)=B%(2)THEN G$=G$+"○ ":D%(1)=255:B%(2)=254
440    IF D%(1)=B%(3)THEN G$=G$+"○ ":D%(1)=255:B%(3)=254
450    IF D%(1)=B%(4)THEN G$=G$+"○ ":D%(1)=255:B%(4)=254
460    IF D%(2)=B%(1)THEN G$=G$+"○ ":D%(2)=255:B%(1)=254
470    IF D%(2)=B%(3)THEN G$=G$+"○ ":D%(2)=255:B%(3)=254
480    IF D%(2)=B%(4)THEN G$=G$+"○ ":D%(2)=255:B%(4)=254
490    IF D%(3)=B%(1)THEN G$=G$+"○ ":D%(3)=255:B%(1)=254
500    IF D%(3)=B%(2)THEN G$=G$+"○ ":D%(3)=255:B%(2)=254
510    IF D%(3)=B%(4)THEN G$=G$+"○ ":D%(3)=255:B%(4)=254
520    IF D%(4)=B%(1)THEN G$=G$+"○ ":D%(4)=255:B%(1)=254
530    IF D%(4)=B%(2)THEN G$=G$+"○ ":D%(4)=255:B%(2)=254
540    IF D%(4)=B%(3)THEN G$=G$+"○ ":D%(4)=255:B%(3)=254
550    PRINT "■ ":FOR X=1 TO ((Y-40)/40):PRINT "■ ";:
       NEXT:PRINT SPC(18)"■ "G$
560    IF G$="● ● ● ● "THEN D$="Y E S ":GOTO 820
570    IF Y=120THEN D$="N O ":GOTO 820
580    Y=Y-120:G$="":R=1
590    GOTO 310
600    IF A$="N "THEN 700
```

Print Instructions; Try Again?

```
610    PRINT "■ ■ ■ ■ ■ ▲ ▲ ▲ ▲ ▲ ▲ ▲ ▲ ▲ ▲ ▲ ▲ ▲ ▲ ▲ ▲ I N S T
       R U C T I O N S ▲ ▲ ▲ ▲ ▲ ▲ ▲ ▲ ▲ ▲ ▲ ▲ ▲ ▲ ▲ ▲ ▲ "
620    PRINT "■ ■ I N ▲ T H I S ▲ G A M E ▲ Y O U ▲ C A N
       ▲ P L A Y ▲ T H E ▲ C O M P U T E R ▲ ▲ ▲ ▲ ▲ ▲ ▲ ▲
        ▲ O R ▲ A ▲ H U M A N ▲ O P P O N E N T "
630    PRINT "■ ▲ Y O U ▲ H A V E ▲ ■ 7 ■ ▲ C H A N C E S
       ▲ T O ▲ C R A C K ▲ T H E ▲ C O D E "
640    PRINT "■ T O ▲ E N T E R ▲ C O L O U R S ▲ U S E ▲
       K E Y S ▲ ▲ ■ 3 ▲ ■ 4 ▲ ■ 5 ▲ ■ 6 ▲ ■ 7 ▲ ■ 8 ■ "
650    PRINT "■ ▲ ▲ ▲ ▲ P R E S S ▲ D E L ▲ I F ▲ Y O U ▲
       M A K E ▲ A ▲ M I S T A K E "
660    PRINT "▲ ▲ ■ ■ ▲ ● ■ ▲ ▲ M E A N S ▲ R I G H T ▲ C
       O L O U R ▲ R I G H T ▲ S P O T "
```

```
670   PRINT "▲▲▲▲▲▲MEANS▲RIGHT▲C
      OLOUR▲WRONG▲SPOT"
680   PRINT "▲▲▲▲▲▲▲▲▲▲▲▲▲▲▲PRESS▲RET
      URN▲TO▲START▲▲▲▲▲▲▲▲▲▲▲▲"
690   GETA$:IF A$<>CHR$(13)THEN 690
700   PRINT "";
710   FOR X=1 TO 8
720   PRINT "▲▲▲▲▲▲▲▲▲▲▲▲▲▲▲▲▲▲▲▲▲
      ▲▲▲▲▲▲▲▲▲▲▲▲▲▲▲▲▲▲▲▲▲▲▲▲▲▲▲▲
      ▲▲▲▲"
730   PRINT "▲▲▲▲▲▲▲▲▲▲▲▲"
740   NEXT
750   PRINT "▲▲▲";
760   PRINT "MIN▲D▲
      QUIZ"
770   FOR X=1 TO 9:FOR Y=0 TO 2:POKE 3074+X+Y*40,160:
      POKE 2069+X+Y*40,14:NEXTY,X
780   RETURN
790   FOR X=1 TO 4
800   FOR Y=1 TO 3:E=RND(1)*5+3:NEXTY
810   A%(X)=E:NEXT:RETURN
820   FOR X=1 TO 4:POKE 3116+C,81:POKE 2092+C,A%(X):C=C
      +2:NEXT
830   PRINT "";:IF D$="NO"THEN PRINT SPC(16)"BAD▲
      LUCK▲IT▲WAS▲THIS"
840   IF D$="YES"THEN PRINT SPC(16)"GOOD▲ON▲Y
      OU▲YOU▲GOT▲IT"
850   PRINT ""SPC(16)"PLAY▲AGAIN▲Y/N▲
      ?"
860   GETA$:IF A$<>"N"ANDA$<>"Y"THEN 860
870   IF A$="N"THEN POKE 0,0:SYS 0
880   RUN
```

ChexSum Tables

10 = 0
20 = 1983
30 = 1439
40 = 1720
50 = 2016
60 = 2016
70 = 1722
80 = 533
90 = 1750
100 = 2294
110 = 1376
120 = 2568
130 = 266
140 = 1693
150 = 2231
160 = 2322
170 = 298
180 = 4416
190 = 2322
200 = 3002
210 = 1684
220 = 312
230 = 670
240 = 4092
250 = 1367
260 = 1761
270 = 770
280 = 303
290 = 7348
300 = 823
310 = 1477
320 = 588
330 = 979
340 = 1398
350 = 1762
360 = 670
370 = 4334
380 = 1968
390 = 3742
400 = 770
410 = 4424
420 = 131
430 = 3439
440 = 3439
450 = 3441
460 = 3439
470 = 3441
480 = 3443
490 = 3439
500 = 3441
510 = 3443
520 = 3441
530 = 3443
540 = 3443
550 = 3301
560 = 2862
570 = 1915
580 = 1542
590 = 526
600 = 938
610 = 2938
620 = 5864
630 = 3494
640 = 3815
650 = 3093
660 = 3447
670 = 3458
680 = 3009
690 = 1711
700 = 435
710 = 678
720 = 4490
730 = 992
740 = 131
750 = 2104
760 = 2940
770 = 5071
780 = 143
790 = 670
800 = 2107
810 = 935
820 = 3572
830 = 3678
840 = 3442
850 = 1979
860 = 2329
870 = 1366
880 = 139
TOTAL = 198346

Penetrator

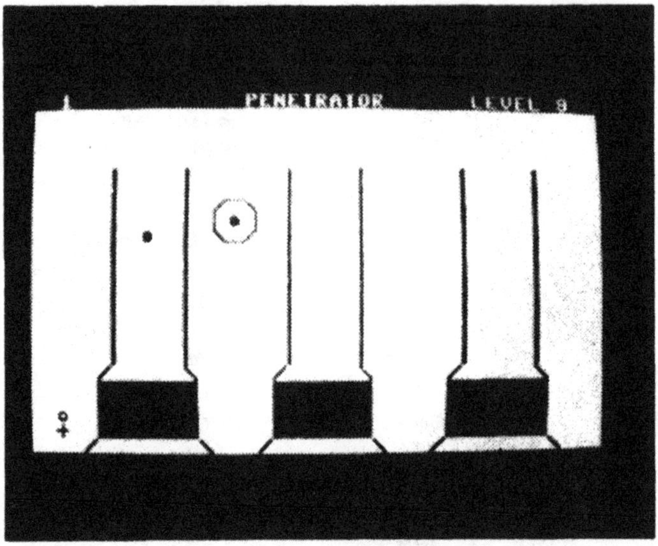

CLASSIFICATION: Shoot Up

You are the pilot of a spaceship which must land and pick up a stranded pilot. In front of your vehicle are three mountains filled with multiplying aliens. You must move your ship up and down with the Q and Z keys to target them, and destroy as many as possible by pressing the SPACE bar.

When the number of aliens gets below five you can land and pick up the pilot — but you must be quick! After picking up the pilot you move onto the next level.

PROGRAMMING SUGGESTIONS

Steadily increase the size of the objects that you must pick up.

Program Variables

S$	Spaceship
T$	Spaceship blanker
D$	Move down a line
B$	Move back a space
BE	Start of screen memory
C	Column position of spaceship
R	Row position of spaceship
PO	Position of multiplying aliens

Listing

```
10    REM PENETRATOR
20    COLOR4,6,3
```

Build the Spaceship, Pilot, Backspace Variable, Column Position

```
30    B$="▌ ":D$="▀ ":S$="/ ▭ \ "+D$+B$+B$+B$+"▯ ▴ ▯ "+D$
      +B$+B$+B$+"\ ▭ / "
40    T$="▴ ▴ ▴ ▴ "+D$+B$+B$+B$+B$+"▴ ▴ ▴ ▴ "+D$+B$+B$+B$
      +B$+"▴ ▴ ▴ ▴ " :BE=3072:GOSUB 570
50    GOSUB 450:G$="▣ ▴ ▴ ▀ ":M$="● "+D$+B$+"+ "
60    V$="▴ "+D$+B$+"▴ ":
70    FOR I=1 TO 40:CC$=CC$+"▐ ":NEXT:FOR I=1 TO 25:RR$
      =RR$+"▀ ":NEXT:POKE 208,12:Q=208
80    C(1)=0:C(2)=12:C(3)=24
90    C1(1)=8:C1(2)=20:C1(3)=32
100   C=C(1):R=3:POKE 202,C:POKE 205,R:PRINT "▴ ";S$;:C1
      =C1(1):E=0:LV=LV-.1
110   FOR I=4032 TO 4032+39:POKE I,160:NEXT
120   PRINT "▣ ";LEFT$(CC$,2);LEFT$(RR$,22);M$;
130   FOR I=1 TO 2 STEP 0
140   A=PEEK(Q):IF A=62THEN GOSUB 330
150   IF A=12THEN GOSUB 350:ELSEIF A=60THEN GOSUB 430
160   IF ETHEN GOTO 190
170   GOSUB 380:SOUND 2,4,4
180   Q=198:NEXT
190   C=C(2):C1=C1(2):E=0:CN=0:R=3
200   PRINT "▣ ";LEFT$(CC$,14);LEFT$(RR$,22);M$;:POKE 400
      4,77:Q=208
210   FOR I=1 TO 2 STEP 0:A=PEEK(Q):IF A=62THEN GOSUB 330
220   POKE 4004,77
230   IF A=12THEN GOSUB 350:ELSEIF A=60THEN GOSUB 430
240   Q=198:IF ETHEN 260
250   GOSUB 380:SOUND 2,4,4:NEXT
260   C=C(3):C1=C1(3):E=0:CN=0:R=3:Q=208
270   PRINT "▣ ";LEFT$(CC$,26);LEFT$(RR$,22);M$;
280   FOR I=1 TO 2 STEP 0:A=PEEK(Q):IF A=62THEN GOSUB 330
290   IF A=12THEN GOSUB 350:ELSEIF A=60THEN GOSUB 430
300   IF ETHEN 100
310   Q=198:GOSUB 380:SOUND 2,4,4:NEXT
320   STOP
330   IF R=1THEN RETURN
340   POKE 202,C:POKE 205,R:PRINT T$;:R=R-1:POKE 205,R:
      POKE 202,C:PRINT "▴ "S$;:RETURN
350   IF R=18THEN IF CN<=5THEN GOSUB 610
360   IF R=18THEN RETURN
```

```
370    POKE 202,C:POKE 205,R:PRINT T$;:R=R+1:POKE 205,R:
       POKE 202,C:PRINT "▲ ";S$;:RETURN
380    N=5+INT(RND(1)*LV*10):IF N<5THEN 380
```

Scan the Keyboard; Move Ship Up or Down

```
390    IF N>18THEN RETURN
400    PO=BE+(N*40)+C1:IF PEEK(PO)=32THEN POKE PO,81:CN=CN
       +1:GOSUB 420:SOUND 1,5,5:RETURN
410    RETURN
420    POKE 205,0:POKE 202,0:PRINT "▲ ";:PRINT USING"▣ # #
       ■ ";CN;:RETURN
430    PE=BE+(R*40)+C1:IF PEEK(PE)=81THEN POKE PE,32:CN=CN
       -1:RETURN
440    RETURN
```

Print the Three Mountains; Set the Difficulty Level

```
450    PRINT "▣ ";
460    PRINT "▲▲▲▲▲▲▲▲▲▲▲▲▲▲▲▲▲▲▣P E N E T R A
       T O R■▲▲▲▣S C O R E■▲▲▲▲▲▲▲▲"
470    PRINT :PRINT :PRINT
480    PRINT
490    FOR HU=1 TO 13:PRINT "▲▲▲▲▲▲▲▲□▲▲▲▲▲□▲▲▲
       ▲▲▲□▲▲▲▲▲□▲▲▲▲▲▲▲▲□▲▲▲▲▲□ ":NEXT
500    PRINT "▲▲▲▲▲▲/▲▲▲▲▲▲▲\▲▲▲▲▲▲▲/▲▲▲▲▲
       ▲\▲▲▲▲▲▲▲/▲▲▲▲▲▲▲\ "
510    PRINT "▲▲▲▲▲▲▣▲▲▲▲▲▲▲▲▲▲■▲▲▲▲▲▲▲▣▲▲
       ▲▲▲▲▲▲■▲▲▲▲▲▲▲▣▲▲▲▲▲▲▲▲▲▲■ "
520    PRINT "▲▲▲▲▲▲▣▲▲▲▲▲▲▲▲▲▲■▲▲▲▲▲▲▲▣▲▲
       ▲▲▲▲▲▲■▲▲▲▲▲▲▲▣▲▲▲▲▲▲▲▲▲▲■ "
530    PRINT "▲▲▲▲▲▲▣▲▲▲▲▲▲▲▲▲▲■▲▲▲▲▲▲▲▣▲▲
       ▲▲▲▲▲▲■▲▲▲▲▲▲▲▣▲▲▲▲▲▲▲▲▲▲■ "
540    PRINT "▲▲▲▲▲▲▣▲▲▲▲▲▲▲▲▲▲■▲▲▲▲▲▲▲▣▲▲
       ▲▲▲▲▲▲■▲▲▲▲▲▲▲▣▲▲▲▲▲▲▲▲▲▲■ "
550    PRINT "▲▲▲▲▲/▲▲▲▲▲▲▲▲▲▲\▲▲▲▲/▲▲▲▲▲▲
       ▲▲\▲▲▲▲/▲▲▲▲▲▲▲▲▲\ "
560    RETURN
570    SCNCLR:PRINT "D I F F I C U L T Y▲L E V E L▲1 -
       H A R D E S T▲9 - E A S I E S T ";
580    GETWE$:IF WE$=""THEN 580
590    IF WE$<"1 "ORWE$>"9 "THEN 580
600    LV=VAL(WE$):RETURN
610    REM
620    IF C1=8THEN PRINT "▣ ";LEFT$(CC$,2);LEFT$(RR$,22);V
       $;
630    IF C1=20THEN POKE 3966,32:POKE 4006,32
```

```
640   IF C1=32THEN PRINT "🅂 ";LEFT$(CC$,26);LEFT$(RR$,22)
      ;V$;
650   PRINT "🅂 ";LEFT$(CC$,10);LEFT$(RR$,2);"P I L O T ▲
      R E S C U E D ";
660   FOR HJ=1 TO 999:NEXT
670   PRINT "🅂 ";LEFT$(CC$,10);LEFT$(RR$,2);"▲ ▲ ▲ ▲ ▲ ▲
      ▲ ▲ ▲ ▲ ▲ ▲ ▲ ";
680   SC=SC+100
690   PRINT "🅂 ";LEFT$(CC$,33);LEFT$(RR$,0);"🅁 ";:
      PRINT USING"# # # # ";SC;:PRINT "▀ ";
700   VE=1:FOR I=1 TO 3
710   PRINT "🅂 ";LEFT$(CC$,VE);LEFT$(RR$,R);T$;:CN=0:E=1:
      VE=VE+12
720   NEXT
730   FOR BV=5 TO 18:DF=BE+(BV*40)+C1:POKE DF,32:NEXT
740   RETURN
```

ChexSum Tables

```
10    =    0          260   = 2889          510   = 2461
20    =  486          270   = 2035          520   = 2461
30    = 6464          280   = 2702          530   = 2461
40    = 6083          290   = 2280          540   = 2461
50    = 2946          300   =  537          550   = 2958
60    = 1379          310   = 1582          560   =  143
70    = 5178          320   =  145          570   = 3635
80    = 1639          330   =  762          580   = 1394
90    = 1819          340   = 4005          590   = 1751
100   = 4726          350   = 1892          600   = 1028
110   = 2053          360   =  824          610   =    0
120   = 1961          370   = 4065          620   = 2706
130   =  886          380   = 2634          630   = 1884
140   = 1681          390   =  820          640   = 2847
150   = 2280          400   = 5336          650   = 3193
160   =  923          410   =  143          660   = 1053
170   =  857          420   = 2771          670   = 2527
180   =  629          430   = 4286          680   =  829
190   = 2382          440   =  143          690   = 3606
200   = 3168          450   =  435          700   = 1143
210   = 2702          460   = 3136          710   = 3944
220   =  525          470   =  585          720   =  131
230   = 2280          480   =  153          730   = 3256
240   = 1070          490   = 3879          740   =  143
250   = 1062          500   = 2961          TOTAL = 154194
```

Dragon's Lair

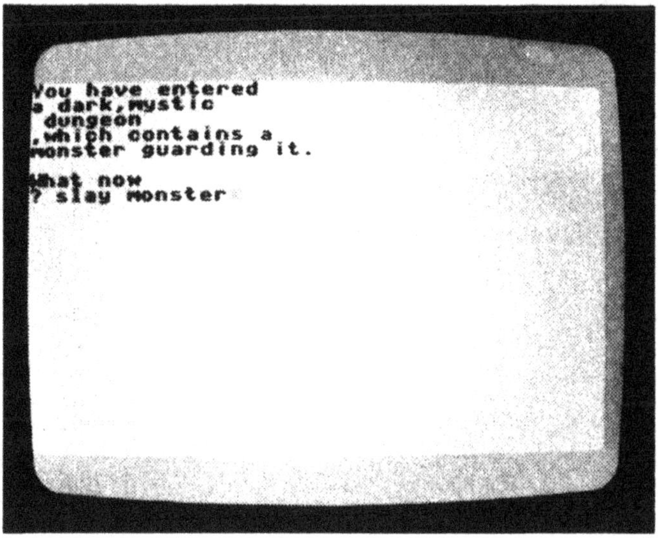

CLASSIFICATION: Adventure

Move through the Dragon's Lair in search of treasure but be careful, a fire breathing nasty is wandering around this place and he isn't too fussy about what or who he eats. You have a number of commands to move to move through this world. They are:

COMMAND	FUNCTION
go left	Move left one location
go right	Move right one location
go forward	Move forward one location
pick-up 'object'	Pick up given object
examine 'object'	Tells you the name of the object
drop 'object'	You guessed it!!
recover treasure	Adds treasure to your hoards
slay monster	Only if you have a weapon
spell monster	Only if you have a magic staff
gaze-into palantir	Reveals important information

PROGRAM
Variables

O%	Number of weapons
O$	Weapons
PO	Strength
TR	Treasure
D	Place
C	Object
N$, V$	Input instructions
P	Flag number of words input

Listing

```
10    COLOR4,8,3: COLOR0,13,3:PRINT CHR$(14)
20    PO=15:DIMO%(3),O$(3):TR=0
```

Read in Objects; Generate a Random Environment

```
30    FOR I=0 TO 3:READO$(I):NEXT
40    DATASWORD,STAFF,PALANTIR,TALISMAN
50    O%(INT(RND(1)*2))=1
60    PRINT "█▙▐O U ▲ H A V E ▲ E N T E R E D ":
      PRINT "A ▲ ";
70    D=INT(RND(1)*4):IF D=0THEN PRINT "█N ▲ E V I L ▲ S
       M E L L I N G "
80    IF D=1THEN PRINT "H O M E L Y "
90    IF D=2THEN PRINT "D A N K ▲ A N D ▲ W E T "
100   IF D=3THEN PRINT "D A R K , M Y S T I C "
110   D=INT(RND(1)*4+1):IF D=1THEN PRINT "▲ B A R N "
120   IF D=2THEN PRINT "▲ D U N G E O N "
130   IF D=3THEN PRINT "▲ C A S T L E "
140   IF D=4THEN PRINT "▲ T O W E R "
150   C=INT(RND(1)*6):PRINT ", W H I C H ▲ C O N T A I N
      S ▲ A ":C1=C
160   IF C=0THEN PRINT "M Y S T E R I O U S ▲ O B J E C T
       . ":O=INT(RND(1)*4)
170   IF C=1THEN PRINT "B O O K ▲ O F ▲ S P E L L S . "
180   IF C=2THEN PRINT "H O R D E ▲ O F ▲ T R E A S U R E
       . "
190   IF C=3THEN PRINT "S M A L L ▲ A N I M A L ▲ R U M A
       G I N G ▲ I N ▲ T H E ▲ C O R N E R . "
200   IF C=4THEN PRINT "M O N S T E R ▲ G U A R D I N G ▲
       I T . "
210   IF C=5THEN PRINT "D R A G O N ▲ B L O C K I N G ▲ Y
       O U R ▲ W A Y . "
220   IF C<3ANDRND(1)>.6THEN PRINT "▐ H E R E ▲ I S ▲ A L
       S O ▲ A ▲ ▲ ▲ ▲ ▲ ▲ ▲ M O N S T E R . ":C1=3
230   IF PO<1THEN PRINT "◣▐ H O U ▲ A R T ▲ S L A I N █
      ":GOTO 1010
240   IF PO<15THEN PO=PO+O%(3)
250   FOR I=0 TO 3:IF RND(1)>.9THEN PO=PO-O%(I)
260   NEXT
```

Input a Response From Player; Check What He Did and Counter

```
270   PRINT :PRINT "● H A T ▲ N O W ":INPUT A$
280   V$="":N$="":P=1:FOR I=1 TO LEN(A$)
```

```
290   IF MID$(A$,I,1)="▲ "THEN P=2:GOTO 320
300   IF P=1THEN V$=V$+MID$(A$,I,1)
310   IF P=2THEN N$=N$+MID$(A$,I,1)
320   NEXTI
330   PRINT "▙ "V$"▲ "N$"▣ "
340   IF V$="S L A Y "THEN 560
350   IF V$="G O "THEN 620
360   IF V$="P I C K - U P "THEN 650
370   IF V$="E X A M I N E "THEN 680
380   IF V$="D R O P "THEN 720
390   IF V$="G A Z E - I N T O "THEN 750
400   IF V$="S P E L L "THEN 830
410   IF V$="R E C O V E R "THEN 920
420   IF V$="R E A D "THEN 970
430   IF V$="I N V E N T O R Y "THEN 1010
440   PRINT "▚ ▒ ▲ D O N ' T ▲ U N D E R S T A N D . ▣ ":
      GOTO 230
450   IF C>3ANDRND(1)>.7THEN C1=C1+1
460   FOR I=1 TO 750:NEXT
```

Print the Countering Message From the Computer

```
470   IF C1=1ANDRND(1)>.9THEN PRINT "▌ H E ▲ R O O F ▲ F
      A L L S ▲ I N ! ":PO=PO-2:GOTO 230
480   IF C1=2ANDRND(1)>.9THEN PRINT "▌ O U ▲ F E L L ▲ D
      O W N ▲ A ▲ P I T ▲ I N ▲ T H E ▲ F L O O R . ":PO
      =PO-3:GOTO 230
490   IF C1=3THEN PRINT "▌ H E ▲ A N I M A L ▲ K E E P S
      ▲ I T S ▲ ▲ D I S T A N C E . "
500   IF C1=4ANDRND(1)>.6THEN PRINT "▌ H E ▲ M O N S T E
      R ▲ A D V A N C E S . "
510   IF C1>5THEN C1=5
520   IF C1<5ORRND(1)<.7THEN 230
530   IF RND(1)>.7THEN PRINT "▌ E ▲ K I L L S ▲ Y O U ! "
      :PO=0:GOTO 1010
540   GOTO 230
550   PRINT "▌ H E ▲ M O N S T E R ▲ A T T A C K S ▲ ▲ ▲
      Y O U . ":PO=PO-INT(RND(1)*4)
560   IF C1<3THEN PRINT "▌ H E R E ▲ I S ▲ N O ▲ M O N S
      T E R . ":GOTO 450
570   IF O%(0)=0THEN PRINT "▣ ▌ O U ▲ H A V E ▲ N O ▲ W E
       A P O N S ! ▣ ":GOTO 450
580   PO=PO-INT(RND(1)*3)
590   IF C=5ANDRND(1)>.6THEN PRINT "▌ H E ▲ D R A G O N ▲
       L I V E S . ":GOTO 450
600   PRINT "▌ H E ▲ B E A S T ▲ I S ▲ D E A D . ":C1=0
610   GOTO 450
```

```
620   IF C1>2ANDRND(1)<C1/7THEN PRINT "▌▒ H E ▲ M O N S T
      E R ▲ W O N ' T ▲ L E T ▲ Y O U . "‡GOTO 450
630   IF N$<>"L E F T "ANDN$<>"R I G H T "ANDN$<>"F O R W
       A R D S "THEN 390
640   PRINT "┏ K "‡GOTO 60
650   IF N$<>O$(O)THEN PRINT "▌▒ H E R E ▲ I S ▲ N O ▲ "N$
      ‡GOTO 450
660   O%(O)=O%(O)+1‡PRINT "┏ K "
670   GOTO 450
680   IF C1>3THEN PRINT "▌▒ H I S ▲ A N G E R S ▲ T H E ▲
      B E A S T . "‡C1=C1+1‡GOTO 460
690   IF C>0THEN PRINT "▌▒ H E R E ▲ I S ▲ N O T H I N G ▲
       T O ▲ ▲ ▲ E X A M I N E . "‡GOTO 450
700   PRINT "▌▒ H E ▲ O B J E C T ▲ T U R N S ▲ O U T ▲ ▲
      T O ▲ B E ▲ A ▲ "O$(O)". "
710   GOTO 450
720   FOR I=0 TO 3‡IF N$=O$(I)ANDO%(I)=0THEN PRINT "▒▌ O U
       ▲ D O N ' T ▲ H A V E ▲ A ▲ "N$‡GOTO 450
730   IF N$=O$(I)THEN O%(I)=O%(I)-1‡O=I‡PRINT "┏ K "
740   NEXT‡GOTO 450
750   IF N$<>"┓ A L A N T I R "THEN PRINT "▒▌ O U ▲ C A N
      ' T ▲ G A Z E ▲ A T ▲ T H A T . "‡GOTO 450


760   IF O%(2)=0THEN PRINT "▒▌ O U ▲ D O N ' T ▲ H A V E ▲
       A ▲ ▲ ▲ ▲ ▲ ▲ ▲ ┓ A L A N T I R . "‡GOTO 450
770   IF RND(1)>.3THEN 810
780   IF RND(1)>.5THEN PRINT "▌▒ H E ▲ G L O B E ▲ R E M A
       I N S ▲ B L A N K . "‡GOTO 450
790   IF RND(1)>.5THEN PRINT   "▒▌ O U ▲ F I N D ▲ A ▲ M O
       N S T E R ▲ L U R K I N G ▲ I N ▲ T H E ▲ S H A D
      O W S . "‡C1=3‡GOTO 490
800   PRINT "▒▌ O U ▲ S E E ▲ A ▲ G
      T R E A S U R E ▲ I N ▲ Y O U R ▲ ▲ ▲ ▲ ▲ ▲ ▒ O U R
       N E Y S . "‡GOTO 230
810   PRINT "▒▌ O U ▲ F E E L ▲ W E A K E R . "
820   PO=PO-1‡GOTO 450
830   IF O%(1)=0THEN PRINT "▒▌ O U ▲ H A V E N ' T ▲ T H E
       ▲ M E A N S ▲ T O ▲ C A S T ▲ S P E L L S . "‡
      GOTO 230
840   IF N$<>"M O N S T E R "THEN PRINT "▒▌ O U ▲ C A N '
      T ▲ S P E L L ▲ T H A T . "‡GOTO 450
850   IF C1<3THEN PRINT "▌▒ H E R E ▲ I S ▲ N O ▲ M O N S
      T E R . "‡GOTO 230
860   IF RND(1)<.8THEN 890
870   PRINT "▒▌ O U R ▲ S P E L L ▲ F A I L E D . "‡
      PRINT "▒ T ▲ H A S ▲ A N G E R E D ▲ T H E ▲ ▲ ▲ ▲
      B E A S T . "‡‡C1=C1+1‡GOTO 460
880   GOTO 450
890   PRINT "▌▒ H E ▲ S P E L L ▲ W O R K E D . "‡C1=0
```

```
900   IF RND(1)>.6THEN PRINT "▌U T ▲ Y O U R ▲ S T A F F
       ▲ S N A P P E D ▲ W I T H ▲ T H E ▲ S T R A I N .
      "‡O%(1)=O%(1)-1
910   GOTO 230
920   IF C<>2THEN PRINT "▌H E R E ▲ I S ▲ N O T H I N G
      ▲ T O ▲ ▲ ▲ R E C O V E R . "‡GOTO 450
930   IF N$<>"T R E A S U R E "THEN PRINT "T H A T ▲ C A
      N N O T ▲ B E ▲ ▲ ▲ ▲ ▲ ▲ ▲ ▲ ▲ R E C O V E R E D . "
      ‡GOTO 400
940   IF C1>2ANDRND(1)>.3THEN PRINT "▌H E ▲ M O N S T E
      R ▲ W O N ' T ▲ L E T ▲ Y O U . "‡C1=C1+1‡GOTO 460
950   TR=TR+INT(RND(1)*101)+100
960   PRINT "T K "‡‡GOTO 230
970   IF C<>1THEN PRINT "▌H E R E ▲ I S ▲ N O ▲ B O O K
      . "‡GOTO 450
980   IF N$<>"B O O K "THEN 440
990   PRINT "▌O U ▲ F E E L ▲ F A I N T "‡PO=PO-2
1000  GOTO 230
1010  PRINT "▌O U ▲ H A V E "PO"S T R E N G T H "
1020  PRINT "▌O U ▲ H A V E "TR"S I L V E R "‡PRINT "C O
       I N S . "
1030  PRINT "▌O U ▲ H A V E "‡FOR I=0 TO 3‡PRINT O%(I)O$
      (I);
1040  IF O%(I)<>1THEN PRINT "S ";
1050  PRINT ‡NEXT
1060  IF PO>0THEN 450
```

ChexSum Tables

Line		Sum	Line		Sum	Line		Sum
10	=	1780	370	=	1422	730	=	3023
20	=	1716	380	=	1215	740	=	719
30	=	1356	390	=	1557	750	=	4675
40	=	2545	400	=	1296	760	=	4486
50	=	1299	410	=	1447	770	=	1108
60	=	2332	420	=	1195	780	=	3984
70	=	3567	430	=	1688	790	=	6524
80	=	1330	440	=	2648	800	=	5475
90	=	1750	450	=	2117	810	=	1565
100	=	1740	460	=	964	820	=	1352
110	=	2707	470	=	4932	830	=	5169
120	=	1462	480	=	6515	840	=	4313
130	=	1384	490	=	3676	850	=	3286
140	=	1330	500	=	3729	860	=	1105
150	=	3315	510	=	1036	870	=	6537
160	=	3558	520	=	1640	880	=	530
170	=	2000	530	=	3509	890	=	2134
180	=	2266	540	=	528	900	=	6245
190	=	3964	550	=	4076	910	=	528
200	=	2497	560	=	3292	920	=	4353
210	=	2894	570	=	3541	930	=	5121
220	=	4637	580	=	1516	940	=	5629
230	=	3113	590	=	3832	950	=	1994
240	=	1748	600	=	2162	960	=	1190
250	=	2759	610	=	530	970	=	3163
260	=	131	620	=	5091	980	=	1366
270	=	1539	630	=	4264	990	=	2248
280	=	2440	640	=	1074	1000	=	528
290	=	2196	650	=	3212	1010	=	1959
300	=	1943	660	=	1625	1020	=	2671
310	=	1920	670	=	530	1030	=	2742
320	=	206	680	=	4255	1040	=	1430
330	=	867	690	=	4132	1050	=	342
340	=	1216	700	=	3119	1060	=	874
350	=	1033	710	=	530	TOTAL	=	310526
360	=	1421	720	=	5160			

Crash Barrier

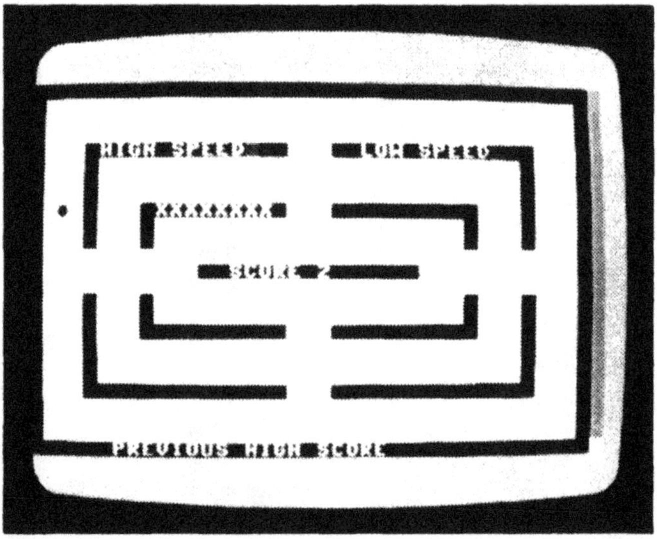

CLASSIFICATION: Evasion COLOUR ILLUSTRATION OBC

Test your skills as a high speed driver. Race around the track swapping lanes whenever you feel like it. Use the I, P, Q and Z keys to move the car around the race track. The longer you can move around the track, the more points you score. Periodically a barrier will appear between the lanes and you will have to swerve to avoid it. The longer you survive, the more frequently crash barriers appear.

PROGRAMMING SUGGESTIONS

Adding a gear stick to the controls of the game would give players more choice of play. Also throw obstacles such as mud slicks into the outer lanes to make the driver's life even more torturous.

PROGRAM
Variables

SC	Start of screen memory
CO	Start of color memory
PO	Car's position on screen
E	Flag to indicate end of game
R	Row position of car
C	Column position of car
QL	Number of barrier to erect (1-17)
R1	Row vector of barrier
C1	Column vector of barrier
PT	Position on screen of barrier
FL	Random flag to place barrier on screen

Listing

Scan Keyboard, Move the Car

```
10     REM CRASH BARRIER
20     DZ$="▣ ":FOR I=1 TO 12:DZ$=DZ$+"▣ ":NEXT
30     FOR I=1 TO 19:DZ$=DZ$+"▣ ":NEXT
40     COLOR4,7,6:COLOR0,2,6:COLOR1,6,2:GOSUB 740:VOL 8
50     DIM C1(25),D1(25),R1(25)
60     FOR I=1 TO 18:READC1(I),R1(I),D1(I):NEXT
70     OA=0:PRINT "▣ ";:GOSUB 430
80     COLOR4,7,5:COLOR0,2,7:COLOR1,6,2:SC=3072:CO=2048:C
       =2:R=2:D=2:E=0:GOSUB 370
90     PRINT "▣ ":POKE PO,81:POKE CC,6
100    A=PEEK(198):IF A=64THEN GOSUB 380
110    IF A=62THEN GOSUB 180:D=1
120    IF A=12THEN GOSUB 200:D=2
130    IF A=33THEN GOSUB 220:D=4
140    IF A=41THEN GOSUB 240:D=8
150    FL=INT(RND(1)*3):IF FL=1THEN GOSUB 260:IF E=1
       THEN GOSUB 350:GOTO 70
160    IF E=1THEN GOSUB 350:GOTO 70
170    SL=SL+.25:PRINT DZ$;"▣ ■ ";INT(SL);"■ ";:GOTO 100
180    POKE PO,32:POKE CC,2:R=R-1:GOSUB 370:IF PEEK(PO)>
       =128THEN E=1:RETURN
190    POKE CC,6:POKE PO,81:RETURN
200    POKE PO,32:POKE CC,2:R=R+1:GOSUB 370:IF PEEK(PO)>
       =128THEN E=1:RETURN
210    POKE CC,6:POKE PO,81:RETURN
220    POKE PO,32:POKE CC,2:C=C-1:GOSUB 370:IF PEEK(PO)>
       =128THEN E=1:RETURN
230    POKE CC,6:POKE PO,81:RETURN
240    POKE PO,32:POKE CC,2:C=C+1:GOSUB 370:IF PEEK(PO)>
       =128THEN E=1:RETURN
250    POKE CC,6:POKE PO,81:RETURN
```

Erect a Barrier Between Two Walls; Check for Collision

```
260    IF OA=1GOTO 320
270    QL=INT(RND(1)*21)
280    R1=R1(QL):C1=C1(QL):D1=D1(QL)
290    ON D1GOTO 300,310:RETURN
300    R1=R1+1:PT=3072+(R1*40)+C1:FOR J=PT TO PT+80
        STEP 40:POKE J,160:NEXT:OA=1:RETURN
310    C1=C1+1:PT=3072+(R1*40)+C1:FOR J=PT TO PT+2:POKE J,
       160:NEXT:OA=1:RETURN
```

```
320    ON D1GOTO 330,340:RETURN
330    FOR J=PT TO PT+80 STEP 40:POKE J,32:NEXT:OA=0:
       RETURN
340    FOR J=PT TO PT+2:POKE J,32:NEXT:OA=0:RETURN
350    FOR I=1 TO 16:FOR J=1 TO 99:NEXT:COLOR4,I,5:
       SOUND 1,17,8:SOUND 2,8,4:NEXT
360    RETURN
370    PO=3072+(R*40)+C:CC=2048+(R*40)+C:RETURN
380    IF D=1THEN A=62:RETURN
390    IF D=2THEN A=12:RETURN
400    IF D=4THEN A=33:RETURN
410    IF D=8THEN A=41:RETURN
420    RETURN
430    REM
```

Draw the Race Track and Instructions For Game; Data for Barriers

```
440    PRINT "◙ ■ ";
450    PRINT "◙ ▲ ▲ ▲ ▲ ▲ ▲ ▲ ▲ ▲ ▲ ▲ ▲ ▲ ▲ ▲ ▲ ▲ ▲ ▲ ▲ ▲
       ▲ ▲ ▲ ▲ ▲ ▲ ▲ ▲ ▲ ▲ ▲ ▲ ▲ ▲ ▲ ▲ ▲ ▲ ◘ ▲ ▬ ";
460    PRINT "◙ ■ ▲ ▬ ▲ ▲ ▲ ▲ ▲ ▲ ▲ ▲ ▲ ▲ ▲ ▲ ▲ ▲ ▲ ▲ ▲ ▲
       ▲ ▲ ▲ ▲ ▲ ▲ ▲ ▲ ▲ ▲ ▲ ▲ ▲ ▲ ▲ ▲ ▲ ▲ ▲ ◙ ▲ ◘ ▲ ▬ ";
470    PRINT "◙ ■ ▲ ▬ ▲ ▲ ▲ ▲ ▲ ▲ ▲ ▲ ▲ ▲ ▲ ▲ ▲ ▲ ▲ ▲ ▲ ▲
       ▲ ▲ ▲ ▲ ▲ ▲ ▲ ▲ ▲ ▲ ▲ ▲ ▲ ▲ ▲ ▲ ▲ ▲ ▲ ◙ ■ ▲ ◘ ▲ ▬ "
       ;
480    PRINT "◙ ■ ▲ ▬ ▲ ▲ ▲ ▲ ▲ ▲ ▲ ▲ ▲ ▲ ▲ ▲ ▲ ▲ ▲ ▲ ▲ ▲
       ▲ ▲ ▲ ▲ ▲ ▲ ▲ ▲ ▲ ▲ ▲ ▲ ▲ ▲ ▲ ▲ ▲ ▲ ▲ ◙ ▲ ◘ ▲ ▬ ";
490    PRINT "◙ ■ ▲ ▬ ▲ ▲ ▲ ◙ ■ ▲ H I G H ▲ S P E E D ◙ ▲
       ■ ▲ ▲ ▬ ▲ ▲ ▲ ◙ ■ ▲ ▲ L O W ▲ S P E E D ◙ ▲ ■ ▲ ▲ ▬
       ▲ ▲ ▲ ◙ ■ ▲ ◘ ▲ ▬ ";
500    PRINT "◙ ■ ▲ ▬ ▲ ▲ ▲ ◙ ▲ ▬ ▲ ▲ ▲ ▲ ▲ ▲ ▲ ▲ ▲ ▲ ▲ ▲
       ▲ ▲ ▲ ▲ ▲ ▲ ▲ ▲ ▲ ▲ ▲ ▲ ▲ ▲ ▲ ◙ ▲ ▬ ▲ ▲ ▲ ◙ ▲ ◘
        ▲ ▬ ";
510    PRINT "◙ ■ ▲ ▬ ▲ ▲ ▲ ◙ ■ ▲ ▬ ▲ ▲ ▲ ▲ ▲ ▲ ▲ ▲ ▲ ▲ ▲
       ▲ ▲ ▲ ▲ ▲ ▲ ▲ ▲ ▲ ▲ ▲ ▲ ▲ ▲ ▲ ▲ ▲   ◙ ■ ▲ ▬ ▲ ▲ ▲ ◙
        ■ ▲ ◘ ▲ ▬ ";
520    PRINT "◙ ■ ▲ ▬ ▲ ▲ ▲ ◙ ▲ ▬ ▲ ▲ ▲ ▲ ▲ ▲ ▲ ▲ ▲ ▲ ▲ ▲
       ▲ ▲ ▲ ▲ ▲ ▲ ▲ ▲ ▲ ▲ ▲ ▲ ▲ ▲ ▲ ◙ ▲ ▬ ▲ ▲ ▲ ◙ ▲ ◘
        ▲ ▬ ";
530    PRINT "◙ ■ ▲ ▬ ▲ ◩ ▲ ▲ ◙ ■ ▲ ▬ ▲ ◩ ▲ ▲ ◙ ■ ▲ X X X
       X X X X X ▲ ▬ ▲ ▲ ▲ ◙ ▲ ▲ ▲ ▲ ▲ ▲ ▲ ▲ ▲ ▲ ▲ ▬ ▲ ◩ ▲ ▲
        ◙ ■ ▲ ▬ ▲ ◩ ▲ ▲ ◙ ■ ▲ ◘ ▲ ▬ ";
540    PRINT "◙ ■ ▲ ▬ ▲ ▲ ▲ ◙ ▲ ▬ ▲ ▲ ▲ ◙ ▲ ▬ ▲ ▲ ▲ ▲ ▲ ▲
       ▲ ▲ ▲ ▲ ▲ ▲ ▲ ▲ ▲ ▲ ▲ ▲ ▲ ▲ ▲ ◙ ▲ ▬ ▲ ▲ ▲ ◙ ▲ ▬ ▲ ▲
        ▲ ◙ ▲ ◘ ▲ ▬ ";
550    PRINT "◙ ■ ▲ ▬ ▲ ◩ ▲ ▲ ◙ ■ ▲ ▬ ▲ ◩ ▲ ▲ ◙ ■ ▲ ▬ ▲ ◩
       ▲ ▲ ▲ ▲ ▲ ▲ ▲ ▲ ▲ ▲ ▲ ▲ ▲ ▲ ▲ ▲ ▲ ▲ ▲ ▲ ◙ ■   ▬ ▲ ◩
        ▲ ▲ ◙ ■ ▲ ▬ ▲ ◩ ▲ ▲ ◙ ■ ▲ ◘ ▲ ▬ ";
```

```
560   PRINT "▣■▲▀▲▲▲▲▲▲▲▲▲▲▲▲▲▲▲▲▲▲
      ▲▲▲▲▲▲▲▲▲▲▲▲▲▲▲▲▲▲▲▣▲◨▲▀";
570   PRINT "▣■▲▀▲▛▲▲▲▲▲▲▲▲▲▲▣■▲▲SC
      ORE▲▲▲▲▲▲▲▲▀▲▛▲▲▲▲▲▲▲▲▲▲▣■
      ▲◨▲▀";
580   PRINT "▣■▲▀▲▲▲▲▲▲▲▲▲▲▲▲▲▲▲▲▲▲
      ▲▲▲▲▲▲▲▲▲▲▲▲▲▲▲▲▲▲▲▣▲◨▲▀";
590   PRINT "▣■▲▀▲▛▲▲▣■▲▀▲▛▲▲▣■▲▀▲▛
      ▲▲▲▲▲▲▲▲▲▲▲▲▲▲▲▲▲▲▲▲▣■ ▀▲▛
      ▲▲▣■▲▀▲▛▲▲▣■▲◨▲▀";
600   PRINT "▣■ ▀▲▲▲▣▲▀▲▲▲▣▲▀▲▲▲▲▲▲
      ▲▲▲▲▲▲▲▲▲▲▲▲▲▲▲▣ ▀▲▲▲▣▲▀▲▲
      ▲▣▲◨▲▀";
610   PRINT "▣■▲▀▲▛▲▲▣■▲▀▲▛▲▲▣■ ▲▲▲
      ▲▲▲▲▲▲▀▲▲▲▣▲▲▲▲▲▲▲▲▲▲▀▲▛▲▲
      ▣■▲▀▲▛▲▲▣■▲◨▲▀";
620   PRINT "▣■▲▀▲▲▲▣▲▀▲▲▲▲▲▲▲▲▲▲▲▲
      ▲▲▲▲▲▲▲▲▲▲▲▲▲▲▲▲▲▣▲▀▲▲▲▣▲◨
      ▲▀";
630   PRINT "▣■▲▀▲▛▲▲▣■▲▀▲▛▲▲▲▲▲▲▲▲
      ▲▲▲▲▲▲▲▲▲▲▲▲▲▲▲▲▲▲▲▲▣■▲▀▲▛
      ▲▲▣■▲◨▲▀";
640   PRINT "▣■▲▀▲▲▲▣▲▀▲▲▲▲▲▲▲▲▲▲▲▲
      ▲▲▲▲▲▲▲▲▲▲▲▲▲▲▲▲▲▣▲▀▲▲▲▣▲◨
      ▲▀";
650   PRINT "▣■▲▀▲▛▲▲▣■▲▲▲▲▲▲▲▲▲▲▲▲
      ▲▲▀▲▲▲▣▲▲▲▲▲▲▲▲▲▲▲▲▲▲▀▲▛▲▲
      ▣■▲◨▲▀";
660   PRINT "▣■▲▀▲▲▲▲▲▲▲▲▲▲▲▲▲▲▲▲▲▲
      ▲▲▲▲▲▲▲▲▲▲▲▲▲▲▲▲▲▲▲▣▲◨▲▀";
670   PRINT "▣■▲▀▲▛▲▲▲▲▲▲▲▲▲▲▲▲▲▲▲▲
      ▲▲▲▲▲▲▲▲▲▲▲▲▲▲▲▲▲▲▲▲▣■▲◨▲▀
      ";
680   PRINT "▣■▲▀▲▲▲▲▲▲▲▲▲▲▲▲▲▲▲▲▲▲
      ▲▲▲▲▲▲▲▲▲▲▲▲▲▲▲▲▲▲▲▣▲◨▲▀";
690   PRINT "▣■▲▲▲▲▲▲PREVIOUS▲HIGH▲
      SCORE▲▲▲▲▲▲▲▲▲▲▲▲▲▲◨▨";
700   PRINT  "▨ "
710   C=0:R=0
720   GETA$:IF A$=""THEN 720
730   RETURN
740   PRINT "♥▥▥▥▥▥▥▥▥▥▥▥▥";
750   PRINT "DO▲YOU▲WANT▲INSTRUCTIO
      NS▲(Y/N)▲:▲";
760   GETA$:IF A$=""THEN 760
770   IF A$="N "THEN RETURN
780   IF A$<>"Y "THEN GOTO 760
790   PRINT "♥ ":PRINT "▲▲▲▲▲▲▲▲▲▲▲▲▣CRAS
      H▲BARRIER▀"
800   PRINT :PRINT :PRINT
```

```
810   PRINT "▲▲▲▲▲▲▲▲STEER▲THE▲CAR▲
      ROUND▲THE▲MAZE"
820   PRINT "▲▲▲▲▲▲▲▲FOR▲AS▲LONG▲AS
      ▲POSSIBLE▲USING"
830   PRINT "▲▲▲▲▲▲▲▲THE▲-"
840   PRINT :PRINT "▲▲▲▲▲▲▲▲▲▲▲▲▲▲▲▲▲▲I
       ▲-▲LEFT▲"
850   PRINT "▲▲▲▲▲▲▲▲▲▲▲▲▲▲▲▲▲▲P▲-▲
      RIGHT"
860   PRINT "▲▲▲▲▲▲▲▲▲▲▲▲▲▲▲▲▲▲Q▲-▲
      UP"
870   PRINT "▲▲▲▲▲▲▲▲▲▲▲▲▲▲▲▲▲▲Z▲-▲
      DOWN"
880   PRINT :PRINT :PRINT "▲▲▲▲▲▲▲▲PRESS▲A
      NY▲KEY▲TO▲START";
890   GETA$:IF A$=""THEN 890
900   RETURN
910   DATA16,0,1,21,0,1,0,10,2,0,14,2,34,14,2,34,10,2,17,
      20,1,21,20,1
920   DATA4,10,2,4,14,2,17,16,1,21,16,1,30,14,2,30,10,2,1
      7,4,1,21,4,1,17,8,1
930   DATA21,8,1,17,13,1,21,13,1
```

ChexSum Tables

Line	ChexSum
10	0
20	2554
30	1931
40	2370
50	1248
60	2233
70	1282
80	5041
90	1280
100	1782
110	1365
120	1364
130	1368
140	1365
150	3916
160	1483
170	3164
180	4000
190	1135
200	4000
210	1135
220	3986
230	1135
240	3986
250	1135
260	1070
270	1239
280	2355
290	1232
300	5724
310	5337
320	1236
330	2878
340	2479
350	3803
360	143
370	3298
380	1184
390	1180
400	1180
410	1187
420	143
430	0
440	584
450	2406
460	2771
470	2962
480	2771
490	5083
500	3221
510	3885
520	3221
530	5437
540	3647
550	5727
560	2771
570	3833
580	2771
590	5727
600	3903
610	5293
620	3221
630	4269
640	3221
650	3855
660	2771
670	3131
680	2771
690	3037
700	244
710	682
720	1216
730	143
740	755
750	2766
760	1216
770	901
780	1525
790	2596
800	585
810	2953
820	3074
830	836
840	1967
850	1752
860	1470
870	1678
880	3025
890	1211
900	143
910	3383
920	4024
930	1332
TOTAL	221692

Hangman

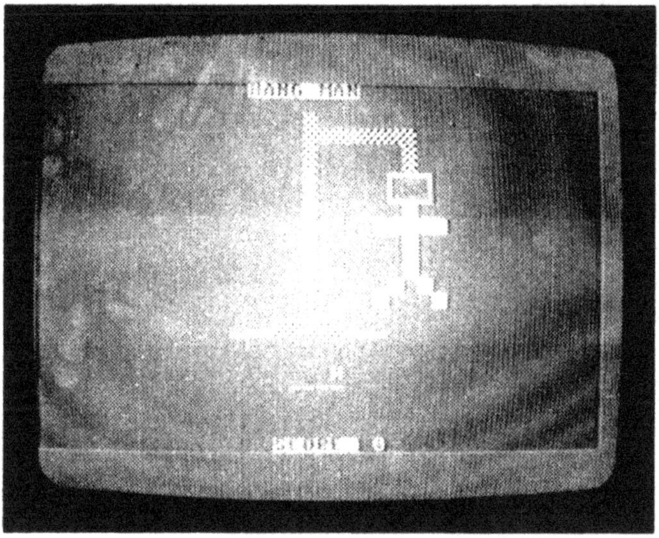

CLASSIFICATION: Educational

The classic word-guessing game in brilliant colour. Guess the word before the computer hangs you.

The computer will print out a line of dashes, each dash representing a letter of the unknown word. Guess a letter by pressing a key. If you guessed correctly, the computer will replace a dash or dashes with the letter. If you were wrong, the computer will begin to build the scaffold and start the execution. Hint: the most common letters in English are E and T.

PROGRAMMING SUGGESTIONS

Add more words to the word bank. Design an edit mode which allows you to change, add or delete words quickly without writing DATA statements. Kids can use this editor to test their parents on their most commonly misspelt words.

Program Variables

W	Pointer to random word
RR$	Move cursor down rows
LE	Length of word
LC	Letter count
CC$	Move cursor across columns
N	Number of words in word bank
W$ ( )	Array for word bank
W$	Word

Listing

```
10     COLOR0,3,3:COLOR4,7,4 :VOL 8:PRINT "■ ";
20     FOR I=1 TO 40:CC$=CC$+"■ ":NEXT:FOR I=1 TO 25:RR$
       =RR$+"■ ":NEXT:N=73:GOSUB 340
30     DIMW$(N):FOR I=0 TO N:READW$(I):NEXT
40     SCNCLR:M$="■ H A N G ▲ M A N ■ ":PRINT TAB((40-
       LEN(M$))/2);M$:LC=0
50     PRINT LEFT$(RR$,23);SPC(17);"■ S C O R E ▲ ■ ";SC;
60     W=INT(RND(1)*N):W$=W$(W):LE=LEN(W$):PE=(40-LE)/2:LV
       =10
70     PRINT "■ ";LEFT$(RR$,20);
80     PRINT SPC(PE);:FOR I=1 TO LE:PRINT "- ";:NEXT:CN=0:
       PT$="0 0 0 0 0 0 0 0 0 0 0 0 0 0 0 0 0 0 0 0 0 0 0
       "
```

Enter the Letters of the Word One by One

```
90     F=0:GETKEYA$
100    IF A$<"A "ORA$>"Z "THEN GOTO 90
110    PRINT "■ ";LEFT$(RR$,19);:F=0
120    FOR I=1 TO LE:L$=MID$(W$,I,1):IF L$=A$THEN IF
       MID$(PT$,I,1)<>"1 "THEN GOSUB 300
130    NEXT
140    IF CN=LE THEN GOSUB 290:GOTO 40
150    IF F=0THEN GOSUB 170
160    GOTO 90
170    IF LC=10THEN GOSUB 310:GOTO 40
180    LC=LC+1:LV=LV-1
```

Print One More Section of the Hangman; Decrement Score

```
190    IF LC=1THEN PRINT "■ ";LEFT$(RR$,16);SPC(14);Y$(1);
       :SOUND 2,7,7:RETURN
200    IF LC=2THEN PRINT "■ ";LEFT$(RR$,15);SPC(19);Y$(2);
       :SOUND 2,9,8:RETURN
210    IF LC=3THEN PRINT "■ ";LEFT$(RR$,3);SPC(19);Y$(3);:
       SOUND 1,5,5:RETURN
220    IF LC=4THEN PRINT "■ ";LEFT$(RR$,3);SPC(26);Y$(4);:
       SOUND 2,6,5:RETURN
230    IF LC=5THEN PRINT "■ ";LEFT$(RR$,6);SPC(25);Y$(5);:
       SOUND 2,5,6:RETURN
240    IF LC=6THEN PRINT "■ ";LEFT$(RR$,8);SPC(26);Y$(6);:
       SOUND 1,8,8:RETURN
250    IF LC=7THEN PRINT "■ ";LEFT$(RR$,9);SPC(24);Y$(7);:
       SOUND 1,6,9:RETURN
```

```
260   IF LC=8THEN PRINT "▣ ";LEFT$(RR$,9);SPC(27);Y$(8);:
      SOUND 1,6,6:RETURN
270   IF LC=9THEN PRINT "▣ ";LEFT$(RR$,12);SPC(26);Y$(9);
      :SOUND 1,6,6:RETURN
280   IF LC=10THEN PRINT "▣ ";LEFT$(RR$,12);SPC(26);Y$(10
      );:SOUND 2,7,6:RETURN
290   PRINT "▣ ";"▌ G O O D ▲ G U E S S ▬ ";:FOR I=1
       TO 100:GETA$:NEXT:SC=SC+LV:RETURN
300   POKE 202,0:PRINT SPC(PE+I-1);L$;:F=1:CN=CN+1:MID$(P
      T$,I,1)="1 ":RETURN
310   PRINT "▣ ";LEFT$(RR$,18);
320   K$="▌ ▣ T H E ▲ W O R D ▲ W A S ▲ "+W$+"▬ ▬ ":KE=
      LEN(K$):TA=(40-KE)/2:PRINT SPC(TA);K$;
330   FOR I=1 TO 50:GETA$:SOUND 1,5,6:SOUND 2,9,2:NEXT:
      RETURN
```

Build the Scaffolding, the Noose and the Hangman

```
340   Y$(1)="▁ ▂ ▃ ✻ ✻ ✻ ✻ ✻ ▃ ▂ ▁ "
350   Y$(2)="✻ □ ▌ ✻ □ ▌ ✻ □ ▌ ✻ □ ▌ ✻ □ ▌ ✻ □ ▌ ✻ □ ▌ ✻
      □ ▌ ✻ □ ▌ ✻ □ ▌ ✻ □ ▌ ✻ ▌ □ ✻ ▌ □ ✻ "
360   Y$(3)="✻ ✻ ✻ ✻ ✻ ✻ ✻ ✻ "
370   Y$(4)="✻ ▣ ▌ ✻ ▣ ▌ ✻ "
380   Y$(5)="┌ □ ┐ ▣ ▌ ▌ ▌ └ □ ┘ "
390   Y$(6)="▣ ▲ ▣ ▌ ▲ ▣ ▌ ▲ ▣ ▌ ▲ ▬ "
400   Y$(7)="▣ ▲ ▲ ▬ "
410   Y$(8)="▣ ▲ ▲ ▬ "
420   Y$(9)="▣ ▲ ▌ ▌ ▣ ▲ ▌ ▌ ▣ ▲ ▌ ▌ ▣ ▬ "
430   Y$(10)="▣ ▲ ▣ ▲ ▣ ▲ ▬ "
440   RETURN
450   DATA DOOR,HOUSE,WALL,BRICK,RETURN,COMPUTER
460   DATA TABLE,KEY,CHAIR,POWER,CURTAIN,CASSETTE,TAPE,CO
      LOR,DATA,STABLE,RUN
470   DATA RECORD,SUPPLY,DEMAND,TREASURE,TITANIC,MELBOURN
      E,PERTH,ECONOMIC
480   DATA CALCULATOR,HELP,HEAD,HIGH,BATTLE,BEEF,BECAUSE,
      EAT,EEL,ETCH,GOLD
490   DATA GATE,GET,JUMP,JUSTICE,JAIL,KILL,KEEPER,LOOK,LE
      ACH,KENNEDY,MORRISON
500   DATA ZEBRA,TEETH,UNIVERSITY,ZOO,CUPBOARD,PERCEPTION
      ,CLARITY,FENCE,VENTILATOR
510   DATA SWITCH,LIGHT,PAPER,PLATE,BRACKET,BUTTON,MACHIN
      E,CURSOR,PLUG
520   DATA CARPET,BAG,RING,LORD,STAR,STATISTICS,CHIP,INTE
      RGRATE,BOTTLE
```

ChexSum Tables

Line		Sum	Line		Sum	Line		Sum
10	=	1942	180	=	1524	350	=	7379
20	=	4935	190	=	3399	360	=	1937
30	=	1968	200	=	3411	370	=	1428
40	=	3744	210	=	3358	380	=	2240
50	=	2367	220	=	3345	390	=	1447
60	=	4623	230	=	3346	400	=	801
70	=	1067	240	=	3370	410	=	806
80	=	4419	250	=	3366	420	=	1884
90	=	897	260	=	3361	430	=	972
100	=	1939	270	=	3405	440	=	143
110	=	1440	280	=	3499	450	=	3372
120	=	4786	290	=	4394	460	=	6162
130	=	131	300	=	4537	470	=	6167
140	=	1654	310	=	1066	480	=	5934
150	=	925	320	=	5720	490	=	6246
160	=	480	330	=	2637	500	=	6800
170	=	1612	340	=	2497	510	=	5668
						520	=	5690
						TOTAL	=	160240

Looney Landa

CLASSIFICATION: Simulation

You have a high-technology exploratory spacecraft at your disposal. Your mission is to land the craft softly on the blue landing pads on the moon. Thrust can be varied up to five without exceeding the safety limits and, in emergencies, you can retro up to nine, risking engine burn-out. Lateral control is achieved by rolling the craft either left or right and thrusting. If you succeed in your mission, you will be given a more difficult task.

The controls are: increase thrust with Z, reduce it with Q, roll left or right with I or P.

PROGRAMMING SUGGESTIONS

Design new environments: create orbiting junk to avoid, different planets with higher gravity and different planetary surfaces. Increase fuel and mass of craft to make manoeuvres more difficult. Invent a new mission — take-off and dock with the mother ship, or land on an asteroid.

PROGRAM
Variables

TL	Toll value
TH	Thrust
FU	Fuel level
M	Mass value
LV	Level
G	Gravity
TM	Timer interval

Listing

Select Graphics Mode and Initialise Game

```
10    COLOR0,1:COLOR4,1:COLOR2,7:COLOR3,10,2:COLOR1,6,5:
      GRAPHIC3,1:VOL 8
20    GOSUB 320:B=1:TL=16:GOSUB 410
30    TH=0:FU%=1000:M=1000:VX=0:VY=0:SX=9600:SY=1080:G=10
      :TM=.1:BO=0
40    CHAR1,34,0,"R O L L ":CHAR1,34,6,"F U E L ":CHAR1,3
      4,10,"V E R T ":CHAR1,34,15,"H O R Z ":COLOR1,4,5
```

Get Player's Input, Update Screen

```
50    GETA$:CHAR1,34,8,STR$(FU%)+"▲ "
60    CHAR1,34,13,STR$(INT(VY))+"▲ "
70    CHAR1,34,19,STR$(INT(VX))+"▲ "
80    IF SX>9120ANDSX<10560ANDSY>16200THEN 450
90    BOX0,INT(SX/120),INT(SY/120)-5,INT(SX/120)+4,INT(SY
      /120),INT(TL*360/32)
100   IF A$<>"P "THEN 130
110   GOSUB 400:TL=TL+1:IF TL>31THEN TL=0
120   B=1:GOSUB 410
130   IF A$<>"I "THEN 160
140   GOSUB 400:TL=TL-1:IF TL<0THEN TL=31
150   B=1:GOSUB 410
160   IF FU%=0THEN GOSUB 200:GOTO 50
170   IF A$="Q "THEN TH=TH-1:IF TH<0THEN TH=0
180   IF A$="Z "THEN TH=TH+1:IF TH>9-BOTHEN TH=9-BO
190   IF TH>FU%THEN TH=FU%
```

Calculate New Position and Velocities
Did Space Craft Crash?

```
200   QY=((TH*9000)/(M+FU%))*COS(((TL-16)*π)/32)
210   QX=((TH*9000)/(M+FU%))*SIN(((TL-16)*π)/32)
220   SX=SX+VX+.005*QX:SY=SY+VY+.005*QY:VY=VY+G-QY:VX=VX
      +QX:FU%=FU%-TH
230   IF (PEEK(8192+INT(SY/960)*320+INT(SX/960)*16+((
      INT(SY/120))AND7))AND30)>0THEN 460
240   IF (PEEK(8196+INT(SY/960)*320+INT(SX/960)*16+((
      INT(SY/120))AND7))AND30)>0THEN 460
250   BOX1,INT(SX/120),INT(SY/120)-5,INT(SX/120)+4,INT(SY
      /120),INT(TL*360/32)
260   IF TH=0THEN 50
```

```
270   SOUND 3,500+30*TH,80:IF TH>5-BOTHEN SOUND 1,990,10
280   IF TH+BO-5<=0ORRND(0)>(TH+BO-5)/30THEN 50
290   BO=BO+1:SOUND 3,1020,20:IF TH>9-BOTHEN TH=TH-1
300   IF BO=9THEN CHAR1,0,22,"R E T R O   F A I L U R E !
       ! "
310   GOTO 50
```

Scenery Information

```
320   DRAW3,0,0 TO 0,159 TO 131,159 TO 131,0
330   DRAW3,0,0 TO 4,8 TO 6,16 TO 7,24 TO 8,32 TO 9,40
       TO 10,48 TO 12,56 TO 7,64 TO 13,72 TO 14,80
340   DRAW3 TO 16,88 TO 14,96 TO 10,104 TO 6,112 TO 8,120
       TO 8,128 TO 10,136 TO 12,144 TO 14,152 TO 18,157
350   DRAW3,37,157 TO 47,152 TO 50,144 TO 52,136 TO 56,12
      8 TO 64,120 TO 72,128 TO 76,136 TO 80,136
360   DRAW3 TO 78,136 TO 90,136 TO 94,130 TO 94,126 TO 90
      ,120 TO 86,115 TO 85,108 TO 90,104 TO 96,95
370   DRAW3 TO 105,90 TO 112,95 TO 116,88 TO 124,80 TO 12
      5,66 TO 118,60 TO 115,48 TO 126,22 TO 128,7 TO 131,
      0
380   DRAW3,18,157 TO 27,130 TO 37,157:DRAW2,78,135 TO 90
      ,135:PAINT3,1,9
390   RETURN
400   B=0
410   DRAWB,147+9*COS(((TL-16)*π)/16),26+18*SIN(((TL-16)
      *π)/16)
420   DRAWB TO 147-9*COS(((TL-16)*π)/16),26-18*SIN(((TL
      -16)*π)/16)
430   DRAWB,147,26 TO 147+9*SIN(((TL-16)*π)/16),26-18*
      COS(((TL-16)*π)/16)
440   RETURN
450   IF TL=16ANDABS(VX)<=10ANDVY<=10THEN END
460   SOUND 3,900,300:FOR I=1 TO 16:COLOR3,I,4:FOR J=1
       TO 200:NEXTJ,I
```

ChexSum Tables

Line		Sum
10	=	3367
20	=	1588
30	=	5652
40	=	5720
50	=	1804
60	=	1766
70	=	1764
80	=	2763
90	=	5529
100	=	1129
110	=	2388
120	=	664
130	=	1125
140	=	2391
150	=	664
160	=	1608
170	=	2757
180	=	3563
190	=	1425
200	=	3795
210	=	3795
220	=	7314
230	=	5861
240	=	5865
250	=	5530
260	=	813
270	=	3138
280	=	3547
290	=	3515
300	=	2655
310	=	476
320	=	1972
330	=	4700
340	=	5386
350	=	4981
360	=	5001
370	=	5773
380	=	3556
390	=	143
400	=	296
410	=	4935
420	=	5116
430	=	5606
440	=	143
450	=	2909
460	=	3552
TOTAL	=	148100

2D Maze

CLASSIFICATION: Evasion

You are placed randomly within a maze and must work your way through to the end.

You can turn left or right with the I and P keys, or move forward to the next junction by hitting the SPACE bar. The end of the maze is a flashing wall of colour.

PROGRAMMING SUGGESTIONS

Put a time limit on solving the maze. Introduce random teleporters which change your position and orientation; once triggered, they disappear. Increase the size of the maze. Have nasty things chase you! Add secret, invisible passageways that change your position but can only be found accidentally.

PROGRAM
Variables

MZ	Maze array
J%	Current junction
D%	Actual orientation
N%	Next junction
M	Number of moves

Listing

Initialise Game and Define Maze

```
10      PRINT "♥ W A I T ":COLOR1,1:DX=9:DY=9:XF=5:YF=9
20      DIMMZ%(DX,DY)
30      RESTORE
40      FOR I=0 TO DY:FOR J=0 TO DX:READMZ%(J,I):NEXTJ,I
50      DATA15,3,4,7,5,7,5,5,15,5,11,14,5,13,5,13,5,3,10,6,
        14,11,6,5,5,5,7,11,8,10
60      DATA10,8,10,6,3,6,11,12,7,9,12,5,9,8,6,12,15,5,13,3
        ,5,5,3,6,15,3,10,2,6,13
70      DATA7,5,9,10,10,12,9,10,12,5,14,7,5,9,12,5,5,15,5,1
        ,11,14,5,7,7,5,3,10,4,5
80      DATA11,8,4,9,8,4,9,12,7,5
90      DEFFNL(X)=((X*2)AND15)+INT((XAND8)/8)
100     DEFFNR(X)=INT(X/2)+(XAND1)*8
110     X=INT(RND(0)*6+2):Y=INT(RND(0)*5):D%=2↑INT(RND(0)
        *4):GRAPHIC2,0:GOSUB 210
```

Get Player's Input; Move Player, Rotate Left or Rotate Right

```
120     GETA$:IF A$<>"I "ANDA$<>"P "ANDA$<>"▲ "THEN 120
130     IF A$="I "THEN D%=FNR(D%):GOSUB 210:GOTO 120
140     IF A$="P "THEN D%=FNL(D%):GOSUB 210:GOTO 120
150     IF (D%ANDMZ%(X,Y))=1THEN X=X-1:IF X<0THEN X=DX
160     IF (D%ANDMZ%(X,Y))=2THEN Y=Y+1:IF Y>DYTHEN Y=0
170     IF (D%ANDMZ%(X,Y))=4THEN X=X+1:IF X>DXTHEN X=0
180     IF (D%ANDMZ%(X,Y))=8THEN Y=Y-1:IF Y<0THEN Y=DY
190     GOSUB 210:IF X=XFANDY=YFTHEN GRAPHIC0:END
200     GOTO 120
```

Draw Player's View; End Game

```
210     SCNCLR:XN=X:YN=Y:IF (D%ANDMZ%(X,Y))=0THEN RETURN
220     IF (D%ANDMZ%(X,Y))=1THEN XN=X-1:IF XN<0THEN XN=DX
230     IF (D%ANDMZ%(X,Y))=2THEN YN=Y+1:IF YN>DYTHEN YN=0
240     IF (D%ANDMZ%(X,Y))=4THEN XN=X+1:IF XN>DXTHEN XN=0
250     IF (D%ANDMZ%(X,Y))=8THEN YN=Y-1:IF YN<0THEN YN=DY
260     DRAW1,0,0 TO 87,57:DRAW1,0,159 TO 87,130:DRAW1,319,
        0 TO 232,57:DRAW1,319,159 TO 232,130
270     IF (MZ%(XN,YN)ANDD%)=0THEN 300
280     BOX1,157,103,162,107:DRAW1,157,103 TO 130,85:DRAW1,
        162,103 TO 189,85
```

```
290    DRAW1,157,107 TO 130,116:DRAW1,162,107 TO 189,116:
       GOTO 310
300    DRAW1,130,85 TO 189,85:DRAW1,130,116 TO 189,116
310    IF (MZ%(XN,YN)ANDFNR(D%))=0THEN 340
320    DRAW1,87,57 TO 87,130:DRAW1,130,85 TO 87,85:DRAW1,1
       30,116 TO 87,116
330    IF (MZ%(XN,YN)ANDD%)>0THEN DRAW1,130,85 TO 130,116
340    IF (MZ%(XN,YN)ANDFNL(D%))=0THEN 370
350    DRAW1,232,57 TO 232,130:DRAW1,189,85 TO 232,85:
       DRAW1,189,116 TO 232,116
360    IF (MZ%(XN,YN)ANDD%)>0THEN DRAW1,189,85 TO 189,116
370    IF (MZ%(XN,YN)ANDFNL(D%))>0THEN 400
380    DRAW1,232,57 TO 189,85:DRAW1,232,130 TO 189,116
390    IF (MZ%(XN,YN)ANDD%)=0THEN DRAW1,189,85 TO 189,116
400    IF (MZ%(XN,YN)ANDFNR(D%))>0THEN 430
410    DRAW1,87,57 TO 130,85:DRAW1,87,130 TO 130,116
420    IF (MZ%(XN,YN)ANDD%)=0THEN DRAW1,130,85 TO 130,116
430    IF XN=XFANDYN=YFTHEN CHAR1,18,11,"H O M E "
440    RETURN
```

ChexSum Tables

10	= 3085	160	= 3286	310	= 2229
20	= 807	170	= 3284	320	= 3669
30	= 141	180	= 3328	330	= 2914
40	= 2902	190	= 2244	340	= 2215
50	= 4511	200	= 527	350	= 3882
60	= 4500	210	= 3077	360	= 2920
70	= 4520	220	= 3625	370	= 2208
80	= 1252	230	= 3604	380	= 2567
90	= 2764	240	= 3602	390	= 2922
100	= 2229	250	= 3634	400	= 2226
110	= 4926	260	= 4807	410	= 2494
120	= 3210	270	= 1801	420	= 2916
130	= 2600	280	= 3813	430	= 2715
140	= 2589	290	= 3332	440	= 143
150	= 3318	300	= 2561	TOTAL	= 125899

Blackjack

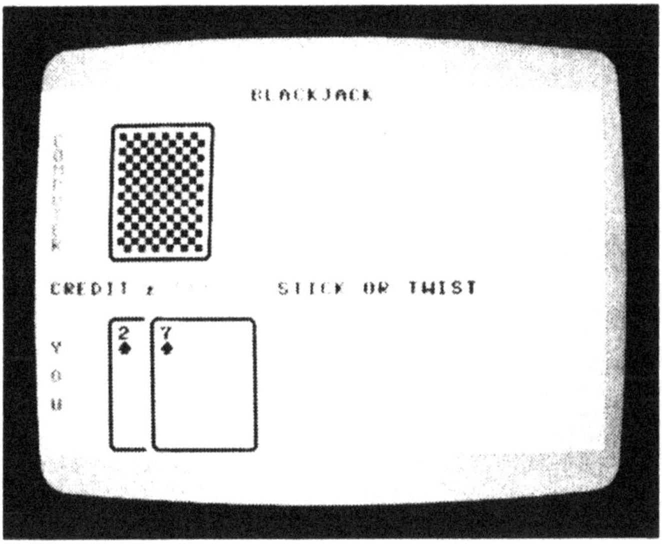

CLASSIFICATION: Gambling

Play Blackjack, the player versus the computer. You start with $50 and can bet up to your credit on one hand.

Enter your bet and hit return, then wait for the computer to deal your card (face down). Use key S to stick, if you think your hand is good enough, or T to twist a new card over. You bust if the total exceeds 21. Try D to double your stake if you feel lucky.

PROGRAM
Variables

CD$	Array of names of cards (A, 2, 3, J, Q, K)
SS$	Suits of deck
CR	Money
CV	Computer's total card value
PV	Player's total card value
NC	Number of cards computer has
NP	Number of cards player has
B	Amount of bet
DT$	Next card
SQ	Stake
DB	Flag of doubling stake
CO%	Computer's card
P%	Player's card
CN%	Array which indicates which cards dealt
C1$, C2$	Computer's first and second cards

Listing

Initialise Game Variables
Draw Screen; Deal First Cards Face Down

```
10    BL$="▚ ▚ ▚ ▚ ▚ ▚ ◘ ▮▮ ▮▮ ▮▮ ▮▮ ▮▮ ▮▮ ":CL$="▴ ▴ ▴ ▴ ▴ ▴ ◘
      ▮▮ ▮▮ ▮▮ ▮▮ ▮▮ ▮▮ ":CN$="◙ ◘ ◘ ◘ ◘ ◘ ◘ ◘ ◘ ◘ ◘ ◘ ◘ ◘ "
20    CA$="◘ ◘ ◘ ◘ ◘ ◘ ◘ ◘ ◘ ◘ ◘ ◘ ◘ ◘ ◘ ◘ ◘ ◘ ◘ ◘ ":NL$="▴ ▴ ▴
      ▴ ▴ ▴ ▴ ▴ ▴ ▴ ▴ ▴ ▴ ▴ ▴ ▴ ▴ ▴ ▴ ▴ ▴ ▴ ▴ ▴ ▴ ▴ ▴ ▴ ▴ ▴ ▴ ▴ ▴ ▴ ▴ ▴ ▴ ▴ ▴ ▴ ▴ ▴ ▴ ▴ ▴ ▴ "
30    C$="═ ═ ═ ═ ═ ═ ":D$="⁞ ◘ ▮▮ ⁞ ◘ ▮▮ ⁞ ◘ ▮▮ ⁞ ◘ ▮▮ ⁞ ◘ ▮▮
      ⁞ ◘ ▮▮ ⁞ ◘ ▮▮ ⁞ ":CR=500:DC$="◘ ◘ "
40    VOL 8:DIMSS$(3):DIMPC(9):DIMCC(9)
50    DIMCD$(12):DIMCN%(12):FOR I=0 TO 12:READCD$(I):CD$(
      I)=CD$(I)+"▴ ":CN%(I)=15:NEXTI
60    DATAA,2,3,4,5,6,7,8,9,10,J,Q,K
70    CD$(9)="1 0 ":SS$(0)="◙ ♥ ":SS$(1)="◙ ♦ ":SS$(2)="■
      ♣ ":SS$(3)="■ ♠ "
80    PRINT "◙ ◙ ▴ ▴ ▴ ▴ ▴ ▴ ▴ ▴ ▴ ▴ ▴ ▴ ▴ ▴ ▴ ▴ B L A C K
      J A C K "
90    PRINT "◙ ◘ ◘ ◘ C ◘ ▮▮ O ◘ ▮▮ M ◘ ▮▮ P ◘ ▮▮ U ◘ ▮▮ T ◘ ▮▮
      E ◘ ▮▮ R ◘ ◘ ◘ ◘ ◘ ◘ ◘ ◘ ▮▮ ◙ Y ◘ ▮▮ ▴ ◘ ▮▮ O ◘ ▮▮ ▴ ◘ ▮▮ U
      "
100   L=0:CX$="◘ ◘ ◘ ◘ ":SQ=0:B=0:CN=-1:PN=-1:DB=0:S=0
110   CY$=CN$+DC$:GOSUB 320:P1$=DT$:PS=X:PN=0:PC(PN)=Y:
      GOSUB 420
120   CY$=DC$:GOSUB 320:C1$=DT$:CS1=X:CN=0:CC(CN)=Y
130   GOSUB 560:CY$=CN$+DC$:DT$=P1$:X=PS:GOSUB 380:RC$=CX
      $:RP$=CX$
```

Flip Over Player's First Card and Enter Bet
Deal Next Two Cards

```
140   PRINT CN$;CA$;"◙ E N T E R ▴ B E T ■ ";:INPUT B
150   PRINT CN$;CA$;NL$
160   IF B<1ORB>CRTHEN 140
170   GOSUB 550
180   CY$=CN$+DC$:GOSUB 320:PN=PN+1:PC(PN)=Y:P1$=DT$:PS
      =X
190   CY$=DC$:CX$=RC$:GOSUB 320:C2$=DT$:CS2=X:CN=CN+1:CC(
      CN)=Y
200   CY$=CN$+DC$:CX$=RP$:DT$=P1$:X=PS:GOSUB 380:GOSUB 42
      0
210   IF PV=21THEN 290
220   PRINT CN$;CA$;"◙ S T I C K ▴ O R ▴ T W I S T ";
230   GETA$:IF A$=""THEN 230
240   IF A$<>"S "ANDA$<>"T "ANDA$<>"D "THEN PRINT CN$;CA$
      ;NL$:SOUND 1,350,5:GOTO 210
```

```
250  IF A$="T "THEN GOSUB 320:PN=PN+1:PC(PN)=Y:GOSUB 380:GOSUB 420:GOSUB 600:GOTO 210
260  IF A$<>"D "ORDB>0ORB>CRTHEN 280
270  GOSUB 550:DB=1:GOTO 210
280  IF A$<>"S "ORPV<12THEN 210
```

Player Sticks, So Reveal Computer's Hand and Play

```
290  S=1:GOSUB 570:GOSUB 480
300  GOSUB 600
310  GOSUB 320:CN=CN+1:CC(CN)=Y:GOSUB 380:GOSUB 480:GOTO 300
320  SOUND 3,700,5:Y=INT(RND(0)*13):IF CN%(Y)=0THEN 320
```

Determine Next Card's Value and Suit; Draw Face Down; Flip Card Over

```
330  DT$=CD$(Y):X=INT(RND(0)*4)
340  IF (CN%(Y)AND(2↑X))=0THEN 320
350  CN%(Y)=CN%(Y)-2↑X
360  PRINT "▣ ■ ";CY$;CX$;"▣ ";C$;"▣ ▣ ▌▌ ";D$;"▣ ";CY$;CX$;"▣ ";D$;"▣ ▌▌ ▣ ";C$;"▣ ";
370  PRINT "▣ ";CY$;CX$;"▣ ▣ ";BL$;BL$;BL$;BL$;BL$;BL$;BL$;BL$;:FOR I=1 TO 100:NEXT:RETURN
380  CC$=LEFT$(SS$(X),1)
390  FOR I=1 TO 500:NEXT:PRINT "▣ ";CY$;CX$;"▣ ▣ ";CC$;DT$;"▲ ▲ ▲ ▲ ▣ ▌▌ ▌▌ ▌▌ ▌▌ ▌▌ ▌▌ ";SS$(X);"▲ ▲ ▲ ▲ ▲ ▣ ▌▌ ▌▌ ▌▌ ▌▌ ▌▌ ▌▌ ";
400  PRINT CL$;CL$;CL$;CL$;CL$;CL$;:CX$=CX$+"▣ ▣ ▣ "
410  SOUND 1,1000,3:FOR I=1 TO 500:NEXT:RETURN
```

Calculate Player's Hand; Calculate Computer's Hand

```
420  PV=0:AC=0:FOR I=0 TO PN:PV=PV+PC(I)+1:IF PC(I)=0 THEN PV=PV+10:AC=AC+1
430  IF PC(I)>9THEN PV=PV-PC(I)+9
440  NEXT
450  IF PV>21ANDAC>0THEN PV=PV-10:AC=AC-1:GOTO 450
460  IF PV>21THEN L=1
470  RETURN
480  IF CN<0THEN RETURN
490  CV=0:AC=0:FOR I=0 TO CN:CV=CV+CC(I)+1:IF CC(I)=0 THEN CV=CV+10:AC=AC+1
500  IF CC(I)>9THEN CV=CV-CC(I)+9
510  NEXT
520  IF CV>21ANDAC>0THEN CV=CV-10:AC=AC-1:GOTO 520
530  IF CV>21THEN L=-1
540  RETURN
```

Draw Credit and Stake

```
550   SQ=SQ+B:PRINT CN$;"  S T A K E   £          ";SQ:CR=CR-B
560   PRINT CN$;"  C R E D I T  £                    ";CR:RETURN
570   PRINT "          ";C1$;"   ";SS$(CS1);"             
                          "
580   SOUND 1,1000,3
590   CV$=DC$:CX$=RC$:DT$=C2$:X=CS1:GOSUB 380:GOSUB 480:
      RETURN
```

Determine Winner and Amount Won or Lost

```
600   IF L=1THEN PRINT CN$;CA$;"   Y O U  B U S T E
       D !     ":SOUND 1,800,10:SOUND 1,700,20:
      GOTO 780
610   IF L<>-1THEN 640
620   PRINT CN$;CA$;NL$;CN$;CA$;"    I  B U S T E D
      ":CR=CR+2*SQ
630   SOUND 1,800,10:FOR I=1 TO 50:NEXT:SOUND 1,900,10:
      GOTO 790
640   IF CV<>21ORCN<>1THEN 670
650   PRINT CN$;CA$;"  I  G O T  B L A C K J A C K !
       ":SOUND 1,900,20:IF PV=21ANDPN=1THEN CR=CR-3*SQ
660   FOR I=1 TO 10:SOUND 1,800+10*I,10:NEXT:CR=CR-SQ:
      GOTO 790
670   IF S=0THEN RETURN
680   IF PV<>21ORPN<>1THEN 710
690   PRINT CN$;CA$;"  Y O U  G O T  B L A C K J A C
      K !  ":CR=CR+3*SQ:GOSUB 570
700   FOR I=1 TO 30:SOUND 1,300+10*I,10:SOUND 2,420+10*I,
      10::FOR J=1 TO 50:NEXTJ:NEXTI:GOTO 790
710   IF CV<17THEN PRINT CN$;CA$;"     I  T W I S T
       . . . .      ":RETURN
720   IF CV<PVTHEN 740
730   PRINT CN$;CA$;"     Y O U  L O S E . . . ":
      SOUND 1,700,10:FOR I=1 TO 50:NEXT:SOUND 1,600,25:
      GOTO 790
740   PRINT CN$;CA$;"     I  L O S E . . .     
       "
750   FOR I=1 TO 10:SOUND 1,900+10*I,10:FOR J=1 TO 50:
      NEXTJ:SOUND 1,1000-10*I,10:NEXT
760   CR=CR+2*SQ
770   GOTO 790
780   GOSUB 570
```

```
790   GOSUB 560:PRINT CN$;"▣ ▌ ";NL$;CN$;CA$;"▣ ▣ ▲ A N O
       T H E R ▲ G A M E ▲ ? "
800   GETA$:IF A$=""THEN 800
810   IF A$="N "THEN END
820   IF CR>0THEN 80
830   PRINT CN$;CA$;"▣ ▌ ▲ ▲ ▲ ▲ B A N K R U P T ! ▬ ":
      END
```

ChexSum Tables

```
10    = 6108
20    = 2532
30    = 6598
40    = 1924
50    = 5345
60    = 1682
70    = 5225
80    = 1897
90    = 4377
100   = 4092
110   = 4303
120   = 3533
130   = 4527
140   = 2124
150   =  844
160   = 1392
170   =  303
180   = 4349
190   = 4733
200   = 3668
210   =  940
220   = 2128
230   = 1215
240   = 5092
250   = 4542
260   = 2311
270   = 1372
280   = 1784
290   = 1067
300   =  298
310   = 3279
320   = 3113
330   = 1965
340   = 1750
350   = 1450
360   = 4995
370   = 5023
380   = 1162
390   = 6940
400   = 2948
410   = 1920
420   = 6113
430   = 2235
440   =  131
450   = 3661
460   = 1088
470   =  143
480   =  831
490   = 6061
500   = 2194
510   =  131
520   = 3634
530   = 1244
540   =  143
550   = 5617
560   = 3683
570   = 5388
580   =  635
590   = 3495
600   = 5046
610   = 1155
620   = 3982
630   = 3029
640   = 1882
650   = 6228
660   = 3884
670   =  762
680   = 1905
690   = 4433
700   = 5669
710   = 3046
720   =  996
730   = 5235
740   = 1941
750   = 4780
760   = 1069
770   =  538
780   =  303
790   = 3470
800   = 1211
810   =  895
820   =  809
830   = 2370
TOTAL = 235915
```

Dungeon

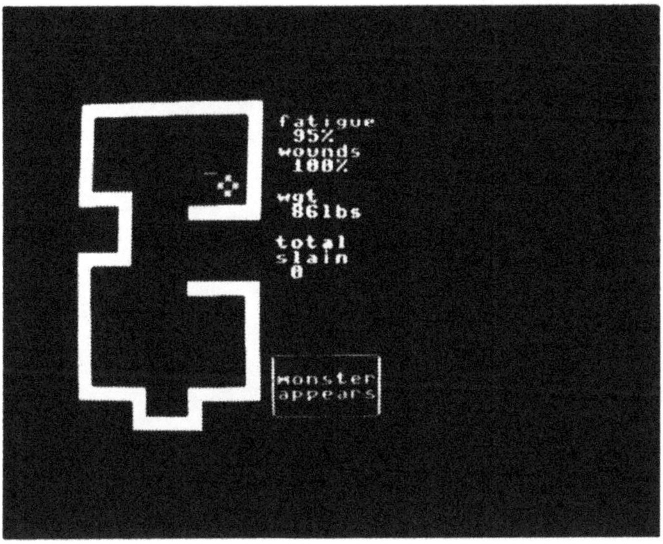

CLASSIFICATION: Adventure

You have been placed in a chamber with a monster and have the following attributes:

Fatigue
Wounds
Weight

You are the red object — explore the rooms and battle the evil monsters. Your controls are R to turn your man right and L to turn your man left. The keys 1 to 9 move you forward the corresponding number of places. The T key thrusts the sword at the monster, but be careful, he fights back. Your wound tolerance must not reach zero or you will die.

PROGRAMMING SUGGESTIONS

Alter the game so if a player stays too long in one position a monster will come after him. Also give the player and the monster more than just the one weapon they currently have. Weapons like a spear or a mace would be useful tools to have.

Program Variables

SC	Screen start
RO	Room number
FA	Fatigue value
X, Y	Player's co-ordinates
MX, MY	Monster's co-ordinates
D	Direction
R$	Room
WO	Wounds value
TS	Total slain
WE	Weight value
V	Steps of movement forward
M	Monster flag

Listing

```
10      REM  DUNGEON
20      DIMR$(4)
```

Define Cursor Movement Variables; Set Colours, Data For Mazes

```
30      Y$="■■■■■■■■■■■■■■■■■■■■■"
        :X$="■■■■■■■■■■■■■■■■■■■■■"
40      COLOR4,6,4:COLOR0,7,5:PRINT CHR$(14):SC=3072
60      SR=INT(RND(1)*11+10)
70      DE=INT(RND(1)*11+10):WE=75+INT(RND(1)*25)
80      TS=0:RO=0:FA=100:WO=100:D=1:X=3:Y=15
90      FOR I=0 TO 4:READR$(I):NEXT
100     DATA093D7L5ED5R104D7L4D2L4U2L4U9R3U4L3U6
110     DATAD10R5E403D991L4U9D9L8U9E406
120     DATA03D5RE5U104R4D7E4092L93U994
130     DATA06D7U7R6D8L2D5R2D8L4E404U91R6D4U4L6U1E40R2L2U6
140     DATA093D9L9R6D9L1D3L1E403U993
150     ON ROGOTO 170,180,190,200
160     MX=10:MY=3:GOTO 210
170     MX=4:MY=3:GOTO 210
180     MX=3:MY=10:GOTO 210
190     MX=10:MY=18:GOTO 210
200     MX=2:MY=18:GOTO 210
210     M=0:IF RND(1)>.5THEN M=INT(RND(1)*3+1):MS=INT(RND(1
        )*10)+5
220     GOSUB 1060:V=0:F=0:GOTO 260
```

Move Your Player Forward, Rotate Him Left or Right

```
230     GETA$:V=VAL(A$):IF V=0THEN 480
240     FA=FA-INT((V/200)*(100-WO)+(V/200)*WE+.5)
250     GOSUB 970:IF M=1ANDRND(1)>.2THEN F=1
260     SW=0:FOR I=1 TO V:PRINT LEFT$(Y$,Y+1);LEFT$(X$,X)"▲
        ▲■▌▌▲▲"
270     X1=X+(D=3)-(D=1):Y1=Y+(D=0)-(D=2)
310     IF  PEEK(SC+Y1*40+X1)<>32ORPEEK(SC+Y1*40+X1+1)<>32
        THEN I=V:GOTO 410
320     IF  PEEK(SC+Y1*40+X1+40)<>32ORPEEK(SC+Y1*40+X1+41)
        <>32THEN I=V:GOTO 410
340     X=X1:Y=Y1:IF X>0ANDX<11ANDY>0ANDY<20THEN 410
350     RO=RO+(X=0)-(X=11)+((Y=20)-(Y=0))*2
360     IF X=0THEN X=10
370     IF X=11THEN X=1
380     IF Y=0THEN Y=19
390     IF Y=20THEN Y=1
```

```
400   GOTO 150
410   PRINT LEFT$(Y$,Y+1);LEFT$(X$,X)"▣ ";
420   ON D+1GOTO 430,440,450,460
430   PRINT "▪ ▲ ◙ ▌▌ ▌▌ ▘ ▘ □ ▌▌ ";:GOTO 470
440   PRINT "◙ ▄ ▀ ▘ ◙ ▌▌ ▌▌ ◙ ▄ ▀ ▲ ▌▌ ";:GOTO 470
```

Print the Player and the Monster

```
450   PRINT "◙ ▘ ▘ ◙ ▌▌ ▌▌ ▀ ▲ ▘ ▌▌ ▌▌ ";:GOTO 470
460   PRINT "▲ ▄ ◙ ▌▌ ▌▌ ▘ ▄ □ ▌▌ ▌▌ ";
470   IF V>0THEN NEXTI
480   IF A$<>"L "ANDA$<>"R "THEN 540
490   IF FA<100THEN FA=FA+1:GOSUB 970
500   SW=0:D=D+(A$="L ")-(A$="R "):IF D<0THEN D=3
510   IF D>3THEN D=0
520   A$=""
530   V=0:GOTO 410
540   IF A$<>"T "THEN 620
550   SW=3:FA=FA-2
560   PRINT LEFT$(Y$,Y+1);LEFT$(X$,X+1);"▣ ";:IF D=0
      THEN PRINT "▘ ":GOTO 600
570   IF D=1THEN PRINT "◙ ▘ ":GOTO 600
580   IF D=2THEN PRINT "◙ ▌▌ ▘ ":GOTO 600
590   PRINT "▌▌ ▘ "
600   X1=X:Y1=Y:X1=X1+((D=3)-(D=1))*2:Y1=Y1+((D=0)-(D=2))
      *2
610   F=1
620   IF SW>0THEN SW=SW-1:IF SW=0THEN GOSUB 970:A$="":
      GOTO 410
630   IF M=0THEN 930
640   IF MS>=SRANDRND(1)>.7THEN F=1
650   IF F=0THEN 770
660   PRINT LEFT$(Y$,MY+1);LEFT$(X$,MX)"▲ ▲ ◙ ▌▌ ▌▌ ▲ ▲ ";:
      IF SM>0ANDMX>=XTHEN PRINT "□ □ ▌▌ ▌▌ ▌▌ ▲ "
690   SM=0:DY=MY+(MY>Y)-(MY<Y):IF PEEK(SC+DY*40+MX)<>32
      ORPEEK(SC+DY*40+MX+1)<>32THEN 730
700   IF PEEK(SC+DY*40+MX+40)<>32ORPEEK(SC+DY*40+MX+41)
      <>32THEN 730
720   MY=DY
730   DY=MX+(MX>X+2)-(MX<X-1):IF ABS(DY-X)<=1THEN DY=DY
      +(DY>1)*2
740   IF PEEK(SC+MY*22+DY)<>32ORPEEK(SC+MY*22+DY+1)<>32
      THEN 770
750   IF PEEK(SC+MY*22+DY+22)<>32ORPEEK(SC+MY*22+DY+23)
      <>32THEN 770
760   MX=DY
770   PRINT LEFT$(Y$,MY+1);LEFT$(X$,MX)"▣ ◙ ▚ ▀ ▘ ◙ ▌▌ ▌▌ ▘
       ";:IF SW=0THEN 820
780   IF  ABS(X1-MX)>1 OR ABS(Y1-MY)>1 THEN  820
```

```
790   SW=1:S=SR/4:S=S+(S*DE)/100:MS=MS-INT(S+.5):IF MS>0
      THEN 820
800   PRINT LEFT$(Y$,MY+1);LEFT$(X$,MX)"▲ ▲ ▣ ▮▮ ▮▮ ▲ "
810   TS=TS+1:M=0:GOTO 930
820   IF SM>0ORRND(1)>.5ORF=0THEN 890
830   X2=MX:Y2=MY
840   PRINT LEFT$(Y$,MY+1);LEFT$(X$,MX);:IF MX<XTHEN
      PRINT "▣ ▣ ◘ ⊡ ";:Y2=Y2+1:X2=X2+1:GOTO 880
850   IF MX=0THEN 930
860   IF PEEK(SC+MY*22+MX-1)=160THEN 930
870   PRINT "▮▮ ◻ ◘ ⊡ ";:X2=X2-1
880   SM=4
890   IF SM=0THEN 930
900   SM=SM-1
910   IF ABS(X2-X)>1ORABS(Y2-Y)>1THEN 930
920   SW=1:S=MS:S=S+(S*2*M)/100:WO=WO-INT(S+.5)
930   IF WO>0ANDFA>0THEN 230
940   FOR I=1 TO 1000:NEXT:PRINT "◣ ▣ ▣ ▣ ◘ T H O U ▲ A R
       T ":PRINT "▲ ▲ ▲ ▲ S L A I N ":M=0
950   GOSUB 970:PRINT "◻ ◻ ";:POKE 198,0:END
960   IF D1=3THEN PRINT "▮▮ ";
970   PRINT LEFT$(Y$,2);LEFT$(X$,14)"◣ F A T I G U E ◘ ▣
      ▮▮ ▮▮ ▮▮ ▮▮ ▮▮ ▮▮ ▮▮ "FA"▮▮ % ▲ "
980   PRINT TAB(14)"◣ W O U N D S ▣ ▮▮ ▮▮ ▮▮ ▮▮ ▮▮ ▮▮ ◘ "WO"▮▮ %
       ▲ "
990   PRINT TAB(14)"▣ ◣ W G T ▣ ▮▮ ▮▮ ▮▮ ◘ "WE"▮▮ L B S ▣ "
1000  PRINT TAB(14)"◣ T O T A L ▣ ▮▮ ▮▮ ▮▮ ▮▮ ▮▮ S L A I N ◘ ▣
       ▮▮ ▮▮ ▮▮ ▮▮ ▮▮ "TS
1010  PRINT LEFT$(Y$,17);LEFT$(X$,14)"◙ ⊡ ⊡ ⊡ ⊡ ⊡ ⊡ ⊡ ▣ ▮▮
       ▮▮ ▮▮ ▮▮ ▮▮ ▮▮ ▮▮ ▮▮ ⊡ ▲ ▲ ▲ ▲ ▲ ▲ ▲ ▲ ⊡ ▣ ▮▮ ▮▮ ▮▮ ▮▮ ▮▮ ▮▮ ▮▮ ▮▮
      ▮▮ ";
1020  PRINT "⊡ ▲ ▲ ▲ ▲ ▲ ▲ ▲ ▲ ⊡ ▣ ▮▮ ▮▮ ▮▮ ▮▮ ▮▮ ▮▮ ▮▮ ▮▮ ▮▮ ⊡ ▲ ▲
      ▲ ▲ ▲ ▲ ▲ ▲ ⊡ ▣ ▮▮ ▮▮ ▮▮ ▮▮ ▮▮ ▮▮ ▮▮ ▮▮ ▮▮ ⊡ ▲ ▲ ▲ ▲ ▲ ▲ ▲ ▲ ⊡ "
      ;
1030  PRINT "▣ ▮▮ ▮▮ ▮▮ ▮▮ ▮▮ ▮▮ ▮▮ ▮▮ ⊡ ⊡ ⊡ ⊡ ⊡ ⊡ ⊡ ◻ ◻ ◻ ◻ ▮▮ ▮▮
      ▮▮ ▮▮ ▮▮ ▮▮ ";
1040  IF  M>0 THEN  PRINT "▣ ▮▮ M O N S T E R ▣ ▮▮ ▮▮ ▮▮ ▮▮ ▮▮
      ▮▮ ▮▮ A P P E A R S "
1050  RETURN
1060  PRINT "◣ ◙ ";:D1=1: FOR I=1 TO LEN(R$(RO))
1070  S$=MID$(R$(RO),I,1):IF VAL(S$)>0THEN FOR J=1 TO
      VAL(S$):GOSUB 1150:NEXT
1080  IF S$="U "THEN D1=0
1090  IF S$="L "THEN D1=3
1100  IF S$="D "THEN D1=2
1110  IF S$="R "THEN D1=1
1120  IF S$="E "THEN PRINT "▀ ";
1130  IF S$="O "THEN  PRINT "◙ ";
1140  NEXT:PRINT "◙ ":GOSUB 970:RETURN
1150  PRINT "▲ ▮▮ ";
```

```
1160  IF D1=0THEN PRINT "□ ";
1170  IF D1=1THEN PRINT "▜ ";
1180  IF D1=2THEN PRINT "▣ ";
1190  IF D1=3THEN PRINT "▐ ";
1200  RETURN
1210  IF S$="O "THEN  PRINT "▣ ";
```

ChexSum Tables

```
10    =    0        440  = 2338       850   =  890
20    =  400        450  = 2308       860   = 2490
30    = 2820        460  = 1667       870   = 1695
40    = 2383        470  =  836       880   =  393
60    = 1558        480  = 1981       890   =  882
70    = 3210        490  = 1910       900   =  735
80    = 3299        500  = 3439       910   = 2570
90    = 1367        510  =  919       920   = 4045
100   = 2802        520  =  359       930   = 1463
110   = 2040        530  =  920       940   = 3842
120   = 2019        540  = 1132       950   = 1696
130   = 3664        550  = 1181       960   = 1123
140   = 1848        560  = 4034       970   = 4198
150   = 1500        570  = 1656       980   = 2958
160   = 1540        580  = 1810       990   = 2406
170   = 1502        590  =  549       1000  = 3615
180   = 1551        600  = 5274       1010  = 6868
190   = 1591        610  =  300       1020  = 5552
200   = 1550        620  = 3767       1030  = 4377
210   = 4283        630  =  790       1040  = 3385
220   = 1735        640  = 2144       1050  =  143
230   = 1885        650  =  773       1060  = 2354
240   = 3701        660  = 5599       1070  = 4207
250   = 2158        690  = 8163       1080  = 1166
260   = 3641        700  = 5195       1090  = 1160
270   = 3346        720  =  508       1100  = 1151
310   = 5600        730  = 5637       1110  = 1166
320   = 5979        740  = 4856       1120  = 1226
340   = 3454        750  = 5193       1130  = 1106
350   = 3425        760  =  507       1140  = 1031
360   = 1018        770  = 4120       1150  =  481
370   = 1019        780  = 2733       1160  = 1117
380   = 1020        790  = 5240       1170  =  993
390   = 1021        800  = 2410       1180  =  991
400   =  526        810  = 1733       1190  = 1123
410   = 1793        820  = 2194       1200  =  143
420   = 1648        830  = 1060       1210  = 1106
430   = 2106        840  = 5837       TOTAL = 262921
```

Warlock

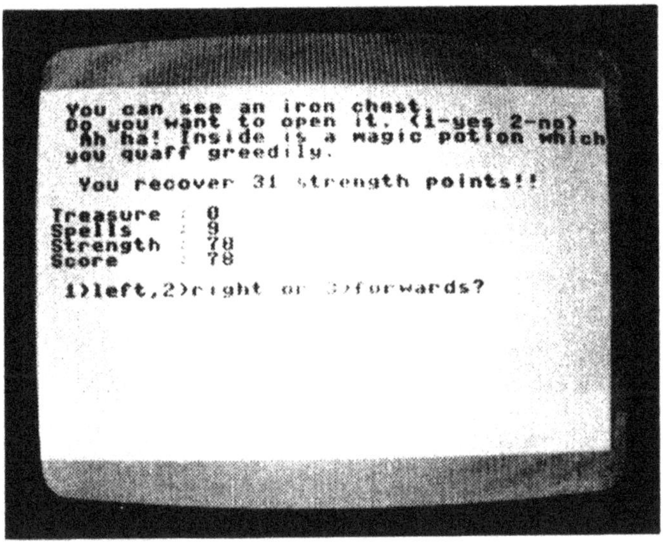

CLASSIFICATION: Adventure

You have been cast into the world of the warlock, a time of dungeons and dragons. The objective of the game is to live as long as possible but at the same time gather as much treasure as you can. You will be confronted with monsters and creatures of all sorts and you will have one of three alternatives: attack, retreat or use a spell. Beware, spells are not always effective against creatures of the night.

PROGRAM
Variables

S	Strength
SP	Spells
TR	Player's treasures
M	Monsters
CO	Colours of monsters
HA	Next event
Z	Up or down stairs
D	Silently or noisily
E	Angry, friendly or dumb looking
MH	Advance or stop
MT	Coins taken by the monster
SS	Metal spikes
TT	Silver or gold
T	Monster's treasure

Listing

```
10    COLOR4,7,3:COLOR0,2,5:S=100:SP=8+INT(RND(1)*4):TR
      =0
20    PRINT CHR$(14)"▚ ▩ ▲ ▲ ▲ ▲ ▲ ▲ ▲ ▲ ▲ ▲ ▲ ▲ - = * ▲ ● ♠ ▬
      ▙ ▛ ▤ ▨ ▲ * = - "
30    PRINT :PRINT "▲ ▲ ▲ ▌O U ' V E ▲ B E E N ▲ T R A N
       S P O R T E D ▲ T O ▲ S O M E W H E R E "
40    PRINT "▲ W I T H I N ▲ T H E ▲ ● A R L O C K ' S ▲
      C A V E S . "
50    PRINT :PRINT "▲ ▲ ▲ L I V E ▲ A S ▲ L O N G ▲ A S ▲
       P O S S I B L E ▲ G A I N I N G "
60    PRINT "▲ T R E A S U R E ▲ A N D ▲ K I L L I N G ▲
      M O N S T E R S . "
70    PRINT :PRINT :PRINT :PRINT "▲ ▲ ▲ ▜ L E A S E ▲ P R
       E S S ▲ A N Y ▲ K E Y ▲ T O ▲ S T A R T . "
80    GETA$:IF A$=""THEN 80
90    PRINT "▚ "
```

Print Message; Press Any Key to Start

```
100   S=S-INT(RND(1)*5)+1:IF S<1THEN 760
110   PRINT :PRINT "▲ ▌R E A S U R E ▲ : "TR:PRINT "▲ ♥
      P E L L S ▲ ▲ ▲ : "SP:PRINT "▲ ♥ T R E N G T H ▲ :
      "S
120   PRINT "▲ ♥ C O R E ▲ ▲ ▲ ▲ : "TR*10+S:POKE 198,0
130   M=INT(RND(1)*13)+1
140   T=INT(RND(1)*20)+1
150   CO=INT(RND(1)*7)+1
160   HA=INT(RND(1)*6)+1
170   PRINT :PRINT "▲ ▲ 1 ) L E F T , 2 ) R I G H T ▲ O R
       ▲ 3 ) F O R W A R D S ? "
180   GETA$:IF A$=""ORA$<>"1 "ANDA$<>"2 "ANDA$<>"3 "
      THEN 180
190   PRINT "▚ "
200   IF RND(1)<.15THEN GOTO 160
210   ON HAGOTO 220,340,460,460,1010,1370
220   PRINT "▲ ▲ ▲ ▌O U ▲ C A N ▲ S E E ▲ A ▲ F L I G H
      T ▲ O F ▲ S T A I R S ▲ G O I N G "
```

Check If You Want to Use the Stairs or Move Into a Room

```
230   Z=INT(RND(1)*2)+1
240   IF Z=1THEN PRINT "▲ ▲ U P W A R D S ▲ I N T O ▲ T H
       E ▲ G L O O M . "
```

```
250  IF Z=2THEN PRINT "▲▲DOWN▲INTO▲BLACKNESS."
260  PRINT :PRINT "▲▲▲▒O▲YOU▲WISH▲TO▲USE▲THEM?":PRINT "▲▲▲▲▲▲▲▲▲1-YES▲2-NO"
270  GETA$:IF A$=""ORA$<>"1 "ANDA$<>"2 "THEN 270
280  IF A$="2 "ORRND(1)<.8THEN 100
290  PRINT :PRINT "▲▲▲**WHOOPS**"
300  FOR I=1 TO 1000:NEXT
310  PRINT :PRINT "▲▲▒OU▲FELL▲DOWN▲THE▲STAIRS!"
320  PRINT :PRINT "▲▲5▲STRENGTH▲POINTS▲TAKEN▲AWAY."
330  S=S-5:GOTO 100
340  PRINT "▲▲▒OU▲CAN▲SEE▲A▲DOOR."
350  PRINT "▲▲▒O▲YOU▲WANT▲TO▲OPEN▲IT▲(1-YES▲2-NO)?"
360  GETA$:IF A$=""ORA$<>"1 "ANDA$<>"2 "THEN 360
370  IF A$="2 "THEN 100
380  PRINT :PRINT "▲▲▒HE▲DOOR▲OPENS";
390  D=INT(RND(1)*2)+1
400  IF D=1THEN PRINT "▲SILENTLY."
410  IF D=2THEN PRINT "▲WITH▲A▲LOUD▲CREAKING."
420  FOR I=1 TO 500:NEXT
430  IF RND(1)<.7THEN 450
440  GOTO 100
```

Print 'Behind a Door You Can See a Creature of Some Sort'

```
450  PRINT "▲▲▒EHIND▲THE▲DOOR-"
460  PRINT "▲▲▒OU▲CAN▲SEE▲A";
470  E=INT(RND(1)*3)+1
480  IF E=1THEN PRINT "N▲ANGRY"
490  IF E=2THEN PRINT "▲FRIENDLY"
500  IF E=3THEN PRINT "▲DUMB"
510  PRINT "▲▲LOOKING▲";
520  ON COGOSUB 1300,1310,1320,1330,1340,1350,1360,1370
530  ON MGOSUB 1160,1170,1180,1190,1200,1210,1220,1230,1240,1250,1260,1270,1280,1290
540  MH=INT(RND(1)*2)+1
550  IF MH=1THEN PRINT :PRINT "▲▲▒E▲ADVANCES!"
560  IF MH=2THEN PRINT :PRINT "▲▲▒E▲STOPS!"
570  PRINT :PRINT "▲▲1)ATTACK,2)RETREAT▲OR▲3)USE▲A▲SPELL"
580  GETA$:IF A$<>"1 "ANDA$<>"2 "ANDA$<>"3 "THEN 580
590  IF A$<>"2 "THEN 640
```

```
600   PRINT :PRINT "▲ ▲ ▲ ▲ ▲ ▒ ▒ ▒ ▒ ▒ ▒ / ! ! "
610   FOR I=1 TO 800:NEXT
620   IF RND(1)<.8THEN 100
630   PRINT :PRINT :PRINT "▲ ▲ ▒ E ▲ D O E S N ' T ▲ L E
      T ▲ Y O U ▲ A N Y H O W ! ":GOTO 570
640   IF A$="1 "THEN 730
650   IF SP=0THEN PRINT "▲ ▲ ▒ O U ▲ H A V E ▲ N O N E .
      ":GOTO 570
660   IF RND(1)<.35THEN 700
670   PRINT : PRINT "▒ ▲ ▲ ▒ H E ▲ S P E L L ▲ W O R K E
      D . ":PRINT
680   SP=SP-1:IF SP<5THEN PRINT "▲ ▲ ▒ U T ▲ Y O U ' R E
      ▲ S H O R T ▲ O N ▲ T H E M ▲ N O W . "
690   GOTO 910
700   PRINT :PRINT "▒ ▲ ▲ ▒ H E ▲ S P E L L ▲ D I D N ' T
       ▲ W O R K . "
710   PRINT "▲ ▲ ▒ T ▲ J U S T ▲ M A D E ▲ H I M ▲ A N G
      R Y . "
720   GOTO 570
730   IF RND(1)<.31ANDINT(RND(1)*10)*10<SORRND(1)<.28
      THEN 900
740   IF RND(1)<.8THEN 790
750   PRINT "▒ "
760   PRINT :PRINT "▲ ▲ ▒ O U ' R E ▲ ▒ ▒ ♠ ▒ ! ! "
770   PRINT :PRINT "▲ ▲ ▲ ▲ ▲ ♥ ▒ ┌ ▒ ▒ ▲ : "TR*10+S
780   END
```

'You Are Dead'; 'You Are Wounded'; 'You Have Lost Your Strength'

```
790   PRINT : PRINT "▒ ▲ ▲ ▒ O U ' V E ▲ B E E N ▲ W O U
      N D E D ▲ A N D ▲ Y O U R ▲ S T R E N G T H ":
      PRINT "▲ ▲ H A S ▲ B E E N ▲ H A L V E D . "
800   S=INT(S/2)
810   IF INT(RND(1))<.4ORSS<>0THEN 100
820   IF RND(1)<.4THEN 870
830   MT=INT(TR/INT(RND(1)*7)):PRINT "▲ ▲ A L S O ▲ T H E
       ▲ M O N S T E R ▲ S T O L E "MT"C O I N S ▲ F R O
      M "
840   PRINT "▲ ▲ Y O U R ▲ P U R S E . . . "
850   TR=TR-MT
860   TR=0:GOTO 100
870   PRINT "▲ ▲ ┌ H ▲ N O ! ▲ ▒ H E ▲ M O N S T E R ▲ S
      T O L E ▲ A L L ▲ Y O U R "
880   PRINT "▲ ▲ C O I N A G E . ▲ ▒ A D ▲ L U C K . "
890   TR=0:GOTO 100
900   PRINT "▒ "
910   PRINT "▲ ▲ ● E L L ▲ D O N E ! ! "
```

```
920   PRINT :PRINT "▲ ▲ ▲ ▮ O U ▲ K I L L E D ▲ H I M , "
      ;
930   PRINT "▲ A N D ▲ H I S ";
940   TT=INT(RND(1)*2)+1
950   PRINT T"C O I N S ▲ O F " '
960   IF TT=1THEN PRINT "▲ ▲ S I L V E R ";
970   IF TT=2THEN PRINT "▲ ▲ G O L D ";
980   PRINT "▲ A R E ▲ N O W ▲ Y O U R S . "
990   TR=TR+T
1000  GOTO 100
1010  IF RND(1)<.3THEN 100
1020  PRINT "▲ ▲ * * W H O O P S * * "
1030  FOR I=1 TO 1000:NEXT
1040  PRINT :PRINT "▲ ▲ ▮ O U ▲ F E L L ▲ D O W N ▲ A ▲ P
       I T ! "
1050  PRINT "▲ ▲ ♠ T ▲ T H E ▲ B O T T O M ";
1060  HN=INT(RND(1)*4)
1070  ON HNGOTO 1080,1090,1110,1130,1130
1080  GOTO 460
1090  PRINT "▲ I S ▲ N O T H I N G . "
1100  GOTO 100
1110  PRINT "▲ I S ▲ A ▲ P O O L ▲ O F ▲ A C I D ! ! "
1120  GOTO 760
1130  SS=INT(RND(1)*10)+1
1140  PRINT "A R E "SS"M E T A L ▲ S P I K E S ! ! "
1150  GOTO 790
1160  PRINT "D E M O G O R G O N ! ":RETURN
1170  PRINT "H Y D R A ! ":RETURN
1180  PRINT "S E R P E N T ! ":RETURN
1190  PRINT "G I A N T ! ":RETURN
1200  PRINT "D R A G O N ! ":RETURN
1210  PRINT "J U B I L E X ! ":RETURN
1220  PRINT "Z O M B I E ! ":RETURN
1230  PRINT "W R A I T H ! ":RETURN
1240  PRINT "M I N O T A U R ! ":RETURN
1250  PRINT "D E V I L ! ":RETURN
1260  PRINT "W E R E W O L F ! ":RETURN
1270  PRINT "O R C ! ":RETURN
1280  PRINT "W A R L O C K ! ":RETURN
1290  PRINT "■ W H I T E ▲ ";:RETURN
1300  PRINT "■ B L A C K ▲ ■ ";:RETURN
1310  PRINT "C O L O U R L E S S ▲ ";:RETURN
1320  PRINT "■ R E D ▲ ■ ";:RETURN
1330  PRINT "■ Y E L L O W ▲ ■ ";:RETURN
1340  PRINT "■ G R E E N ■ ▲ ";:RETURN
1350  PRINT "■ P U R P L E ▲ ■ ";:RETURN
1360  PRINT "■ B L U E ▲ ■ ";:RETURN
1370  PRINT "▲ ▲ ▮ O U ▲ C A N ▲ S E E ▲ A ";
1380  Z=INT(RND(1)*2+1)
1390  IF Z=1THEN PRINT "▲ W O O D E N ";
```

```
1400  IF Z=2THEN PRINT "N ▲ I R O N ";
1410  PRINT "▲ C H E S T . "
1420  PRINT "▲ ▲ ▒ O ▲ Y O U ▲ W A N T ▲ T O ▲ O P E N ▲
      I T . ▲ ( 1 - Y E S ▲ 2 - N O ) "
1430  GETA$:IF A$=""ORA$<>"1 "ANDA$<>"2 "THEN 1430
1440  IF A$="2 "THEN 100
1450  Z=INT(RND(1)*10+1)
1460  IF Z=1THEN ? "▲ ▲ ┏ H ▲ D E A R ! ▲ ▒ T ▲ W A S ▲ B
       O O B Y ▲ T R A P P E D ! ":? "▲ ▲ ▒ O U ▲ C H O K
       E ▲ O N ▲ P O I S O N ▲ G A S . ":S=S-10
1470  IF Z<3THEN 100
1480  IF Z<8THEN PRINT "▲ ▲ ▒ T ▲ W A S ▲ E M P T Y . ":
      GOTO 100
1490  PRINT "▲ ▲ ▲ ♠ H ▲ H A ! ▲ ▒ N S I D E ▲ I S ▲ A ▲
      M A G I C ▲ P O T I O N ▲ W H I C H "
1500  PRINT "▲ ▲ Y O U ▲ Q U A F F ▲ G R E E D I L Y . "
1510  Z=INT(RND(1)*20+16)
1520  PRINT :PRINT "▲ ▲ ▲ ▒ O U ▲ R E C O V E R "Z"S T R
      E N G T H ▲ P O I N T S ! ! ":S=S+Z:GOTO 100
```

ChexSum Tables

10	= 3629		290	= 1287		570	= 3340
20	= 3229		300	= 1021		580	= 3162
30	= 3938		310	= 2665		590	= 1104
40	= 2585		320	= 2955		600	= 2204
50	= 3435		330	= 1187		610	= 971
60	= 2770		340	= 1874		620	= 1106
70	= 3716		350	= 3163		630	= 3616
80	= 1149		360	= 2942		640	= 916
90	= 372		370	= 908		650	= 2956
100	= 2472		380	= 1826		660	= 1176
110	= 4756		390	= 1316		670	= 2405
120	= 2283		400	= 1622		680	= 4646
130	= 1389		410	= 2618		690	= 534
140	= 1396		420	= 964		700	= 2589
150	= 1407		430	= 1120		710	= 2265
160	= 1401		440	= 525		720	= 532
170	= 2804		450	= 1648		730	= 3747
180	= 3744		460	= 1449		740	= 1110
190	= 372		470	= 1317		750	= 372
200	= 1551		480	= 1396		760	= 2125
210	= 2084		490	= 1545		770	= 2560
220	= 3541		500	= 1225		780	= 129
230	= 1338		510	= 952		790	= 6417
240	= 2868		520	= 2612		800	= 846
250	= 2634		530	= 4820		810	= 2174
260	= 4119		540	= 1408		820	= 1113
270	= 2941		550	= 2331		830	= 5915
280	= 1709		560	= 2067		840	= 1323

```
850   =  863
860   = 1007
870   = 3290
880   = 1785
890   = 1007
900   =  372
910   = 1196
920   = 1938
930   =  821
940   = 1428
950   =  918
960   = 1608
970   = 1419
980   = 1341
990   =  778
1000  =  525
1010  = 1109
1020  =  994
1030  = 1021
1040  = 2213
1050  = 1510
1060  = 1174
1070  = 2010
1080  =  531
1090  = 1074
1100  =  525
1110  = 1611
1120  =  531
1130  = 1482
1140  = 1806
1150  =  538
1160  = 1272
1170  =  866
1180  = 1045
1190  =  854
1200  =  925
1210  = 1033
1220  =  944
1230  =  951
1240  = 1138
1250  =  857
1260  = 1116
1270  =  702
1280  = 1028
1290  =  948
1300  =  960
1310  = 1379
1320  =  811
1330  = 1222
1340  =  976
1350  = 1224
1360  =  896
1370  = 1449
1380  = 1337
1390  = 1456
1400  = 1379
1410  =  709
1420  = 3190
1430  = 3002
1440  =  908
1450  = 1402
1460  = 7880
1470  =  796
1480  = 2777
1490  = 3723
1500  = 1841
1510  = 1463
1520  = 4723
TOTAL = 279355
```

Reel Thing

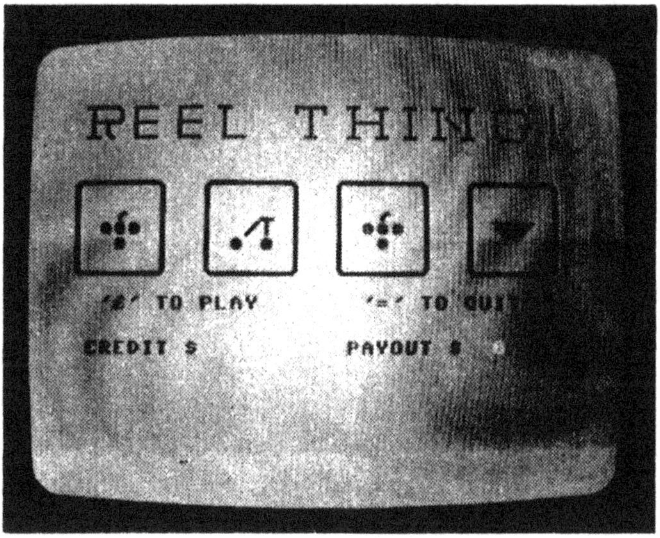

CLASSIFICATION: Gambling

Play a four wheel poker machine. You start with ten dollars and can win up to $2000. There are five different symbols — cherries, grapes, pine-apples, watermelons and, for big dollars, dollar signs. Spin the wheels and try your luck. There are different combinations in every game. Controls are £ to spin wheels and = to exit.

PROGRAMMING SUGGESTIONS

The odds of the wheels can be adjusted in this game. New symbols could be designed. Finally, the payout could be changed, for example, if cherry, cherry, dollar, dollar was to pay $3Ø, then this could be inserted after line 63:

If R(Ø) = Ø and R(1) = Ø and R(2) = 4 and
R(3) = 4 then W = 3Ø

Program Variables

WH	Weighting of each symbol on each wheel
R	Symbol currently showing
SC	Screen memory
CL	Colour memory
CR	Money
W	Amount won
WT	Weighting of wheel
FT	Random function to select symbol

Listing

Initialise Game and Draw Title Screen

```
10    VOL 8:COLOR0,2,6:COLOR4,2,6:COLOR1,14,4
20    PRINT "▖▣ ▴ ▴ ▴ ▴ ┳ ═ ▜ ┏ ═ ▴ ┏ ═ ▴ ┳ ▴ ▴ ▴ ▴ ┏ ┳
      ▜ ▴ ┳ ▴ ┳ ▴ ┳ ▴ ┳ ▴ ┳ ▴ ▛ ═ ▜ ▴ ▐ "
30    PRINT "▴ ▴ ▴ ▴ ┣ ┳ ▟ ┣ ═ ▴ ┣ ═ ▴ ▐ ▴ ▴ ▴ ▴ ▴ ▴ ▐ ▴ ▴
      ┣ ═ ┫ ▴ ▐ ▴ ▐ ╲ ▐ ▴ ▐ ▴ ┳ ▴ ▐ "
40    PRINT "▴ ▴ ▴ ▴ ┻ ▙ ▴ ▙ ═ ▴ ▙ ═ ▴ ▙ ═ ▴ ▴ ▴ ▴ ▴ ┻ ▴ ▴
      ┻ ▴ ┻ ▴ ┻ ▴ ┻ ▴ ┻ ▴ ▙ ═ ▟ ▴ ● "
50    DIMWH(3,4):DIMR(3):SC=1024:CL=55296:CR=10:W=0:
      GOSUB 680:FOR I=0 TO 3:R(I)=0:NEXT
60    COLOR1,2,3:PRINT "▣ ▣ ▴ ▴ ▴ ▛ ═ ═ ═ ═ ═ ▜ ▴ ▴ ▛ ═ ═
      ═ ═ ═ ▜ ▴ ▴ ▛ ═ ═ ═ ═ ═ ▜ ▴ ▴ ▛ ═ ═ ═ ═ ═ ▜ "
70    PRINT "▣ ▣ ▣ ▐ ▚ ▚ ▚ ▚ ▚ ▐ ▴ ▴ ▐ ▚ ▚ ▚ ▚ ▚ ▐ ▴ ▴ ▐
      ▚ ▚ ▚ ▚ ▚ ▐ ▴ ▴ ▐ ▚ ▚ ▚ ▚ ▚ ▐ "
80    PRINT "▣ ▣ ▣ ▐ ▚ ▚ ▚ ▚ ▚ ▐ ▴ ▴ ▐ ▚ ▚ ▚ ▚ ▚ ▐ ▴ ▴ ▐
      ▚ ▚ ▚ ▚ ▚ ▐ ▴ ▴ ▐ ▚ ▚ ▚ ▚ ▚ ▐ "
90    PRINT "▣ ▣ ▣ ▐ ▚ ▚ ▚ ▚ ▚ ▐ ▴ ▴ ▐ ▚ ▚ ▚ ▚ ▚ ▐ ▴ ▴ ▐
      ▚ ▚ ▚ ▚ ▚ ▐ ▴ ▴ ▐ ▚ ▚ ▚ ▚ ▚ ▐ "
100   PRINT "▣ ▣ ▣ ▐ ▚ ▚ ▚ ▚ ▚ ▐ ▴ ▴ ▐ ▚ ▚ ▚ ▚ ▚ ▐ ▴ ▴ ▐
      ▚ ▚ ▚ ▚ ▚ ▐ ▴ ▴ ▐ ▚ ▚ ▚ ▚ ▚ ▐ "
110   PRINT "▣ ▣ ▣ ▐ ▚ ▚ ▚ ▚ ▚ ▐ ▴ ▴ ▐ ▚ ▚ ▚ ▚ ▚ ▐ ▴ ▴ ▐
      ▚ ▚ ▚ ▚ ▚ ▐ ▴ ▴ ▐ ▚ ▚ ▚ ▚ ▚ ▐ "
120   PRINT "▣ ▣ ▣ ▙ ═ ═ ═ ═ ═ ▟ ▴ ▴ ▙ ═ ═ ═ ═ ═ ▟ ▴ ▴ ▙
      ═ ═ ═ ═ ═ ▟ ▴ ▴ ▙ ═ ═ ═ ═ ═ ▟ "
130   PRINT :COLOR1,2,4:PRINT "▣ ▣ ▴ ▴ ▴ ' £ ' ▴ T O ▴ P
      L A Y ▴ ▴ ▴ ▴ ▴ ▴ ▴ ' = ' ▴ T O ▴ Q U I T "
140   GOSUB 210:GOSUB 240
```

Get input

```
150   GETA$:IF A$=""THEN 150
160   IF A$="= "THEN 200
170   IF A$<>"£ "THEN 150
180   CR=CR-1:GOSUB 210:GOSUB 240:GOSUB 280:GOSUB 580:
      IF CR=0THEN 200
190   GOTO 150
```

End Game

```
200   COLOR1,6:PRINT "S Q Q Q Q Q Q Q Q Q Q Q Q Q Q Q Q Q
      Q Q Q ] ] ] ] ] ] ] W E L L , ▲ T H A N K ▲ Y O U ▲
      F O R ▲ P L A Y I N G ! ":END
```

Print Credit Rating

```
210   COLOR1,13,4:PRINT "S Q Q Q Q Q Q Q Q Q Q Q Q Q Q Q Q
      Q Q ▲ ▲ ▲ ▲ C R E D I T ▲ $ ▲ ▲ ▲ ▲ ▲ ▲ ▲ II II II II II
      II ";CR
220   COLOR1,8:PRINT "S Q Q Q Q Q Q Q Q Q Q Q Q Q Q Q Q Q
      ] ] ] ] ] ] ] ] ] ] ] ] ] ";CR
230   RETURN
```

Print Payout

```
240   COLOR1,13,4:PRINT "S Q Q Q Q Q Q Q Q Q Q Q Q Q Q Q Q
      Q Q ] ] ] ] ] ] ] ] ] ] ] ] ] ] ] ] ] ] ] ] ] ] ] P A
      Y O U T ▲ $ ▲ ▲ ▲ ▲ ▲ ▲ ▲ II II II II II II "
250   RETURN
260   COLOR1,8:PRINT "S Q Q Q Q Q Q Q Q Q Q Q Q Q Q Q Q Q
      ] ] ] ] ] ] ] ] ] ] ] ] ] ] ] ] ] ] ] ] ] ] ] ] ] ]
      ] ] ] ] ] ] ";W
270   RETURN
```

Spin Wheels

```
280   FOR I=1 TO 4:COLOR1,10
290   PRINT "S Q Q Q Q Q Q Q ";:FOR K=1 TO 5:FOR J=1
      TO 4:IF I<=JTHEN PRINT "≡ ] ] ] ] ▚ ▚ ▚ ▚ ▚ ";:
      GOTO 310
300   PRINT "] ] ] ] ] ] ] ] ] ] ";
310   NEXTJ:PRINT :NEXTK
320   PRINT "S Q Q Q Q Q Q Q ";:FOR K=1 TO 5:FOR J=1
      TO 4:IF I<=JTHEN PRINT "13 ] ] ] ] ▚ ▚ ▚ ▚ ▚ ";:
      GOTO 340
330   PRINT "] ] ] ] ] ] ] ] ] ] ";
340   NEXTJ:PRINT :NEXTK
350   IF I=1THEN PRINT "S Q Q Q Q Q Q Q ] ] ] ] ";:
      GOSUB 410
360   IF I=2THEN PRINT "S Q Q Q Q Q Q Q ] ] ] ] ] ] ] ] ]
      ] ] ] ] ";:GOSUB 410
370   IF I=3THEN PRINT "S Q Q Q Q Q Q Q ] ] ] ] ] ] ] ] ]
      ] ] ] ] ] ] ] ] ] ] ] ] ] ] ";:GOSUB 410
380   IF I=4THEN PRINT "S Q Q Q Q Q Q Q ] ] ] ] ] ] ] ] ]
      ] ] ] ] ] ] ] ] ] ] ] ] ] ] ] ] ] ] ] ] ] ] ";:
      GOSUB 410
```

```
390   SOUND 1,200,5:NEXTI
400   RETURN
```

Select and Draw Symbol

```
410   WT=0:FOR J=0 TO 4:WT=WT+WH(I-1,J):NEXT
420   FT=INT(RND(0)*WT+1):J=0
430   FT=FT-WH(I-1,J):IF FT<=0THEN R(I-1)=J:GOTO 470
440   J=J+1:IF J<4THEN 430
450   R(I-1)=4
460   PRINT "◙▲▲▲▲▲▲◙‖‖‖‖‖▲▨+▧▲◙‖‖‖‖
      ‖▲▧+▧▲◙‖‖‖‖‖▲▧+▨▲◙‖‖‖‖‖▲▲▲
      ▲▲":RETURN
470   IF J>0THEN 500
480   COLOR1,10,4:PRINT "▲▲▲▲▲◙‖‖‖‖‖▲▲▲☐▲
      ◙‖‖‖‖‖▲▲/▥▲";
490   COLOR1,3,4:PRINT "◙‖‖‖‖‖▲●▲●▲◙‖‖‖‖‖
      ▲▲▲▲▲":RETURN
500   IF J>1THEN 530
510   COLOR1,10,4:PRINT "▲▲▲▲▲◙‖‖‖‖‖▲▲▨▲▲
      ";
520   COLOR1,5,4:PRINT "◙‖‖‖‖‖▲●●●▲◙‖‖‖‖‖
      ▲▲●▲▲◙‖‖‖‖‖▲▲▲▲▲":RETURN
530   IF J>2THEN 560
540   COLOR1,6,4:PRINT "▲▲▲▲▲◙‖‖‖‖‖▲▧V▨▲"
      ;
550   COLOR1,9,4:PRINT "◙‖‖‖‖‖▲▲※▲▲◙‖‖‖‖‖
      ▲▲※▲▲◙‖‖‖‖‖▲▲▲▲▲":RETURN
560   COLOR1,3,6:PRINT "▲▲▲▲▲◙‖‖‖‖‖▲☐☐☐▲"
      ;
570   COLOR1,16,4:PRINT "◙‖‖‖‖‖▲◥◙▲▀◤▲◙‖‖
      ‖‖‖▲▲☐▲▲◙‖‖‖‖‖▲▲▲▲▲":RETURN
```

Calculate Payout

```
580   W=0
590   IF R(0)=0THEN W=W+1:IF R(1)=0THEN W=W+1:IF R(2)=0
      THEN W=W+4:IF R(3)=0THEN W=W+17
600   IF R(0)=1ANDR(1)=1THEN W=W+3:IF R(2)=1THEN W=W+13:
      IF R(3)=1THEN W=W+80
610   IF R(0)=2ANDR(1)=2THEN W=W+4:IF R(2)=2THEN W=W+60:
      IF R(3)=2THEN W=W+80
620   IF R(0)=3ANDR(1)=3ANDR(2)=3THEN W=W+176:IF R(3)=3
      THEN W=W+154
630   IF R(0)=4ANDR(1)=4ANDR(2)=4THEN W=W+120:IF R(3)=4
      THEN W=W+2000
640   GOSUB 260:P=W
```

```
650     IF W>10THEN FOR J=1 TO INT(P/10):CR=CR+10:W=W-10:
        GOSUB 220:SOUND 1,990,1:NEXT
660     IF W>0THEN FOR J=1 TO W:CR=CR+1:W=W-1:GOSUB 220:
        SOUND 1,1000,1:NEXT
670     RETURN
```

Establish Weighting of Wheels

```
680     WH(0,0)=8:WH(0,1)=8:WH(0,2)=5:WH(0,3)=3:WH(0,4)=1
690     WH(1,0)=4:WH(1,1)=4:WH(1,2)=3:WH(1,3)=3:WH(1,4)=1
700     WH(2,0)=3:WH(2,1)=4:WH(2,2)=3:WH(2,3)=4:WH(2,4)=2
710     WH(3,0)=2:WH(3,1)=4:WH(3,2)=3:WH(3,3)=5:WH(3,4)=1
720     RETURN
```

ChexSum Tables

Line	Sum	Line	Sum	Line	Sum
10	= 2040	250	= 143	490	= 3514
20	= 5176	260	= 3062	500	= 778
30	= 4948	270	= 143	510	= 2387
40	= 4709	280	= 1179	520	= 5044
50	= 5489	290	= 5352	530	= 779
60	= 7613	300	= 567	540	= 2539
70	= 6157	310	= 697	550	= 4673
80	= 6157	320	= 5223	560	= 2570
90	= 6157	330	= 567	570	= 5030
100	= 6157	340	= 697	580	= 316
110	= 6157	350	= 1670	590	= 6033
120	= 6661	360	= 1944	600	= 5293
130	= 3334	370	= 2402	610	= 5293
140	= 672	380	= 2962	620	= 4503
150	= 1212	390	= 858	630	= 4556
160	= 919	400	= 143	640	= 725
170	= 1141	410	= 2975	650	= 4905
180	= 3207	420	= 1921	660	= 4196
190	= 526	430	= 3786	670	= 143
200	= 4714	440	= 1443	680	= 3673
210	= 3984	450	= 718	690	= 3680
220	= 2028	460	= 7048	700	= 3681
230	= 143	470	= 777	710	= 3684
240	= 5181	480	= 3756	720	= 143
				TOTAL	= 222653

Road Patrol

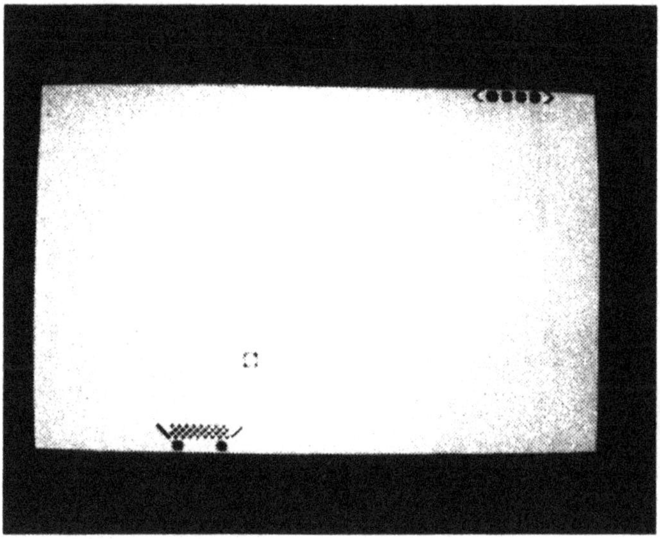

CLASSIFICATION: Shoot Up

Move your vehicle left and right along the bottom of the screen, avoiding the aliens' bombs descending upon you. You can fire at the aliens by pressing the SPACE bar. Move left and right using the I and P keys.

PROGRAMMING SUGGESTIONS

Increase the speed of the missiles so that the player's reactions have to be swifter. Occasionally place barriers around the patrol car so that it is paralyzed.

PROGRAM
Variables

PA$	Patrol car
SA$	Alien ship
MS	Missile in flight flag
SV	Start of screen
SC	Score
K1	Start of machine language routine
E	Flag to indicate end of game

Listing

```
10    REM ROAD PATROL
20    RESTORE:FOR I=1 TO 40:LN$=LN$+"▲ ":NEXT:PA$="\ ※ ※
      ※ ※ ⁄ ▣ ▮▮▮▮▮▮ ▲ ● ▲ ▲ ● ":LT$="▣ "
30    FOR I=1 TO 23:LT$=LT$+"▣ ":NEXT
40    FOR I=1 TO 40:J$=J$+"▣ ":NEXT:FOR I=1 TO 25:H$=H$
      +"▣ ":NEXT
50    RT$="▲ ▲ ▲ ▲ ▲ ▲ ":K1=12000:SV=3072
```

Read In Machine Language Program; Define the Ship and Alien

```
60    FOR I=0 TO 10:READA:POKE 12000+I,A:NEXT
70    PRINT "▣ ";:GOSUB 420:SA$="▲ ( ● ● ● ● > ▲ "
80    GOSUB 490:PRINT "▣ ";
90    PRINT "▣ ";:E=0:PO=17:PRINT LT$;LEFT$(LN$,PO);PA$;:
      F=0:F1=0:RO=2
100   MS=0:ML=0
110   PRINT "▣ ";"S C O R E : ▲ ";:PRINT USING"# # # ";SC
      ;:A=PEEK(198):IF A=33THEN GOSUB 190
```

Main Logic Loop; Move Your Ship Backwards and Forwards

```
120   IF A=41THEN GOSUB 220
130   IF A=60THEN F=1
140   IF FTHEN GOSUB 250:IF ETHEN GOTO 90
150   GOSUB 310
160   JC=INT(RND(1)*LV):IF JC=1THEN F1=1
170   IF F1THEN GOSUB 330:IF ETHEN 90
180   GOTO 110
190   PRINT LT$;:SYS K1
200   IF PO>1THEN PO=PO-1
210   PRINT LEFT$(LN$,PO);PA$;:RETURN
220   PRINT LT$;:SYS K1
230   IF PO<35THEN PO=PO+1:PRINT LEFT$(LN$,PO);PA$;:
      RETURN
240   RETURN
250   IF MS=1THEN 270
260   PT=PO+2:R=20:MS=1
270   POKE TM,32:TM=(SV+(R*40)+PT)
280   IF PEEK(TM)<>32THEN GOSUB 390:E=1:MS=0:RETURN
290   IF R=0THEN MS=0:POKE TM,32:F=0:RETURN
300   POKE TM,209:R=R-1:RETURN
310   IF CO=30THEN GOSUB 570
320   PRINT "▣ ";LEFT$(H$,RO);LEFT$(J$,CO);SA$;:CO=CO+1:
      RETURN
```

Alien Drops Bombs On You; You Fire Up at Alien, Check for Crash

```
330   IF ML=1THEN 350
340   ZN=CO+2:PF=RO+1:ML=1
350   POKE RD,32:RD=SV+(PF*40)+ZN
360   IF PEEK(RD)<>32THEN GOSUB 540:E=1:RETURN
370   IF PF=24THEN ML=0:F1=0:RETURN
380   POKE RD,209:PF=PF+1:RETURN
390   FOR I=1 TO 15:FOR J=1 TO 20:COLOR4,I,4:NEXT:NEXT:E
      =1
400   FOR I=390 TO 1023:SOUND 3,I,5:NEXT
410   SC=SC+20:COLOR4,1,3:COLOR0,4,5:RETURN
420   PRINT "▚ ";TAB(13);"P A T R O L ▲ C A R "
430   PRINT :PRINT :PRINT "A V O I D ▲ T H E ▲ A L I E N
      ▲ U S I N G ▲ T H E ▲ I ▲ K E Y ▲ T O ▲ M O V E ":
      PRINT
440   PRINT "L E F T , ▲ T H E ▲ P ▲ K E Y ▲ T O ▲ M O V
      E ▲ R I G H T ▲ A N D ▲ T H E ▲ ":PRINT
450   PRINT "S P A C E B A R ▲ T O ▲ F I R E ▲ A T ▲ T H
      E ▲ A L I E N . G O O D ▲ L U C K ! ":PRINT :
      PRINT :PRINT
460   PRINT TAB(8);"P R E S S ▲ R E T U R N ▲ T O ▲ S T A
       R T ";
470   GETA$:IF A$<>CHR$(13)THEN 470
480   RETURN
490   PRINT "▚ E N T E R ▲ L E V E L ▲ O F ▲ D I F F I C
      U L T Y ▲ 8 - E A S Y ▲ 1 - H A R D ";
500   GETA$:IF A$=""THEN 500
510   IF A$<"0 "ORA$>"9 "THEN 500
520   LV=VAL(A$):RETURN
530   DATA162,79,169,32,157,152,15,202,208,250,96
540   PRINT "▚ ";TAB(12);"▌ P A T R O L ▲ C A R ▲ D E S T
       R O Y E D ▀ ";:SC=SC-10
550   FOR I=1 TO 10:SOUND 1,5,8:SOUND 2,5,4:NEXT:FOR I=1
       TO 1000:NEXT:COLOR0,2,5:COLOR0,4,5
560   PRINT "▚ ";TAB(12);"▲ ▲ ▲ ▲ ▲ ▲ ▲ ▲ ▲ ▲ ▲ ▲ ▲ ▲ ▲ ▲ ▲
       ▲ ▲ ▲ ▲ ";:RETURN
570   PRINT "▚ ";LEFT$(H$,RO);LEFT$(J$,CO);RT$;
580   RO=INT(RND(1)*20):IF RO<=1THEN 580:ELSECO=1
590   RETURN
```

ChexSum Tables

```
10     =    0        210    = 1402        410    = 2154
20     = 6267        220    =  770        420    = 1764
30     = 1914        230    = 3159        430    = 4225
40     = 3636        240    =  143        440    = 3485
50     = 2030        250    =  878        450    = 4251
60     = 2122        260    = 1656        460    = 2394
70     = 2476        270    = 2199        470    = 1707
80     =  824        280    = 2644        480    =  143
90     = 4485        290    = 2170        490    = 3682
100    =  855        300    = 1399        500    = 1212
110    = 4004        310    = 1067        510    = 1530
120    =  975        320    = 3192        520    =  936
130    =  973        330    =  872        530    = 2301
140    = 1639        340    = 2026        540    = 3869
150    =  295        350    = 2195        550    = 4361
160    = 2447        360    = 2158        560    = 2126
170    = 1309        370    = 1809        570    = 2084
180    =  526        380    = 1557        580    = 3113
190    =  770        390    = 2392        590    =  143
200    = 1459        400    = 1766        TOTAL  = 120540
```

Letterbox

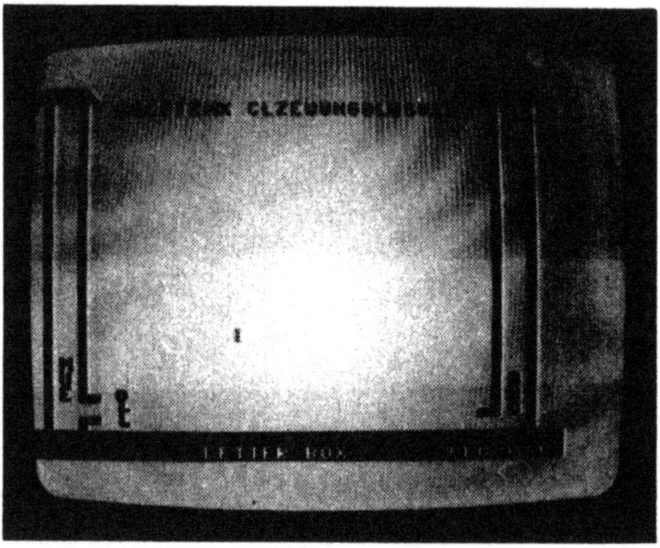

CLASSIFICATION: Educational

Catch the falling letters and post them in the letterbox on the left. If you do not catch them, they will go into the dead-letter box on the right. If you fill the good-letter box before the dead-letter box, then you will go to the next of the five floors. However, should the dead-letter box be filled first, you will go back to the previous floor. The letters fall faster for each higher floor.

Move the mailman left and right with the left and right cursor keys prior to the letter falling. When the letter is falling the mailman can only be moved right by pressing the key that matches the letter that is falling. To move the mailman left, use the same key and the shift key.

PROGRAMMING SUGGESTIONS

Have more than one letter falling to the ground and award bonus points if the player catches the letters.

PROGRAM
Variables

A$(24)	Random letter table
A$(0)	Used for mailman movement with cursor key
C$	Colour table
LM$	Left facing mailman
RM$	Right facing mailman
LV	Floor level
S	Sound register
SL	Good letter stack (number from top)
SR	Missed letter stack (number from top)
X4	Horizontal location of mailman
DX	Direction of mailman
N	Number of dropped letters
K	Row number of dropped letters
M$	Key pressed
M	ASC value of pressed key
K1	Screen location for stacking letters
F	Colour of dropped letters

Listing

```
10    REM LETTER BOX
```

Define Variables; Draw the Post Office

```
20    VOL 8
30    DN$="▣ ◘ ◘ ◘ ◘ ◘ ◘ ◘ ◘ ◘ ◘ ◘ ◘ ◘ ◘ ◘ ◘ ◘ ◘ ◘ ◘ ◘ ◘ ◘
      ◘ "
40    BL$="▬ ▌ ▌ ▌ ▌ ▌ ▲ ▲ ▲ ▲ ▲ ▲ ▲ ▲ ▲ ▲ ▲ ▲ ▲ ▲ ▲ ▲ ▲ ▲
      ▲ ▲ ▲ ▲ ▲ ▲ ▲ ▲ ▲ ▲ ▲ ▲ ▲ ▲ ▲ ▲ ▲ ▲ ▲ ▲ "
50    RT$="▣ ▌ ▌ ▌ ▌ ▌ ▌ ▌ ▌ ▌ ▌ ▌ ▌ ▌ ▌ ▌ ▌ ▌ ▌ ▌ ▌ ▌ ▌ ▌
      ▌ ▌ ▌ ▌ ▌ ▌ ▌ ▌ ▌ ▌ ▌ ▌ ▌ ▌ ▌ ▌ ▌ ▌ ▌ ▌ ▌ "
60    DIMA$(24)‡A$(0)="▌ "‡C$="▣ ◣ ▣ ▣ ▣ ▣ ▣ ▣ ▣ "
70    LM$="■ ● ▲ ◘ ▌▌ ▌▌ ┤ ▲ ◘ ▌▌ ▌▌ ▣ ▲ "‡RM$="■ ▲ ● ◘ ▌▌ ▌▌ ▲
      ├ ◘ ▌▌ ▌▌ ▲ ▣ "‡LV=1
80    SL=20‡SR=21‡X1=INT(RND(.)*8)+10‡DX=1
90    IF LV<1THEN LV=1
100   IF LV>5THEN LV=5
110   GOSUB 340
120   FOR L=1 TO 24‡A$(L)=CHR$(INT(RND(.)*26+65))‡NEXT
130   PRINT LEFT$(DN$,21)RIGHT$(RT$,X1)RM$;
140   E=INT(RND(.)*4)+1‡F=E+6-LV
150   FOR J=E TO F‡PRINT "▣ ▌ ▌ ▌ ▌ ▌ ▲ ▲ ▲ ▲ ▲ ▲ ▲ ▲ ▲ ▲ ▲ ▲ ▲
      ▲ ▲ ▲ ▲ ▲ ▲ ▲ ▲ ▲ ▲ ▲ ▲ ▲ ▲ ▲ ▲ ▲ ▲ ▲ "
160   N=0‡FOR I=1 TO 24
170   GOSUB 440
180   PRINT "▣ ◘ "MID$(C$,J,1)TAB(I+5)A$(I);
190   NEXT‡NEXT
200   PRINT "▣ ";‡N=INT(RND(.)*24)+1
210   FOR K=1 TO 22
220   PRINT LEFT$(DN$,K)TAB(5+N)"▲ ◘ ▌▌ "MID$(C$,F,1)A$(N)
      "▌▌ ";
230   FOR T=1 TO 85-(LV*12)‡NEXT‡GOSUB 440
240   IF SL=0THEN LV=LV+1‡N=SR‡GOSUB 700‡GOTO 80
250   IF K=23THEN 120
260   NEXT
270   FOR T=4+N TO 32
280   IF T=X1THEN GOSUB 310‡T=I+1‡GOTO 300
290   PRINT TAB(T)"▲ "MID$(C$,F)A$(N)‡PRINT "□ ";
300   NEXT
310   GOSUB 760
320   IF SR=0THEN LV=LV-1‡N=SL‡GOSUB 730‡GOTO 80
330   GOTO 120
340   COLOR0,7,5‡COLOR4,7,5‡PRINT "▣ "
350   PRINT "▣ ▣ ▣ ◤ ▲ ▲ ▲ ◥ ▬ ▲ ▲ ▲ ▲ ▲ ▲ ▲ ▲ ▲ ▲ ▲ ▲ ▲ ▲
      ▲ ▲ ▲ ▲ ▲ ▲ ▲ ▲ ▲ ▲ ▲ ▲ ▲ ▲ ▲ ▲ ▲ ▣ ▣ ◤ ▲ ▲ ▲ ◥ "
```

```
360   FOR I=1 TO 22
370   PRINT "■■■■■■■▲▲▲▲▲▲▲▲▲▲▲▲▲▲▲▲▲▲▲
      ▲▲▲▲▲▲▲▲▲▲▲▲▲▲▲▲■■■■■"
380   NEXT
390   PRINT "■■▲▲▲▲▲▲▲▲▲▲▲▲▲▲▲▲▲▲▲▲▲▲▲▲▲
      ▲▲▲▲▲▲▲▲▲▲▲▲▲▲▲▲▲▲▲▲▲▲▲▲▲"
400   PRINT "■■▲▲▲▲▲▲▲▲▲▲▲▲▲▲▲▲▲▲LETTER▲B
      OX▲▲▲▲▲▲▲▲▲▲FLOOR▲▲▲■■■"LV"■"
410   PRINT LEFT$(DN$,21)"■■■■■■■■▲■■■";
420   PRINT LEFT$(BL$,29)"■■■■"
430   RETURN
```

Move Mailman Left or Right, Depending on Key Pressed

```
440   REM MOVE MAILMAN
450   GETM$:IF M$=""THEN 540
460   IF M$="■"THEN PRINT "■":END
470   IF M$=A$(N)THEN MM$=RM$:DX=1:GOTO 510
480   M=ASC(M$):M=M-128
490   IF M=ASC(A$(N)+CHR$(0))THEN MM$=LM$:DX=-1:GOTO 510
500   M$="":GOTO 540
510   PRINT LEFT$(DN$,21)RIGHT$(RT$,X1)MM$;
520   X1=X1+DX:IF X1<5THEN X1=5
530   IF X1>29THEN X1=29
540   IF K<20ORK>22THEN RETURN
550   IF DX=-1AND(X1<(N+3)ORX1>(N+5))THEN RETURN
560   IF DX=1AND(X1<(N+4)ORX1>(N+6))THEN RETURN
570   FOR T=5+N TO 5 STEP -1
580   PRINT LEFT$(DN$,22)TAB(T)MID$(C$,F)A$(N)"■"LM$
590   NEXT
600   FOR T=5 TO 2 STEP -1
610   PRINT LEFT$(DN$,22)TAB(T)MID$(C$,F)A$(N)"▲"
620   NEXT
630   PRINT LEFT$(DN$,22)TAB(5)"■"LM$
640   REM GOT LETTER STACK
650   FOR K1=3074+SL*40 TO 3074+20*40 STEP 40
660   POKE K1,PEEK(K1+40)
670   NEXT
680   POKE K1,32:SL=SL-1
690   N=1:GOSUB 700:K=23:X1=5:RETURN
```

Make Sound for Dead and Live Stacks; Put Letter in Dead Stack

```
700   REM SOUND
710   SOUND 1,25,25
720   RETURN
730   REM SOUND
740   SOUND 2,50,15
```

```
750     RETURN
760     REM MISSED LETTER STACK
770     FOR K1=3105+SR*40 TO 3105+21*40 STEP 40
780     POKE K1,PEEK(K1+40)
790     NEXT
800     POKE K1,32:SR=SR-1
810     N=1:GOSUB 730:RETURN
```

ChexSum Tables

Line		Sum	Line		Sum	Line		Sum
10	=	0	280	=	2318	550	=	3050
20	=	277	290	=	1981	560	=	2853
30	=	1061	300	=	131	570	=	1327
40	=	2317	310	=	303	580	=	2576
50	=	2115	320	=	2939	590	=	131
60	=	2588	330	=	527	600	=	1069
70	=	4790	340	=	1528	610	=	2229
80	=	3110	350	=	3171	620	=	131
90	=	1126	360	=	710	630	=	1565
100	=	1128	370	=	2957	640	=	0
110	=	299	380	=	131	650	=	2599
120	=	3090	390	=	2111	660	=	1039
130	=	1826	400	=	3765	670	=	131
140	=	2327	410	=	1859	680	=	1252
150	=	2418	420	=	1529	690	=	1780
160	=	1116	430	=	143	700	=	0
170	=	302	440	=	0	710	=	586
180	=	1888	450	=	1232	720	=	143
190	=	320	460	=	1435	730	=	0
200	=	1767	470	=	2647	740	=	584
210	=	710	480	=	1421	750	=	143
220	=	3059	490	=	3667	760	=	0
230	=	2037	500	=	994	770	=	2609
240	=	2921	510	=	1833	780	=	1039
250	=	839	520	=	1946	790	=	131
260	=	131	530	=	1197	800	=	1284
270	=	984	540	=	1380	810	=	878
						TOTAL	=	117530

Ganymede

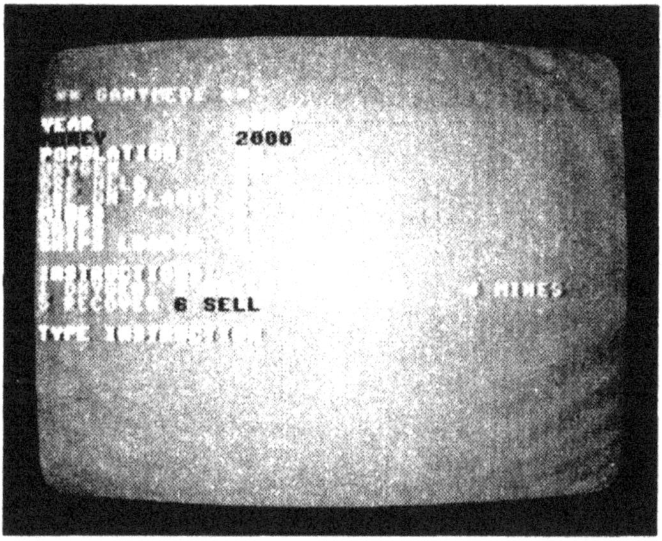

CLASSIFICATION: Strategy

The purpose of this game is to run a small moon base on Jupiter's satellite, Ganymede. You must attempt to set up a mine on Jupiter's surface and collect the valuable ore deposited there.

This treasure means life to you as you must sell it to Earth to obtain money to buy supplies and the vital oxygen which your people need. You must also build more mines as they can be destroyed by storms on Jupiter's surface. Can you sell enough ore to Earth to buy the oxygen you need, or will you suffocate?

Commands are:

1. Import oxygen from earth.
2. Build spaceships.
3. Load spaceships with mining equipment and personnel.
4. Send your loaded ship to set up mines.
5. Recover some mined ore from the surface of Jupiter.
6. Sell recovered ore to Earth.

PROGRAM
Variables

MI	Mines
M	Money
S	Ships
L	Ships loaded
OB	Ore held
OM	Ore on planet
P	Population
Y	Year
O	Oxygen
OS	Total ore sold
F	Fuel
N	Number of aliens

Listing

```
10      REM GANYMEDE
20      MI=0:M=2000:S=1:L=0:OBB=0
30      OM=0:P=50:Y=0:O=200
40      DEFFNR(R)=INT(RND(R)*R+1):OS=0
50      COLOR4,7,4:COLOR0,13,3
```

Clear All Variables; Print Instructions and Supplies

```
60      PRINT "■■▲**▲GANYMEDE▲**"
70      PRINT :PRINT "■YEAR▲▲▲▲▲▲▲▲▲▲"2000+Y:
        PRINT "■MONEY▲▲▲▲▲▲▲▲▲"M
80      PRINT "■POPULATION▲▲▲"P:PRINT "■OX
        YGEN▲▲▲▲▲▲▲▲"O
90      PRINT "■ORE▲HELD▲▲▲▲▲▲"OB:PRINT "ORE
        ▲ON▲PLANET"OM
100     PRINT "■MINES▲▲▲▲▲▲▲▲▲▲"MI
110     PRINT "■SHIPS▲▲▲▲▲▲▲▲▲▲"S:PRINT "SHI
        PS▲LOADED▲"L
120     PRINT :PRINT "■INSTRUCTIONS: "
130     PRINT "■1▲OXYGEN","■2▲BUILD","■3
        ▲LOAD","■4▲MINES"
140     PRINT "■5▲RECOVER","■6▲SELL":
        PRINT :PRINT "■TYPE▲INSTRUCTION"
150     GETA$:IF A$="" THEN 190
160     IF A$<"1"ORA$>"6"THEN 150
170     PRINT "■":ON VAL(A$)GOSUB 360,430,480,540,670,830:
        PRINT "■PRESS▲A▲KEY"
180     GETA$:IF A$=""THEN 180
```

Print Report for Game, Amount of Oxygen Left, Supplies Used

```
190     PRINT "■■▲▲▲REPORT▲FOR▲YEAR":Y
        =Y+1:PRINT
200     R=FNR(P/3):P=P+R:PRINT "■"R"CHILDREN▲WE
        RE▲BORN":O=O-P
210     IF O<PTHEN PRINT "■"P-O"PEOPLE▲DIED":
        PRINT "OF▲OXYGEN▲STARVATION":P
        =0
220     IF MI>0ANDFNR(10)=10THEN PRINT "■MINE"FNR(MI)"
        WAS▲DESTROYED":MI=MI-1
230     IF MI>0ANDFNR(10)>5THEN 220
```

```
240   IF P<2THEN PRINT :PRINT "■ L I F E ▲ O N ▲ B A S E
       ▲ ▲ ▲ ▲ ▲ ▲ ▲ ▲ ▲ ▲ E X T I N G U I S H E D ":
      GOTO 920
250   IF MI>0THEN R=FNR(MI*4)*FNR(MI):PRINT "■ "R"K G ′ S
       ▲ O F ▲ O R E ▲ W E R E ":PRINT "M I N E D ":OM=OM
      +R
260   IF OS>3000THEN PRINT "◣ T H E ▲ G O V E R N M E N T
       ▲ H A S ▲ A L L ▲ T H E ▲ O R E ▲ I T ▲ W A N T S
      ":GOTO 920
270   R=FNR(P):PRINT "◣ "R"U N I T S ▲ O F ▲ O X Y G E N
      ":PRINT "▲ W E R E ▲ R E C Y C L E D ":O=O+R
280   IF P*1.3<=OORFNR(5)<3THEN 330
290   PRINT :PRINT "■ T H E ▲ P E O P L E ▲ R E V O L T E
       D "
300   IF M>200ANDP<75THEN 320
310   PRINT "◣ T H E Y ▲ O V E R - R A N ▲ T H E ▲ B A S
      E ▲ A N D ▲ ■ K I L L E D ■ ▲ Y O U ":GOTO 920
320   PRINT :PRINT "■ Y O U ▲ S T O P P E D ▲ T H E M ":M
      =M-200:P=P-FNR(P/2):PRINT "■ T H E R E ▲ W E R E ▲
      C A S U A L T I E S "
330   PRINT :PRINT :PRINT "■ P R E S S ▲ A ▲ K E Y "
340   GETA$:IF A$=""THEN 340
350   GOTO 60
360   PRINT "■ ▲ ▲ ▲ ▲ ▲ ▲ ▲ ▲ ▲ ▲ O X Y G E N ":PRINT "■ Y O
       U ▲ H A V E "O"U N I T S "
370   R=FNR(15)+15:PRINT :PRINT "■ C O S T "R"F O R ▲ S H
       I P P I N G "
380   R1=FNR(2)+1:PRINT "A N D "R1"P E R ▲ U N I T ":
      PRINT :INPUT "■ B U Y ▲ H O W ▲ M U C H ";N
390   IF N=0THEN RETURN
400   IF N*R1+R>MTHEN PRINT "■ N O T ▲ E N O U G H ▲ M O
      N E Y ":GOTO 370
410   M=M-(N*R1+R):O=O+N
420   RETURN
430   PRINT "▲ ▲ ▲ ▲ ▲ ▲ ▲ ▲ ▲ ▲ ◣ S H I P S ":PRINT "■ Y O U
       ▲ H A V E "S"S H I P S "
440   R=FNR(15)+15:PRINT "■ C O S T "R"I N ▲ L A B O U R
       ▲ A N D ▲ M A T E R I A L S "
450   INPUT "■ B U I L D ▲ H O W ▲ M A N Y ";N:IF N*R>M
      THEN PRINT "■ N O T ▲ E N O U G H ▲ M O N E Y ":
      GOTO 450
460   M=M-R*N:S=S+N
470   RETURN
480   PRINT "▲ ▲ ▲ ▲ ▲ ▲ ▲ ▲ ▲ ▲ ◣ S H I P S ":PRINT "■ Y O U
       ▲ H A V E "S:PRINT L"A R E ▲ L O A D E D "
490   R=FNR(10)+25:PRINT :PRINT "◣ C O S T S "R"T O ▲ L O
       A D ▲ A ":PRINT "S H I P "
500   INPUT "L O A D ▲ H O W ▲ M A N Y ";N:IF N+L>S
      THEN PRINT "■ N O T ▲ E N O U G H ▲ S H I P S ":
      GOTO 500
```

```
510   IF R*N>MTHEN PRINT "N O T ▲ E N O U G H ▲ M O N E Y
       "‡GOTO 500
520   M=M-R*N‡L=L+N
530   RETURN
```

Send Ships to Set Up Mines; Check If Any Ships to Send

```
540   PRINT "■ Y O U ▲ H A V E "L"S H I P S "‡PRINT "L O
      A D E D ▲ A N D ▲ R E A D Y "
550   INPUT "■ S E N D ▲ H O W ▲ M A N Y ";N‡IF N>LORP/2
      <NTHEN PRINT "■ T O O ▲ M A N Y "‡GOTO 550
560   IF N=0THEN RETURN
570   L=L-N
580   PRINT ‡PRINT "■ H O W ▲ M U C H ▲ F U E L ▲ F O R ▲
       ▲ ▲ ▲ ▲ M I S S I O N "‡INPUT F
590   IF F>MTHEN PRINT "■ N O T ▲ E N O U G H ▲ M O N E Y
       "‡GOTO 580
600   M=M-F
610   R=2/(FNR(4)+.5)‡IF R*10*N<=FTHEN 650
620   PRINT "■ N O T ▲ E N O U G H ▲ F U E L "‡R=INT((R
      *10*N-F)/10)‡IF R=0THEN R=1
630   IF R>NTHEN R=N
640   S=S-R‡PRINT "■ "R"S H I P S ▲ A R E ▲ S T R A N D E
       D "‡N=N-R
650   PRINT ‡PRINT "■ "N"M I N E S ▲ W E R E "‡PRINT "E S
       T A B L I S H E D ▲ O N ▲ ▲ ▲ ▲ ▲ ▲ ▲ ▲ ▲ ■ J U P I
      T E R "
660   MI=MI+N‡RETURN
670   PRINT "■ Y O U ▲ H A V E "S"S H I P S "
680   INPUT "S E N D ▲ H O W ▲ M A N Y ";N‡IF N>SORP/2<N
      THEN PRINT "■ T O O ▲ M A N Y "‡GOTO 680
690   IF N=0THEN RETURN
700   IF N>S-LTHEN L=S-N
710   PRINT ‡PRINT "■ H O W ▲ M U C H ▲ F U E L ▲ F O R ▲
       ▲ ▲ ▲ ▲ M I S S I O N "‡INPUT F
720   IF F>MTHEN PRINT "■ N O T ▲ E N O U G H ▲ M O N E Y
       "‡GOTO 710
730   M=M-F‡IF OM=0THEN R=0‡GOTO 800
740   R=FNR(OM*2)/OM‡IF R*10*N<=FTHEN 780
750   PRINT "■ N O T ▲ E N O U G H ▲ F U E L "‡R=INT((R
      *10*N-F)/10)‡IF R=0THEN R=1
760   IF R>NTHEN R=N
770   S=S-R‡PRINT "■ "R"S H I P S ▲ A R E ▲ S T R A N D E
       D "‡N=N-R
780   R=INT(N*10*R+.5)
790   IF R>OMTHEN R=OM
800   PRINT "■ "R"K G ' S ▲ O F ▲ O R E ▲ W E R E "‡
      PRINT "R E C O V E R E D "
810   OM=OM-R‡OB=OB+R
```

```
820   RETURN
830   PRINT "▲ ▲ ▲ ■ S E L L ▲ ▲ T O ▲ ▲ ■ E A R T H "‡
      PRINT ‡PRINT "Y O U ▲ H A V E "OB"K G ' S "‡
      PRINT "T O ▲ S E L L "
840   F=FNR(5)+5‡PRINT "■ T H E ▲ G O V E R N M E N T ▲ P
       A Y S "F‡PRINT "P E R ▲ K G "‡R=FNR(20)+25‡R1=FNR(
      3)+3
850   PRINT "■ T R A N S P O R T A T I O N ▲ C O S T S "‡
      PRINT R"F O R ▲ F U E L "‡PRINT "■ A N D "R1"P E R
      ▲ K G "‡PRINT "O F ▲ O R E "
860   PRINT "■ H O W ▲ M U C H ▲ D O ▲ Y O U ▲ W A N T "‡
      INPUT "T O ▲ S E L L ";N
870   IF N>OBTHEN PRINT "■ Y O U ▲ D O N ' T ▲ H A V E ▲
      T H A T ▲ ▲ ▲ M U C H "‡GOTO 860
880   IF N=0THEN RETURN
890   IF R1*N+R>MTHEN PRINT "■ N O T ▲ E N O U G H ▲ M O
      N E Y "‡GOTO 860
900   OB=OB-N‡M=M-(R1*N+R)‡PRINT "■ T H E ▲ G O V E R N M
       E N T ▲ O F "‡PRINT "■ E A R T H ■ ▲ T H A N K S ▲
       Y O U "
910   M=M+F*N‡OS=OS+N‡RETURN
```

Print Message Thanking Player for Saving the Planet

```
920   FOR I=1 TO 5000‡NEXT‡PRINT "■ ■ T H E ▲ G O V E R N
       M E N T ▲ O F ▲ ▲ ▲ ▲ ▲ ■ E A R T H ■ ▲ T H A N K
      S ▲ Y O U "
930   PRINT "F O R ▲ Y O U R ▲ S E R V I C E ▲ O F "Y‡
      PRINT "Y E A R S "
940   PRINT ‡PRINT "■ Y O U ▲ M A D E ▲ £ "M‡PRINT ‡
      PRINT "■ A N D ▲ S O L D "OS"K G ' S "‡PRINT "O F ▲
       O R E "
950   END
```

ChexSum Tables

Line		ChexSum
10	=	0
20	=	2303
30	=	1710
40	=	2402
50	=	1121
60	=	1401
70	=	3139
80	=	2607
90	=	3125
100	=	1181
110	=	2794
120	=	1706
130	=	3481
140	=	4082
150	=	1311
160	=	1533
170	=	4156
180	=	1212
190	=	2781
200	=	4752
210	=	5301
220	=	5494
230	=	1741
240	=	4583
250	=	6676
260	=	5561
270	=	5198
280	=	2181
290	=	2033
300	=	1497
310	=	4425
320	=	6801
330	=	1587
340	=	1214
350	=	476
360	=	2942
370	=	3411
380	=	4406
390	=	757
400	=	3503
410	=	1969
420	=	143
430	=	3058
440	=	4088
450	=	5259
460	=	1528
470	=	143
480	=	3874
490	=	3873
500	=	4953
510	=	3127
520	=	1502
530	=	143
540	=	3448
550	=	4880
560	=	757
570	=	588
580	=	3116
590	=	2872
600	=	580
610	=	2970
620	=	4671
630	=	992
640	=	3530
650	=	4369
660	=	939
670	=	1640
680	=	4673
690	=	757
700	=	1506
710	=	3244
720	=	2875
730	=	2332
740	=	3016
750	=	4671
760	=	992
770	=	3530
780	=	1440
790	=	1154
800	=	2947
810	=	1580
820	=	143
830	=	4728
840	=	6625
850	=	6084
860	=	2925
870	=	3898
880	=	757
890	=	3502
900	=	6564
910	=	1891
920	=	5508
930	=	2633
940	=	4353
950	=	129
TOTAL	=	270053

Snakepit

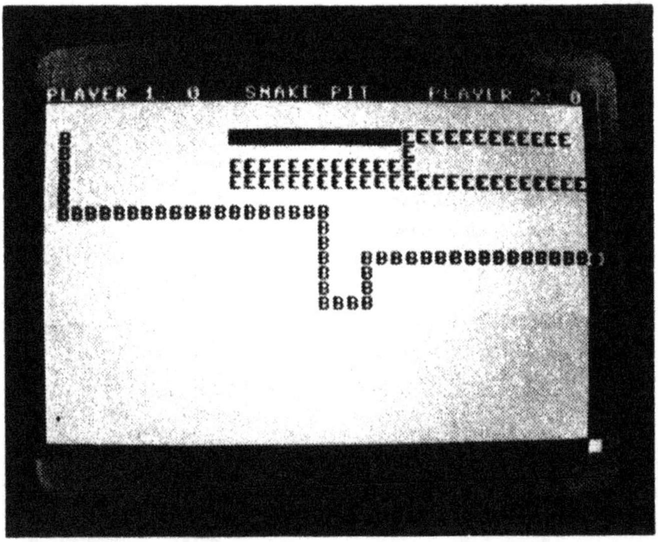

CLASSIFICATION: Evasion

You are one of two snakes placed in a pit, each trying to bite the other's tail off. The other snake can be either the computer or another opponent. Biting your own tail, turning back on yourself and running into the wall are all fatal to you. Try to block the other snake's path so that he runs into your tail. Seven bites of the tail determine the winner of each game. It is not necessary to hold keys down or hold the joystick in a fixed position, as the snake will continue travelling in the last direction it was pointed. For player 1 the keys to move up, left, right and down are W, A, S and Z. For player 2 they are I, J, K and M.

PROGRAMMING SUGGESTIONS

Give the opposing snake intelligence so that he can counteract your moves. Place obstacles on the board at random to make play more difficult.

PROGRAM
Variables

CO	Color offset address
UL	Left joystick
UR	Right joystick
X1	Left joystick X direction increment
Y1	Left snake Y direction increment
X2	Right snake X direction increment
Y2	Right snake Y direction increment
PI	Screen location of left snake
P2	Screen location of right snake
N	Number of players
F	Speed variable
S1	Left snake score
S2	Right snake score

Listing

```
10    REM   SNAKEPIT
20    VOL 8:GOTO 780
30    REM  GET DIRECTION
```

Scan Both Joystick Ports and the Keyboard; Call Move Snake

```
40    IF N=1THEN 60
50    IF JL<>0THEN 130
60    JL=JOY(1)
70    JL=15-(JLAND15)
80    IF JL=0THEN 130
90    IF JL=1THEN X1=0:Y1=-1:GOTO 290
100   IF JL=2THEN X1=0:Y1=1:GOTO 290
110   IF JL=8THEN X1=1:Y1=0:GOTO 290
120   IF JL=4THEN X1=-1:Y1=0:GOTO 290
130   JL=0:JR=JOY(2)
140   JR=15-(JRAND15)
150   IF JR=0THEN 200
160   IF JR=1THEN X2=0:Y2=-1:GOTO 290
170   IF JR=2THEN X2=0:Y2=1:GOTO 290
180   IF JR=8THEN X2=1:Y2=0:GOTO 290
190   IF JR=4THEN X2=-1:Y2=0:GOTO 290
200   GETA$:IF A$=""THEN 290
210   IF A$="I "THEN X2=0:Y2=-1:GOTO 290
220   IF A$="W "THEN X1=0:Y1=-1:GOTO 290
230   IF A$="M "THEN X2=0:Y2=1:GOTO 290
240   IF A$="Z "THEN X1=0:Y1=1:GOTO 290
250   IF A$="K "THEN X2=1:Y2=0:GOTO 290
260   IF A$="S "THEN X1=1:Y1=0:GOTO 290
270   IF A$="J "THEN X2=-1:Y2=0:GOTO 290
280   IF A$="A "THEN X1=-1:Y1=0:GOTO 290
```

Plot the Player on Screen and Check for Collision

```
290   REM PLOT PLAYER POSITION
300   P1=P1+X1+(Y1*40):P=P1:S=1:GOSUB 380
310   IF S=0THEN 990
320   IF N=1THEN GOSUB 610
330   P2=P2+X2+(Y2*40):P=P2:S=2:GOSUB 380
340   IF S=0THEN 990
350   POKE P1,81:POKE P1+CO,2
360   POKE P2,87:POKE P2+CO,5
370   FOR T=1 TO F*F+F*20:NEXT:GOTO 30
380   REM CHECK FOR HIT
390   IF PEEK(P)=32THEN RETURN
```

```
400   FOR I=5 TO 1 STEP -1:COLOR4,I,5:GOSUB 580
410   POKE P,81:FOR T=1 TO 60:NEXT
420   POKE P,81:NEXT
430   IF S=1THEN S2=S2+1:S=0
440   IF S=2THEN S1=S1+1:S=0
450   FOR T=1 TO 200:NEXT
460   IF S1<7ANDS2<7THEN RETURN
```

Print Out Who Won the Game and Prompt For Another

```
470   REM WINNERS ROUTINE
480   GOSUB 720:PRINT "PLAYER 1:  PLAYER 2:  "
490   PRINT ""SPC(10)S1SPC(24)""S2
500   IF S1<S2THEN N=2:PRINT ""
510   IF S2<S1THEN N=1:PRINT ""
520   PRINT "WINNER....PLAYER ";
530   PRINT N
540   PRINT "ANOTHER GAME? (Y/N)"
550   GET A$:IF A$="Y"THEN RUN
560   IF A$<>"N"THEN 550
570   END
580   REM SOUND
590   FOR T=1 TO 10:SOUND 2,15,2:SOUND 1,30,4:NEXT
600   RETURN
610   REM COMPUTERS MOVE
620   IF PEEK(P2+X2+Y2*40)=32ANDRND(.)<.85THEN RETURN
630   XN=X2:YN=Y2:Y2=0
640   X2=1-(INT(RND(.)*3)):IF X2=0THEN 640
650   X=PEEK(P2+X2+Y2*40):IF X=32THEN IF X2=1THEN A$="K"
      :RETURN
660   IF X=32THEN IF X2=-1THEN A$="J":RETURN
670   X2=0
680   Y2=1:X=PEEK(P2+X2+Y2*40):IF X=32THEN A$="M":
      RETURN
690   Y2=-1:X=PEEK(P2+X2+Y2*40):IF X=32THEN A$="I":
      RETURN
700   X2=XN:Y2=YN
710   RETURN
720   COLOR4,11,4:COLOR0,4,5
```

Draw Pit, Print Player Instructions and Enter Number of Players

```
730   PRINT "                    SNAKE PIT                    "
```

```
740   FOR I=1 TO 22:PRINT "▮▮ ◙ ▲ ▲ ":NEXT
750   PRINT "◙ ▮▮ ▲ ▲ ▲ ▲ ▲ ▲ ▲ ▲ ▲ ▲ ▲ ▲ ▲ ▲ ▲ ▲ ▲ ▲ ▲ ▲ ▲ ▲ ▲
      ▲ ▲ ▲ ▲ ▲ ▲ ▲ ▲ ▲ ▲ ▲ ▲ ▲ ▲ ▲ ▲ ▲ ▲ ▲ ▲ ▲ ▲ ▲ ▲ ▲ ◙ ";"◙ "
760   POKE 4031,160
770   RETURN
780   GOSUB 720
790   PRINT "◙ ◙ ◙ ◙ ◙ P L A Y E R ▲ 1 ' S ▲ K E Y S ▲ ▲
      ▲ P L A Y E R ▲ 2 ' S ▲ K E Y S "
800   PRINT "◙ ◙ U P "SPC(9)"W "SPC(17)"I "
810   PRINT "◙ ◙ L E F T "SPC(7)"A "SPC(17)"J "
820   PRINT "◙ ◙ R I G H T "SPC(6)"S "SPC(17)"K "
830   PRINT "◙ ◙ D O W N "SPC(7)"Z "SPC(17)"M "
840   PRINT "◙ ◙ ◙ J O Y S T I C K ( P O R T ▲ B ) ▲ ▲ ▲
      J O Y S T I C K ( P O R T ▲ A ) "
850   PRINT "◙ ◙ ◙ E N T E R ▲ N U M B E R ▲ 1 ▲ O R ▲ 2
      ▲ F O R "
860   PRINT "◙ ◙ ◙ ◙ ◙ ◙ ◙ ◙ ◙ ◙ N U M B E R ▲ O F ▲ P L A
      Y E R S . "
870   PRINT "◙ ◙ ◙ T H E ▲ C O M P U T E R ▲ W I L L ▲ B
      E ▲ P L A Y E R ▲ 2 "
880   PRINT "◙ ◙ ◙ ◙ ◙ ◙ ◙ ◙ ◙ ◙ W H E N ▲ O N L Y ▲ 1 ▲ P
      L A Y E R ▲ A V A I L A B L E . "
890   PRINT "◙ ◙ ◙ N U M B E R ▲ O F ▲ P L A Y E R S : ▲
      ";
900   PRINT "◙ ▲ ■ ";:FOR T=1 TO 80:NEXT:POKE 3072+999,16
      0
910   GETA$:IF A$="1 "ORA$="2 "THEN 930
920   PRINT "▮▮ ▲ ▮▮ ";:FOR T=1 TO 80:NEXT:GOTO 900
930   N=VAL(A$)
940   PRINT "◙ ◙ ◙ ◙ ◙ ◙ ◙ ◙ ◙ ◙ ◙ ◙ ◙ ◙ ◙ ◙ ◙ ◙ ◙ ◙ ◙ ◙ ◙
      ◙ ◙ ◙ E N T E R ▲ S P E E D ▲ ( 1 : F A S T ▲ - ▲ 9
       : S L O W ) ▲ ";:GOTO 970
950   PRINT "◙ ▲ ■ ";:FOR T=1 TO 80:NEXT
960   PRINT "▮▮ ▲ ▮▮ ";:FOR T=1 TO 80:NEXT
970   GETA$:IF A$<"1 "ORA$>"9 "THEN 950
980   F=VAL(A$):GOSUB 1140
990   GOSUB 720:PRINT "◙ ◙ ◙ ◙ P L A Y E R ▲ 1 : ▲ ▲ ◙ ◙
      ◙ ◙ ◙ ◙ ◙ ◙ ◙ ◙ ◙ ◙ ◙ ◙ ◙ ◙ ◙ ◙ ◙ ◙ ◙ P L A Y E R ▲ 2 : ▲ ▲
       "
1000  PRINT "◙ ◙ ◙ "SPC(10)S1SPC(24)"◙ "S2
1010  REM SET RANDOM WALLS
1020  NW=INT(RND(.)*4):PRINT "◙ ";
1030  IF NW=0THEN 1090
1040  FOR I=1 TO NW
1050  FOR J=1 TO RND((.)*6)+3
1060  PRINT :NEXT
1070  PRINT SPC((RND(.)*8)+8):FOR K=1 TO RND(.)*16+8:
      PRINT "■ ◙ ▲ ";:NEXT
1080  NEXT
1090  REM SET INITIAL POSITIONS
```

```
1100  P1=3154:P2=3189:X1=0:X2=0:Y1=1:Y2=1:S=9
1110  IF N=2THEN 1120
1120  REM
1130  GOTO 150
1140  RETURN
```

ChexSum Tables

Line		Sum	Line		Sum	Line		Sum
10	=	0	390	=	1117	770	=	143
20	=	882	400	=	2026	780	=	299
30	=	0	410	=	1431	790	=	3003
40	=	725	420	=	590	800	=	1460
50	=	1051	430	=	1727	810	=	1604
60	=	686	440	=	1729	820	=	1719
70	=	1151	450	=	974	830	=	1619
80	=	865	460	=	1398	840	=	3196
90	=	2348	470	=	0	850	=	2075
100	=	2183	480	=	3236	860	=	2004
110	=	2190	490	=	1402	870	=	2652
120	=	2350	500	=	1493	880	=	3023
130	=	1151	510	=	1493	890	=	1854
140	=	1169	520	=	2208	900	=	2568
150	=	866	530	=	231	910	=	1919
160	=	2355	540	=	2193	920	=	2307
170	=	2190	550	=	1263	930	=	654
180	=	2197	560	=	1129	940	=	4313
190	=	2354	570	=	129	950	=	1534
200	=	1213	580	=	0	960	=	1680
210	=	2426	590	=	2164	970	=	1924
220	=	2435	600	=	143	980	=	1084
230	=	2231	610	=	0	990	=	3236
240	=	2247	620	=	3073	1000	=	1402
250	=	2232	630	=	1521	1010	=	0
260	=	2241	640	=	2436	1020	=	1576
270	=	2400	650	=	3915	1030	=	932
280	=	2393	660	=	2285	1040	=	766
290	=	0	670	=	370	1050	=	1487
300	=	2746	680	=	3666	1060	=	342
310	=	802	690	=	3858	1070	=	3752
320	=	928	700	=	1061	1080	=	131
330	=	2753	710	=	143	1090	=	0
340	=	802	720	=	1109	1100	=	3408
350	=	1252	730	=	2724	1110	=	842
360	=	1251	740	=	1495	1120	=	0
370	=	2249	750	=	2530	1130	=	526
380	=	0	760	=	584	1140	=	143
						TOTAL	=	179337

Break-In

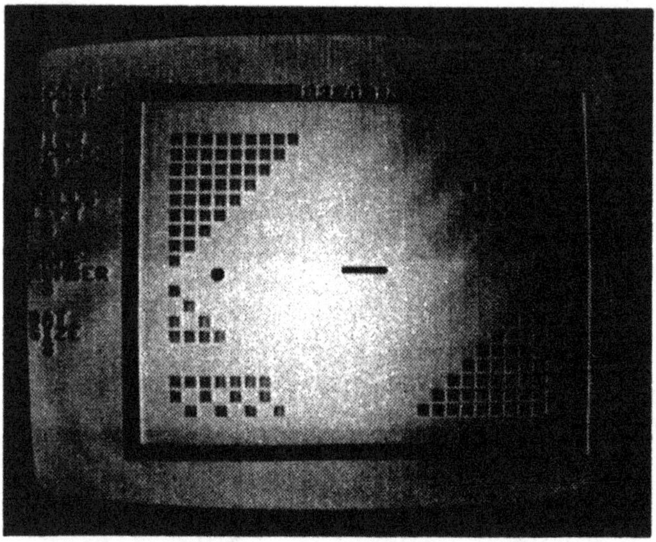

CLASSIFICATION: Co-ordination

You are inside a four-walled container with a series of brick walls, a moving ball and a bat. The ball is bouncing off the bricks and you must use your bat to stop it getting past you and hitting the wall. You are given nine balls for each game and you lose a ball each time one gets past your bat. The bat can be moved left and right using the I and P keys. There are three different brick wall configurations and two bat sizes. The smaller the bat, the more points scored.

PROGRAMMING SUGGESTIONS

Add more courts to the game so that the player has a greater choice of games. Make the ball change speed in midflight, i.e. accelerate or decelerate.

PROGRAM
Variables

SC	Start address of screen
CB	Color offset value
GM	Game number
BS	Bat size
GS	Game score
HS	High score
BV	Vertical position of bat
BH	Horizontal position of bat
BY	Vertical position of ball
BX	Horizontal position of ball
BA	Screen position of ball
DX	Horizontal movement value of ball
DY	Vertical movement value of ball
SW	Switch to allow screen refresh

Listing

```
10      REM  BREAKIN
```

Set Volume, Move Bat Left or Right; Check If Ball Hits Boundary

```
20      DN$="[HOME][DOWN][DOWN][DOWN][DOWN][DOWN][DOWN][DOWN][DOWN][DOWN][DOWN][DOWN][DOWN][DOWN][DOWN][DOWN][DOWN][DOWN][DOWN][DOWN][DOWN][DOWN][DOWN]
        [DOWN][DOWN][RIGHT][RIGHT][RIGHT][RIGHT][RIGHT][RIGHT][RIGHT][RIGHT][RIGHT][RIGHT][RIGHT][RIGHT][RIGHT][RIGHT][RIGHT][RIGHT][RIGHT][RIGHT][RIGHT][RIGHT][RIGHT][RIGHT][RIGHT][RIGHT]
         [RIGHT][RIGHT][RIGHT][RIGHT][RIGHT][RIGHT][RIGHT][RIGHT][RIGHT][RIGHT][RIGHT][RIGHT][RIGHT][RIGHT][RIGHT] "
30      SC=3072:NB=9:GOTO 330
40      GOTO 20
50      VOL 8:SOUND 2,1,5:RETURN
60      REM  MOVE BAT
70      GETA$:IF A$=""THEN A=64
80      IF A$="I "THEN A=12
90      IF A$="P "THEN A=36
100     IF A=64THEN 170
110     PRINT LEFT$(DN$,BV)RIGHT$(DN$,BH);:FOR I=1 TO BS:
        PRINT "▲ ";:NEXT
120     BH=BH+((A=12)-(A=36))*2
130     IF BH<8THEN BH=8
140     IF BH>38-BSTHEN BH=38-BS
150     PRINT LEFT$(DN$,BV)RIGHT$(DN$,BH);:FOR I=1 TO BS:
        PRINT "■ ▔ ";:NEXT:
160     REM CHECK BOUNDARY HIT
170     BX=BX+DX:BY=BY+DY:FF=21
180     IF BX<9THEN DX=-DX:GOSUB 50:GOTO 230
190     IF BX>36THEN DX=-DX:GOSUB 50:GOTO 230
200     IF BY<1THEN BY=1:DY=-DY:GOSUB 50:GOTO 230
210     IF BY>23THEN BY=23:DY=-DY:GOSUB 50
220     REM CHECK BAT/BRCK HIT & PRINT BALL
230     POKE BA,32:BA=SC+BY*40+BX
240     IF PEEK(BA)=120THEN BA=B1:DY=-DY:FF=133:GOSUB 50:
        GOTO 60
250     IF PEEK(BA)=207THEN DY=-DY:FF=35:GOSUB 50:GS=GS+1:
        PRINT "[HOME] ■ [DOWN] "GS
260     POKE BA,81
270     REM CHECK FOR MISSED BALL
280     IF GM=1ANDBY>22ANDDY=-1THEN NB=NB-1:PRINT "[HOME][DOWN][DOWN][DOWN]
        [DOWN][DOWN][DOWN][DOWN][DOWN][DOWN] ■ "NB
290     IF GM<>1ANDBY=12THEN NB=NB-1:PRINT "[HOME][DOWN][DOWN][DOWN][DOWN][DOWN][DOWN][DOWN]
         [DOWN][DOWN] ■ "NB
300     IF NB<1THEN 1090
310     IF INT(GS/100)-(GS/100)<>0THEN 60
320     ON GMGOSUB 830,900,990
```

Draw Title Screen; Select the Game Number and Bat Size

```
330    REM TITLE SCREEN
340    COLOR4,3,6:COLOR0,3,6:PRINT "▙ ▣ ▣ ▣ ▣ ■ ▲ ▲ ▲ ▲ ▲
       ▲ ▲ ▲ ▲ ▲ ▲ ▲ ▲ ▲ ▲ ▲ ▲ ▲ ▲ ● "
350    FOR T=1 TO 100:NEXT
360    PRINT "▙ ▣ ▣ ▣ ▣ ▣ ▣ ▲ ▲ ▲ ▲ ▲ ▲ ▲ ▲ ▲ ▲ ▲ ▲ ▲ ▲ ▲ ▲ ▲ ▲ ▲
       ▲ ▲ ● ■ ● ▜ ● "
370    FOR T=1 TO 100:NEXT
380    PRINT "▙ ▣ ▣ ▣ ▣ ▣ ▣ ▣ ▲ ▲ ▲ ▲ ▲ ▲ ▲ ▲ ▲ ▲ ▲ ▲ ▲ ▲ ▲ ▲ ▲ ▲
       ▲ ▲ ● ▲ ■ ● ▲ ▜ ● "
390    FOR T=1 TO 100:NEXT
400    PRINT "▙ ▣ ▣ ▣ ▣ ▣ ▣ ▣ ▣ ▛ ▲ ▲ ▲ ▲ ▲ ▲ ▲ ▲ ▲ ▲ ▲ ▲ ▲ ▲ ▲ ▲ ▲
       ▲ ▲ ● ▣ ● ▲ ■ ● ▲ ▜ ● ▙ ● "
410    FOR T=1 TO 100:NEXT
420    PRINT "▙ ▣ ▣ ▣ ▣ ▣ ▣ ▣ ▣ ▣ ▛ ▲ ▲ ▲ ▲ ▲ ▲ ▲ ▲ ▲ ▲ ▲ ▲ ▲ ▲ ▲
       ▲ ▲ ● ▲ ▣ ● ▲ ■ ● ▲ ▜ ● ▲ ▙ ● "
430    FOR T=1 TO 100:NEXT
440    PRINT "▙ ▣ ▣ ▣ ▣ ▣ ▣ ▣ ▣ ▣ ▣ ▙ ▲ ▲ ▲ ▲ ▲ ▲ ▲ ▲ ▲ ▲ ▲ ▲ ▲ ▲
       ▲ ▲ ● ▛ ● ▲ ▣ ● ▲ ■ ● ▲ ▜ ● ▲ ▙ ● ▢ ● "
450    FOR T=1 TO 100:NEXT
460    PRINT "▙ ▣ ▣ ▣ ▣ ▣ ▣ ▣ ▣ ▣ ▣ ▣ ▙ ▲ ▲ ▲ ▲ ▲ ▲ ▲ ▲ ▲ ▲ ▲ ▲ ▲
       ▲ ▲ ● ▲ ▛ ● ▲ ▣ ● ▲ ■ ● ▲ ▜ ● ▲ ▙ ● ▲ ▢ ● "
470    FOR T=1 TO 200:NEXT:FF=35:GOSUB 50
480    PRINT "▙ ▣ ▣ ▣ ▣ ▣ ▣ ▣ ▣ ▣ ▣ ▣ ▙ ▲ ▲ ▲ ▲ ▲ ▲ ▲ ▲ ▲ ▲ ▲ ▲ ▲
       ▲ ▲ B ▲ ▛ ● ▲ ▣ ● ▲ ■ ● ▲ ▜ ● ▲ ▙ ● ▲ ▢ ● "
490    FOR T=1 TO 200:NEXT:FF=21:GOSUB 50
500    PRINT "▙ ▣ ▣ ▣ ▣ ▣ ▣ ▣ ▣ ▣ ▣ ▣ ▙ ▲ ▲ ▲ ▲ ▲ ▲ ▲ ▲ ▲ ▲ ▲ ▲ ▲
       ▲ ▲ B ▲ ▛ R ▲ ▣ ● ▲ ■ ● ▲ ▜ ● ▲ ▙ ● ▲ ▢ ● "
510    FOR T=1 TO 200:NEXT:FF=35:GOSUB 50
520    PRINT "▙ ▣ ▣ ▣ ▣ ▣ ▣ ▣ ▣ ▣ ▣ ▣ ▙ ▲ ▲ ▲ ▲ ▲ ▲ ▲ ▲ ▲ ▲ ▲ ▲ ▲
       ▲ ▲ B ▲ ▛ R ▲ ▣ E ▲ ■ ● ▲ ▜ ● ▲ ▙ ● ▲ ▢ ● "
530    FOR T=1 TO 200:NEXT:FF=21:GOSUB 50
540    PRINT "▙ ▣ ▣ ▣ ▣ ▣ ▣ ▣ ▣ ▣ ▣ ▣ ▙ ▲ ▲ ▲ ▲ ▲ ▲ ▲ ▲ ▲ ▲ ▲ ▲ ▲
       ▲ ▲ B ▲ ▛ R ▲ ▣ E ▲ ■ A ▲ ▜ ● ▲ ▙ ● ▲ ▢ ● "
550    FOR T=1 TO 200:NEXT:FF=35:GOSUB 50
560    PRINT "▙ ▣ ▣ ▣ ▣ ▣ ▣ ▣ ▣ ▣ ▣ ▣ ▙ ▲ ▲ ▲ ▲ ▲ ▲ ▲ ▲ ▲ ▲ ▲ ▲ ▲
       ▲ ▲ B ▲ ▛ R ▲ ▣ E ▲ ■ A ▲ ▜ K ▲ ▙ ● ▲ ▢ ● "
570    FOR T=1 TO 200:NEXT:FF=21:GOSUB 50
580    PRINT "▙ ▣ ▣ ▣ ▣ ▣ ▣ ▣ ▣ ▣ ▣ ▣ ▙ ▲ ▲ ▲ ▲ ▲ ▲ ▲ ▲ ▲ ▲ ▲ ▲ ▲
       ▲ ▲ B ▲ ▛ R ▲ ▣ E ▲ ■ A ▲ ▜ K ▲ ▙ I ▲ ▢ ● "
590    FOR T=1 TO 200:NEXT:FF=35:GOSUB 50
600    PRINT "▙ ▣ ▣ ▣ ▣ ▣ ▣ ▣ ▣ ▣ ▣ ▣ ▙ ▲ ▲ ▲ ▲ ▲ ▲ ▲ ▲ ▲ ▲ ▲ ▲ ▲
       ▲ ▲ B ▲ ▛ R ▲ ▣ E ▲ ■ A ▲ ▜ K ▲ ■ I ▲ ▢ N "
610    FOR T=1 TO 200:NEXT:FF=21:PRINT "▣ ▣ "
620    GOSUB 50
630    PRINT "■ ▲ ▲ ▲ ▲ ▲ ▲ ▲ ▲ ▲ ▲ ▣ S E L E C T ▲ G A M E ▲
       N U M B E R ( 1 - 3 ) ":FOR T=1 TO 90:NEXT
```

```
640  PRINT "□▀▲▲▲▲▲▲▲▲▲▲S E L E C T▲G A M E▲
     N U M B E R ( 1 - 3 ) ";:FOR T=1 TO 90:NEXT
650  GETGM$:IF GM$<"1 "THEN PRINT :PRINT "□ ";:GOTO 620
660  IF GM$>"3 "THEN PRINT :PRINT "□ ";:GOTO 620
670  GM=VAL(GM$):PRINT "▲ "GM:PRINT :FF=35
680  GOSUB 50
690  PRINT "■▲▲▲▲▲▲▲▲▲▲▲◪S E L E C T▲B A T▲
     S I Z E ( 2 - 3 ) ":FOR T=1 TO 90:NEXT
700  PRINT "□▀▲▲▲▲▲▲▲▲▲▲▲▲S E L E C T▲B A T▲
     S I Z E ( 2 - 3 ) ";:FOR T=1 TO 90:NEXT
710  GETBS$:IF BS$<"2 "THEN PRINT :PRINT "□ ";:GOTO 680
720  IF BS$>"3 "THEN PRINT :PRINT "□ ";:GOTO 680
```

> Draw Court, Print Score, High Score, Balls Left and Game Number

```
730  BS=VAL(BS$):PRINT "▲ "BS
740  NB=9:GS=100*(4-BS)
750  FOR T=1 TO 500:NEXT
760  PRINT "◪■▲▲▲▲▲▲▲▲▲◪▲▲▲▲▲▲▲▲▲▲▲▲▲▲▲▲▲▲
     B R E A K I N▲▲▲▲▲▲▲▲▲▲▲▲▲▲▲▲▲▲▲▲"
770  FOR I=1 TO 23:PRINT "▲▲▲▲▲▲▲▲▲◪▲▀▲▲▲▲▲▲▲
     ▲▲▲▲▲▲▲▲▲▲▲▲▲▲▲▲▲▲▲▲▲▲▲▲▲▲▲▲▲▲▲▲▲▲▲◪
     ▲ ":NEXT
780  PRINT "■▲▲▲▲▲▲▲▲▲◪▲▲▲▲▲▲▲▲▲▲▲▲▲▲▲▲▲▲
     ▲▲▲▲▲▲▲▲▲▲▲▲▲▲▲▲▲▲▲▲▲▲▲▲▲▲▲▲▲▲▲◪ "
790  PRINT "◪S C O R E ":PRINT GS:PRINT "◪H I G H ":
     PRINT "S C O R E ":PRINT HS:PRINT "◪B A L L S "
800  PRINT "L E F T ":PRINT NB:PRINT "◪G A M E ":
     PRINT "N U M B E R ":PRINT GM
810  PRINT "◪B A T ":PRINT "S I Z E ":PRINT BS
820  ON GMGOTO 830,900,990
```

> Print Out the Courts for Games One, Two and Three

```
830  REM   GAME 1
840  PRINT "◪◪◪◪ "
850  FOR J=1 TO 4:PRINT "◪◪◪◪◪◪◪◪◪◪◪┌┌┌┌┌┌┌
     ┌┌┌┌┌┌┌┌┌┌┌┌┌┌┌┌┌┌┌┌┌┌┌┌ ":
     NEXT
860  IF GS>0THEN GS=GS+1
870  IF SW>0THEN 60
880  SW=1:BV=21:BH=17:BY=15:BX=18:BA=SC+BY*40+BX:DX=-1:D
     Y=-1
890  GOTO 110
900  REM GAME2
910  PRINT "◪◪◪◪ "
```

```
920   FOR J=1 TO 3:PRINT "▮▮▮▮▮▮▮▮▯┌┌┌┌┌┌
      ┌┌┌┌┌┌┌┌┌┌┌┌┌┌┌┌┌┌┌ ":
      NEXT
930   PRINT "▯▯▯▯▯▯▯▯▯▯▯▯▯ "
940   FOR J=1 TO 3:PRINT "▮▮▮▮▮▮▮▮▯┌┌┌┌┌┌
      ┌┌┌┌┌┌┌┌┌┌┌┌┌┌┌┌┌┌┌ ":
      NEXT
950   IF GS>0THEN GS=GS+1
960   IF SW>0THEN 60
970   SW=1:BV=13:BH=20:BY=10:BX=21:BA=SC+BY*40+BX:DX=1:DY
      =-1
980   GOTO 110
990   REM GAME3
1000  PRINT "▮▯▯ "
1010  FOR I=0 TO 8:PRINT "▮▮▮▮▮▮▮▮▮▮ ";:FOR J=9
      -I TO 1 STEP -1:PRINT "▯▮┌ ";:NEXT
1020  PRINT SPC(I*2+8);:FOR J=9-I TO 1 STEP -1:PRINT "┬ "
      ;:NEXT:PRINT :NEXT:PRINT
1030  FOR I=0 TO 8:PRINT "▮▮▮▮▮▮▮▮▮▮ ";:FOR J=1
      TO I+1:PRINT "▯▮┌ ";:NEXT
1040  PRINT SPC(((8-I)*2)+8);:FOR J=1 TO I+1:PRINT "┬ ";:
      NEXT:PRINT :NEXT:PRINT "▮ "
1050  IF GS>0THEN GS=GS+1
1060  IF SW>0THEN 60
1070  SW=1:BV=13:BH=16:BY=9:BX=24:BA=SC+BY*40+BX:DX=1:DY
      =-1
1080  GOTO 110
```

Check for Another Game

```
1090  REM END GAME
1100  PRINT "▮▯▯▯▯▯▯▯▯▯▯▯▯▯▯▮▮▮▮▮▮▮
      ▮▮    ANOTHER GAME(Y/N)"
1110  GETA$
1120  IF A$="N "THEN PRINT "▯ ":END
1130  IF A$<>"Y "THEN 1110
1140  IF GS>HSTHEN HS=GS
1150  SW=0:GOTO 600
```

ChexSum Tables

Line		Sum
10	=	0
20	=	3709
30	=	1603
40	=	472
50	=	1020
60	=	0
70	=	1421
80	=	1139
90	=	1146
100	=	834
110	=	3210
120	=	2108
130	=	1079
140	=	1914
150	=	3604
160	=	0
170	=	2291
180	=	2336
190	=	2373
200	=	2844
210	=	2332
220	=	0
230	=	2008
240	=	3889
250	=	4413
260	=	444
270	=	0
280	=	4078
290	=	3307
300	=	913
310	=	2400
320	=	1056
330	=	0
340	=	2812
350	=	975
360	=	2337
370	=	975
380	=	2495
390	=	975

Line		Sum
400	=	3037
410	=	975
420	=	3147
430	=	975
440	=	3941
450	=	975
460	=	4073
470	=	1821
480	=	3945
490	=	1817
500	=	3816
510	=	1821
520	=	3676
530	=	1817
540	=	3532
550	=	1821
560	=	3396
570	=	1817
580	=	3252
590	=	1821
600	=	3232
610	=	1853
620	=	247
630	=	3625
640	=	3827
650	=	2596
660	=	2123
670	=	2072
680	=	247
690	=	3391
700	=	3593
710	=	2610
720	=	2128
730	=	1325
740	=	1644
750	=	975
760	=	2593
770	=	3324
780	=	2264

Line		Sum
790	=	3959
800	=	2957
810	=	1488
820	=	1282
830	=	0
840	=	317
850	=	8437
860	=	1448
870	=	821
880	=	5699
890	=	526
900	=	0
910	=	317
920	=	8438
930	=	534
940	=	8438
950	=	1448
960	=	821
970	=	5500
980	=	526
990	=	0
1000	=	286
1010	=	3802
1020	=	3941
1030	=	3397
1040	=	4143
1050	=	1448
1060	=	821
1070	=	5463
1080	=	526
1090	=	0
1100	=	2726
1110	=	267
1120	=	1359
1130	=	1199
1140	=	1328
1150	=	1015
TOTAL	=	248333

Minotaur

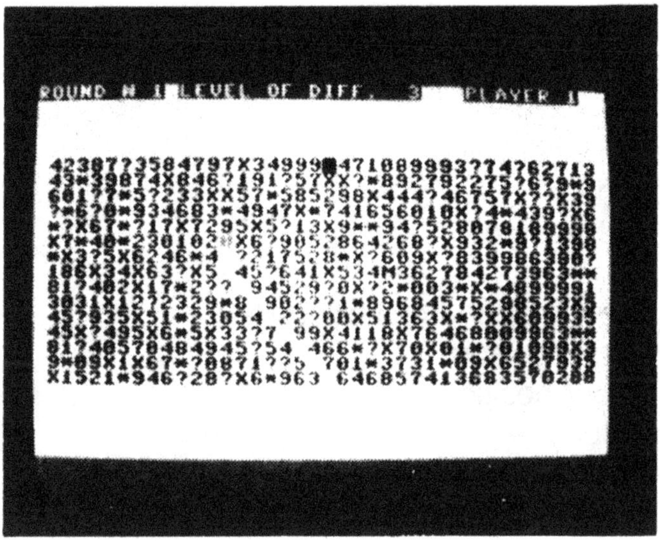

CLASSIFICATION: Educational

You are placed at the bottom centre of a matrix of numbers and symbols which you can move through by pressing keys as follows: W-up, X-down, A-left, D-right, Q-up left, E-up right, Z-down left and C-down right. It is easy to remember the keys because they form a diamond round the S key and each key points in the correct direction with reference to the S key. Your objective is to guess an integer (a whole number) in the range of Ø to 1ØØØ. You can get clues by moving over the X squares but in the least number of moves. Each number you move over is added to your score. If the number is too large, you are pursued by a minotaur which is placed in the centre of the screen at the start of each game, and which gradually creeps closer as you play. If he catches you, the game ends and you lose. When you think you have the number, move to the white block at the top of the matrix.

PROGRAMMING SUGGESTIONS

Make the board multilevel, and give the player and minotaur the ability to travel from level to level by landing on an appropriate spot.

PROGRAM

Variables

LD%	Level of difficulty
R%	Round
SN%	Secret number
D1%, D2%, D3%	Digits of a secret number (SN%)
PP%	Players' position
M%	Minotaur position
LS%	Last score
TS%	Total score
CU	Character under minotaur
NC%	Number of clues
T% ( )	Truth array for clues
MR%, MC	Minotaur row, colour
PR%, PC%	Player's row, colour

Listing

```
10     REM MINOTAUR
```

Set Screen Colours; Input the Difficulty Level; Print Board

```
20     PRINT "■ ";:COLOR4,9,4:COLOR0,7,5:PRINT TAB(10);"■
       M I N O T A U R ▲ M A S T E R - M I N D ":
30     PRINT :PRINT :PRINT
40     PRINT :PRINT "L E V E L ▲ O F ▲ D I F F I C U L T Y
        ? ( 1 - 9 ) ";
50     GETX$:IF X$=""THEN 50
60     IF VAL(X$)<1ORVAL(X$)>9THEN 50
70     LD%=VAL(X$):PRINT LD%
80     FOR T=1 TO 1000:NEXT
90     GOTO 250
100    FOR I=3273 TO 3833 STEP 40
110    FOR J=0 TO 37
120    K1=INT(RND(0)*13)
130    IF K1>9THEN 160
140    POKE I+J,K1+48
150    GOTO 220
160    IF K1<>10THEN 190
170    POKE I+J,24
180    GOTO 220
190    IF K1<>11THEN 210
200    POKE I+J,63:GOTO 220
210    POKE I+J,42
220    NEXT:NEXT
230    POKE 3292,160
240    RETURN
250    R%=1:SN%=INT(RND(0)*999+1)
260    D1%=INT(SN%/100):D2%=INT((SN%-D1%*100)/10):D3%=SN%
       -D1%*100-D2%*10
270    PRINT "■ ";:COLOR4,4,3:COLOR0,7,5:GOSUB 100
280    PP%=3852:M%=3572:IF PEEK(3852)>48THEN LS%=PEEK(3852
       )-48
290    IF PEEK(3852)=63ORPEEK(3852)=42ORPEEK(3852)=24
       THEN LS%=0:POKE 3852,48
300    TS%=TS%+LS%:CU=PEEK(3572):POKE 3572,13:POKE 3292,16
       0
```

Print Difficulty Level, Score and Total Score; Scan Keyboard

```
310    PRINT "■■R O U N D ▲ # ";R%;"■ L E V E L ▲ O F ▲
       D I F F . ▲ ";LD%;"■ ";TAB(30);"■ P L A Y E R ▲ 1 ■
        "
320    FOR I=1 TO 21:PRINT :NEXT:PRINT "■ ▲ T O T A L ▲ S
       C O R E ▲ ";TS%;TAB(21);"L A S T ▲ S C O R E ";LS%;
```

```
330    C=0:Q=1
340    GETX$:C=C+1
350    IF C=7THEN Q=1-Q:C=0
360    IF Q<>0THEN 390
370    IF PEEK(PP%)>63THEN POKE PP%,PEEK(PP%)-128:Q=1:
       GOTO 390
380    POKE PP%,PEEK(PP%)+128:Q=1
390    IF X$=""THEN 340
400    GOSUB 1940:IF PEEK(PP%)>64THEN POKE PP%,PEEK(PP%)
       -128
410    IF X$="W "THEN 510
420    IF X$="A "THEN 550
430    IF X$="D "THEN 590
440    IF X$="X "THEN 630
450    IF X$="E "THEN 670
460    IF X$="Q "THEN 710
470    IF X$="Z "THEN 750
480    IF X$="C "THEN 790
490    IF X$="T "THEN 830
500    GOTO 340
510    IF PEEK(PP%-40)=32THEN 340
520    LS%=PEEK(PP%)-48
530    POKE PP%,32:PP%=PP%-40
540    GOTO 850
550    IF PEEK(PP%-1)=32THEN 340
560    LS%=PEEK(PP%)-48
570    POKE PP%,32:PP%=PP%-1
580    GOTO 850
590    IF PEEK(PP%+1)=32THEN 340
600    LS%=PEEK(PP%)-48
610    POKE PP%,32:PP%=PP%+1
620    GOTO 850
630    IF PEEK(PP%+40)=32THEN 340
640    LS%=PEEK(PP%)-48
650    POKE PP%,32:PP%=PP%+40
660    GOTO 850
670    IF PEEK(PP%-39)=32THEN 340
680    LS%=PEEK(PP%)-48
690    POKE PP%,32:PP%=PP%-39
700    GOTO 850
710    IF PEEK(PP%-41)=32THEN 340
720    LS%=PEEK(PP%)-48
730    POKE PP%,32:PP%=PP%-41
740    GOTO 850
750    IF PEEK(PP%+39)=32THEN 340
760    LS%=PEEK(PP%)-48
770    POKE PP%,32:PP%=PP%+39
780    GOTO 850
790    IF PEEK(PP%+41)=32THEN 340
800    LS%=PEEK(PP%)-48
810    POKE PP%,32:PP%=PP%+41
```

```
820   GOTO 850
830   PR%=INT((PP%-3072)/40) :PC%=PP%-PR%*40-3072:
      GOSUB 1590:IF PP%<>M%THEN 830
840   GOTO 1770
850   PR%=INT((PP%-3072)/40) :PC%=PP%-PR%*40-3072
860   K1=PEEK(PP%):IF K1=63THEN GOSUB 950
870   IF PP%=M%THEN 1770
880   IF K1=24THEN GOSUB 970
890   IF K1=42THEN GOSUB 1440
900   IF K1=160THEN 1490
910   K1=PEEK(PP%)-48:IF LS%+K1>=10-LD%THEN GOSUB 1590
920   TS%=TS%+K1:GOSUB 1860
930   IF PP%=M%THEN 1770
940   GOTO 330
950   I=INT(RND(1)*10):POKE PP%,I+48
960   RETURN
970   POKE PP%,48
980   IF NC%>=9THEN GOTO 1430
990   K2=INT(RND(0)*9+1):IF T%(K2)=1THEN 990
1000  T%(K2)=1:NC%=NC%+1
```

At Random, Print a Clue at the Top of the Screen

```
1010  ON K2GOTO 1020,1050,1090,1130,1170,1210,1260,1290,1
      340
1020  GOSUB 1890:PRINT "S U M ▲ O F ▲ D I G I T S ▲ O F ▲
       S E C R E T ":PRINT TAB(9);"N U M B E R ▲ E Q U A
      L S ▲ ";
1030  PRINT D1%+D2%+D3%
1040  GOSUB 1910:RETURN
1050  GOSUB 1890:PRINT "S E C R E T ▲ N U M B E R ▲ I S ▲
       ";
1060  IF SN%/2=INT(SN%/2)THEN PRINT "E V E N ":GOTO 1080
1070  PRINT "O D D "
1080  PRINT :GOSUB 1910:RETURN
1090  K=INT(RND(1)*200)+SN%:J=K-200:IF J<0THEN J=0
1100  IF K>1000THEN K=1000
1110  GOSUB 1890:PRINT "N U M B E R ▲ I S ▲ B E T W E E N
       ";J:PRINT TAB(9);"A N D ";K
1120  GOSUB 1910:RETURN
1130  GOSUB 1890:PRINT "N U M B E R ▲ I S ▲ ";
1140  IF SN%/5=INT(SN%/5)THEN PRINT "D I V I S I B L E ":
      GOTO 1160
1150  PRINT "N O T ▲ D I V I S I B L E "
1160  PRINT TAB(9);"B Y ▲ 5 ":GOSUB 1910:RETURN
1170  L=D1%:IF D2%>LTHEN L=D2%
1180  IF D3%>LTHEN L=D3%
1190  GOSUB 1890:PRINT "L A R G E S T ▲ D I G I T ▲ I N ▲
```

```
      T H E ":PRINT TAB(9);"S E C R E T ▲ N U M B E R ▲
      I S ";L
1200  GOSUB 1910:RETURN
1210  GOSUB 1890:PRINT "F I R S T ▲ D I G I T ▲ I N ▲ T H
      E ▲ S E C R E T ":PRINT TAB(9);"N U M B E R ▲ I S
      ▲ ";
1220  IF D1%>5THEN PRINT "L A R G E R ▲ T H A N ▲ 5 ":
      GOTO 1250
1230  IF D1%<5THEN PRINT "L E S S ▲ T H A N ▲ 5 ":GOTO 12
      50
1240  PRINT "E Q U A L ▲ T O ▲ 5 "
1250  GOSUB 1910:RETURN
1260  GOSUB 1890:PRINT "S U M ▲ O F ▲ F I R S T ▲ A N D ▲
      T H I R D ":PRINT TAB(9);"D I G I T S ▲ I S ▲ ";
1270  PRINT D1%+D3%
1280  GOSUB 1910:RETURN
1290  GOSUB 1890:PRINT "O N E ▲ O F ▲ T H E ▲ D I G I T S
      ▲ I N ▲ T H E ":PRINT TAB(9);"S E C R E T ▲ N U M
      B E R ▲ I S ▲ ";
1300  K=INT(RND(1)*3):IF K=0ANDSN%>99THEN PRINT D1%:
      GOTO 1330
1310  IF K=1ANDSN%>9THEN PRINT D2%:GOTO 1330
1320  PRINT D3%
1330  GOSUB 1910:RETURN
1340  GOSUB 1890:PRINT "P R O D U C T ▲ O F ▲ T H E ▲ N O
      N - Z E R O ":PRINT TAB(9);"D I G I T S ▲ I S ";
1350  IF D1%=0ANDD2%=0THEN PRINT D3%:GOTO 1420
1360  IF D1%=0ANDD3%=0THEN PRINT D2%:GOTO 1420
1370  IF D1%=0THEN PRINT D2%*D3%:GOTO 1420
1380  IF D2%=0ANDD3%=0THEN PRINT D1%:GOTO 1420
1390  IF D2%=0THEN PRINT D1%*D3%:GOTO 1420
1400  IF D3%=0THEN PRINT D1%*D2%:GOTO 1420
1410  PRINT D1%*D2%*D3%
1420  GOSUB 1910:RETURN
1430  GOTO 1090
1440  POKE PP%,48
1450  IF TS%<11THEN RETURN
1460  I=INT(RND(0)*100):IF I>50THEN TS%=TS%-10:RETURN
1470  IF I<10THEN TS%=TS%+50:RETURN
1480  TS%=TS%+10:RETURN
```

Input the Secret Number; If Wrong, Then Give Player Clue

```
1490  GOSUB 1890:PRINT "G U E S S ▲ A T ▲ T H E ▲ S E C R
      E T ▲ N U M B E R ":PRINT TAB(9);
1500  INPUT "A N D ▲ H I T ▲ ▣R E T U R N■ ";K$
1510  I=VAL(K$):IF I=SN%THEN 1770
1520  G1%=INT(I/100):G2%=INT((I-G1%*100)/10):G3%=I-G1%*10
      0-G2%*10
```

```
1530  PRINT "[CLR] ":PRINT :IF D1%=G1%THEN PRINT "F I R S T ▲
       D I G I T ▲ C O R R E C T ":PRINT
1540  IF D2%=G2%THEN PRINT "S E C O N D ▲ D I G I T ▲ C O
       R R E C T ":PRINT
1550  IF D3%=G3%THEN PRINT "T H I R D ▲ D I G I T ▲ C O R
       R E C T "
1560  IF D1%<>G1%ANDD2%<>G2%ANDD3%<>G3%THEN PRINT "N O ▲
      D I G I T S ▲ C O R R E C T "
1570  FOR T=1 TO 2000:NEXT
1580  R%=R%+1:GOTO 270
1590  MR%=INT((M%-1024)/40):MC%=M%-MR%*40-3072
1600  IF MC%<>PC%THEN 1630
1610  IF MR%>PR%THEN MR%=MR%-1:GOTO 1700
1620  MR%=MR%+1:GOTO 1700
1630  IF MR%<>PR%THEN 1660
1640  IF MC%>PC%THEN MC%=MC%-1:GOTO 1700
1650  MC%=MC%+1:GOTO 1700
1660  IF M%>PP%THEN 1690
1670  IF MC%<PC%THEN MC%=MC%+1:GOTO 1700
1680  MC%=MC%-1:GOTO 1700
1690  MR%=MR%-1
1700  K=3072+40*MR%+MC%:IF PEEK(K)=160THEN RETURN
1710  POKE M%,CU:IF CU=63THEN GOTO 1740
1720  IF CU>=48THEN GOTO 1740
1730  IF CU=24THEN GOTO 1740
1740  M%=K:CU=PEEK(M%)
1750  POKE M%,13
1760  RETURN
1770  PRINT "[CLR] ";:IF M%=PP%THEN 1810
```

Print the Score and Who Won, You or Minotaur; Print Magic Number

```
1780  FOR I=1 TO 18:PRINT "▲ ▲ ▲ C O N G R A T U L A T I
      O N S ! ▲ ▲ ▲ C O N G R A T U L A T I O N S ! ":
      NEXT:PRINT
1790  PRINT "Y O U ▲ H A V E ▲ D E F E A T E D ▲ T H E ▲
      M I N O T A U R ! ! ":PRINT "Y O U R ▲ S C O R E ▲
      I S ▲ ";TS%;
1800  PRINT "I N ▲ ";R%;"▲ R O U N D S ":GOTO 1830
1810  FOR I=1 TO 18:PRINT "■ ▲ ▲ ▲ M I N O T A U R ▲ W I
      N S ! ▲ ▲ ▲ ▲ M I N O T A U R ▲ W I N S ! ":NEXT:
      PRINT
1820  PRINT "T H E ▲ S E C R E T ▲ N U M B E R ▲ W A S ▲
      ";SN%
1830  PRINT :PRINT "H I T ▲ A N Y ▲ K E Y ▲ F O R ▲ A N O
       T H E R ▲ G A M E "
1840  GETX$:IF X$=""THEN 1840
1850  RUN
```

```
1860 PRINT CHR$(13);CHR$(145);"▲ T O T A L ▲ S C O R E ▲
     ▲ ▲ ▲ ▲ ▲ ▲ ▲ ▲ ▲ ▲ ";TAB(21);"L A S T ▲ S C O R E ▲ ▲
     ▲ ▲ ▲ ";
1870 PRINT CHR$(13);CHR$(145);"▲ T O T A L ▲ S C O R E ▲
     ";TS%;TAB(21);"L A S T ▲ S C O R E ";LS%;
1880 RETURN
1890 PRINT CHR$(13);:FOR I=1 TO 21:PRINT CHR$(145);:
     NEXT:PRINT "■ ";
1900 PRINT TAB(9);:RETURN
1910 FOR I=1 TO 18:PRINT CHR$(17);:NEXT
1920 PRINT TAB(35);"◣ ";
1930 RETURN
1940 FOR I=3160 TO 3186:POKE I,32:NEXT
1950 FOR I=3200 TO 3226:POKE I,32:NEXT
1960 RETURN
1970 K1=INT(RND(0)*14):PRINT K1,:GOTO 1970
```

ChexSum Tables

Line		Sum	Line		Sum	Line		Sum
10	=	0	310	=	4779	610	=	1451
20	=	4621	320	=	4912	620	=	534
30	=	585	330	=	680	630	=	1571
40	=	2389	340	=	903	640	=	1181
50	=	1196	350	=	1587	650	=	1505
60	=	1953	360	=	971	660	=	534
70	=	1204	370	=	3514	670	=	1570
80	=	1032	380	=	1638	680	=	1181
90	=	526	390	=	872	690	=	1513
100	=	1312	400	=	2944	700	=	534
110	=	709	410	=	969	710	=	1571
120	=	1207	420	=	957	720	=	1181
130	=	848	430	=	952	730	=	1507
140	=	943	440	=	978	740	=	534
150	=	527	450	=	959	750	=	1570
160	=	1089	460	=	971	760	=	1181
170	=	629	470	=	982	770	=	1512
180	=	527	480	=	955	780	=	534
190	=	1091	490	=	964	790	=	1571
200	=	1246	500	=	525	800	=	1181
210	=	629	510	=	1571	810	=	1506
220	=	320	520	=	1181	820	=	534
230	=	589	530	=	1506	830	=	5454
240	=	143	540	=	534	840	=	584
250	=	2063	550	=	1513	850	=	3533
260	=	5528	560	=	1181	860	=	1955
270	=	1987	570	=	1452	870	=	1060
280	=	3734	580	=	534	880	=	1043
290	=	4346	590	=	1513	890	=	1104
300	=	3293	600	=	1181	900	=	1022

```
910   =  3336
920   =  1338
930   =  1060
940   =   528
950   =  2055
960   =   143
970   =   515
980   =  1543
990   =  2619
1000  =  1484
1010  =  3081
1020  =  4787
1030  =  1009
1040  =   562
1050  =  2128
1060  =  2977
1070  =   441
1080  =   779
1090  =  3495
1100  =  1286
1110  =  3349
1120  =   562
1130  =  1513
1140  =  3423
1150  =  1236
1160  =  1472
1170  =  1700
1180  =  1168
1190  =  4879
1200  =   562
1210  =  4573
1220  =  2670
1230  =  2519
1240  =   941
1250  =   562
1260  =  4211
1270  =   656
1280  =   562
1290  =  5167
1300  =  3577
1310  =  2268
1320  =   311
1330  =   562
1340  =  4265
1350  =  2330
1360  =  2329
1370  =  2066
1380  =  2328
1390  =  2067
1400  =  2066
1410  =  1009
1420  =   562
1430  =   587
1440  =   515
1450  =   956
1460  =  3178
1470  =  1812
1480  =  1086
1490  =  3464
1500  =  1679
1510  =  1723
1520  =  5020
1530  =  3812
1540  =  3022
1550  =  2710
1560  =  4953
1570  =  1031
1580  =  1271
1590  =  3341
1600  =  1316
1610  =  2469
1620  =  1477
1630  =  1347
1640  =  2405
1650  =  1447
1660  =  1061
1670  =  2407
1680  =  1448
1690  =   810
1700  =  2898
1710  =  1928
1720  =  1571
1730  =  1370
1740  =  1195
1750  =   421
1760  =   143
1770  =  1569
1780  =  4920
1790  =  4976
1800  =  2036
1810  =  4653
1820  =  2254
1830  =  2713
1840  =  1321
1850  =   139
1860  =  4669
1870  =  4697
1880  =   143
1890  =  2969
1900  =   688
1910  =  1619
1920  =   828
1930  =   143
1940  =  1682
1950  =  1683
1960  =   143
1970  =  2328
TOTAL = 346832
```

Star Trader

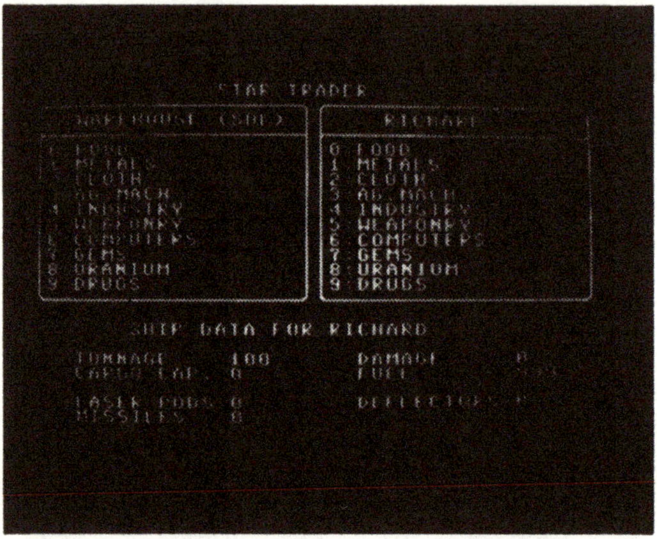

CLASSIFICATION: Strategy

You are the pilot of an interstellar merchant vessel. Using all of your charm and intelligence, you secure a loan from the Solar Interstellar Bank (Sol branch) to purchase a second-hand merchant ship. With the little cash left over, you decide to enter the hazardous world of interstellar speculation. Use your cash to purchase various items at cheap prices, then travel to worlds where the demand for these items is great and sell them at a profit. You must repay the bank your massive loan or risk repossession. Beware of pirates and space storms. Full instructions are contained within the game. May you make a gigabuck or two!

PROGRAMMING SUGGESTIONS

Limit the supply of goods available on each planet. Introduce random patrols searching for gems, drugs or uranium among the inner worlds. Add random events such as black holes, or robbers who attack you and try to steal your cash.

PROGRAM Variables

S$	Ship name
GD	Goods in warehouse and ship
TP	Trade prices
T$	Trade items
CC	Cargo capacity
SS	Ship size
LP	Laser pods
MS	Missiles
DF	Deflectors
P%	Planetary data
PL$	Planetary names
CS	Cash
CR	Bank balance
DM	Damage to ship
DR	Current real damage
PF	Pirate fleet
SN	Number of pirates in fleet
SD	Star data
L	Current planetary system

Important Note

Star Trader is such a large program that it leaves no room for ChexSum to be merged with it.

You must therefore type in Star Trader in two sections, run ChexSum on each half in turn, then merge the two halves:

1. Enter lines 10 to 1440 of the first half of Star Trader which follow.

Listing

Initialise Game Variables

```
10  N$="╚■▲▲▲▲▲▲▲▲▲▲▲▲▲▲▲▲▲▲STAR▲TRADER"÷S$="BOLT▲BIN▲▲"÷VOL 8
20  PRINT "■ ";N$÷PRINT "▣▲▲▲▲▲▲▲▲▲▲▲▲▲▲▲PLEASE▲WAIT..."
30  RC$="▣▣▣▣▣▣▣▣▣▣▣▣▣▣▣▣▣▣▣▣▣▣▣▣▣"
40  NL$="▲▲▲▲▲▲▲▲▲▲▲▲▲▲▲▲▲▲▲▲▲▲▲▲▲▲▲▲▲▲▲▲▲▲▲▲▲▲▲▲"
50  CY$="▣▣▣▣▣▣▣▣▣▣▣▣▣▣▣▣"÷L$="╪╪╪╪╪╪╪╪╪╪╪╪╪╪╪╪╪╪╪╪╪╪╪"÷CD$="▣▣▣▣▣▣▣▣▣▣"
60  L1$="╪╪╪╪╪╪╪╪╪╪╪╪╪+╪╪╪╪╪╪╪╪╪╪╪╪+╪╪╪╪╪╪╪╪╪╪╪╪╪╪"
70  LP=0÷MS=0÷DF=0÷DIMW%(9,1)÷DIMP(9,6)÷DIMPL$(9)÷SS=100÷L=0
80  DIMPF(9,3)÷DIMGD(8,1)÷DIMTP(8)
90  DEFFNX(D)=INT(RND(0)*D*8-D*3)
100 DEFFNDS(D)=INT(SQR(ABS(P(D,0)-P(L,0))↑2+ABS(P(D,1)-P(L,1))↑2+ABS(P(D,2)-P(L,2))↑2))
110 RESTORE
120 DATASIRIUS,PROCYON,WESEN,ALTAIR,DENEB,DUBHE,VEGA,CAPELLA,CASTOR,POLLUX,ANTARES
130 DATAZOSMA,RIGEL,MEGREZ,MINTAKA,SAIPH,KOCHAB,PHAEDA
140 DATAETAMIN,ERIDANE,WOLF,HAMAL,ARIADNE
150 FOR I=1 TO 9÷IF RND(0)<.333THEN READPL$(I)÷READD$÷GOTO 180
160 IF RND(0)<.333THEN READD$÷READPL$(I)÷GOTO 180
170 READD$÷READPL$(I)
180 P(I,0)=FNX(I)÷P(I,1)=FNX(I)÷P(I,2)=FNX(I)
190 P(I,3)=91-10*I+INT(RND(0)*15)+INT(RND(0)*15)
200 P(I,4)=21-2*I-INT(RND(0)*3)÷P(I,5)=INT(2000/(P(I,3)*P(I,4))+1)
210 P(I,6)=FNDS(I)
220 NEXTI÷PL$(0)="SOL"÷P(0,3)=110+INT(RND(0)*20)÷P(0,4)=20÷P(0,5)=1
230 DIMT$(9)÷T$(0)="▌0÷FOOD▲▲▲▲"÷T$(1)="▌1÷METALS▲▲"
240 T$(6)="▌6÷GEMS▲▲▲▲"
250 T$(2)="▌2÷WEAPONS▲"÷T$(3)="▌3÷CYBORGS▲"
260 T$(4)="▌4÷URANIUM▲"÷T$(5)="▌5÷DRUGS▲▲▲"
270 T$(7)="▌7÷FUEL▲▲▲▲"÷T$(8)="▌8÷REPAIRS▲"
```

```
280   COLOR0,2:COLOR4,2
290   PRINT "♥▲▲▲▲▲▲▲W E L C O M E▲T O▲S T A R
      ▲T R A D E R ! "
300   INPUT "ⓠ▲▲▲▲▲▲▲E N T E R▲N A M E▲O F▲Y
      O U R▲S H I P ";S$:PRINT "♥ "
310   GD(7,1)=10:CS=5000:CR=-5000:SD=5+INT(RND(0)*200)/10
      0:GOSUB 2200:GOSUB 690:B=2*CS+500
```

Get Player's Command and Help Table

```
320   GETA$:IF A$=""THEN 320
330   IF A$="Q "THEN 530
340   IF A$="I "THEN GOSUB 690:GOTO 320
350   IF A$="M "THEN GOSUB 870:GOTO 320
360   IF A$="J "THEN GOSUB 990:GOTO 320
370   IF A$="B "ANDL=0ANDB>0THEN GOSUB 2400:GOTO 320
380   IF A$="D "ANDL=0ANDCS>0THEN GOSUB 2480:GOTO 320
390   IF A$="T "THEN GOSUB 1270:GOTO 320
400   IF A$="U "ANDL=0THEN GOSUB 570:GOTO 320
410   IF A$="L "ANDL=0THEN GOSUB 630:GOTO 320
420   IF ASC(A$)=13THEN 320
430   PRINT N$;"ⓠⓠⓠⓠ▲▲▲▲▲▲▲▲▲▲▲V A L I D▲C
       O M M A N D S▲A R E▲: ":PRINT "ⓠ▲'I'▲▲C
       A R G O▲A N D▲S H I P▲S T A T U S"
440   PRINT "ⓠ▲'J'▲▲H Y P E R▲J U M P▲C H A R
      T ":PRINT "ⓠ▲'T'▲▲T R A D E▲T A B L E"
450   PRINT "ⓠ▲'M'▲▲S Y S T E M▲L I B R A R Y"
460   PRINT "ⓠ▲'Q'▲▲T O▲Q U I T▲G A M E"
470   PRINT "ⓠ▲'U'▲▲U N L O A D▲S H I P▲T O▲
      W A R E H O U S E"
480   PRINT "ⓠ▲'L'▲▲L O A D▲S H I P▲F R O M▲
      W A R E H O U S E"
490   PRINT "ⓠ▲'B'▲▲B O R R O W▲C A S H▲F R O
      M▲B A N K"
500   PRINT "ⓠ▲'D'▲▲D E P O S I T▲C A S H▲I N
      ▲B A N K"
510   GETA$:IF A$=""THEN 510
520   GOTO 330
530   PRINT "ⓠⓠⓠ▲▲▲Q U I T T I N G :▲A R E▲Y O
      U▲S U R E▲? ";
```

Quitting, Loading and Unloading, Inventory

```
540   GETA$:IF A$=""THEN 540
550   IF A$="Y "THEN 2860
560   GOSUB 690:GOTO 320
```

```
570   IN=-1‡I$=""‡PRINT "▣ ";CV$;NL$
580   PRINT CV$;"▒ ▲U N L O A D I N G ▲";
590   GOSUB 1620‡IF IN>6THEN SOUND 1,200,5‡GOTO 590
600   PRINT RIGHT$(T$(IN),8);‡INPUT N‡IF INT(N)>GD(IN,1)
      ORN<0THEN SOUND 1,200,5‡GOTO 570
610   GD(IN,0)=GD(IN,0)+INT(N)‡GD(IN,1)=GD(IN,1)-INT(N)
620   PRINT CV$;NL$‡GOSUB 2360‡GOSUB 850‡RETURN
630   IN=-1‡I$=""‡PRINT CV$;NL$
640   PRINT CV$;"▒ ▲L O A D I N G ▲";
650   GOSUB 1620‡IF IN>6THEN SOUND 1,200,5‡GOTO 650
660   PRINT RIGHT$(T$(IN),8);‡INPUT N‡IF INT(N)>GD(IN,0)
      ORN<0THEN SOUND 1,200,5‡GOTO 630
670   GD(IN,1)=GD(IN,1)+INT(N)‡GD(IN,0)=GD(IN,0)-INT(N)
680   PRINT CV$;NL$‡GOSUB 2360‡GOSUB 850‡RETURN
690   PRINT N$‡PRINT "▞ ";L$;"▚ ▞ ";L$;"▚ ";
700   PRINT "▌ ▲ ▲ W A R E H O U S E ▲ ( S O L ) ▲ ▌ ▌ ▲
      ▲ ▲ ▲ ▲ ▲ ▲ ▲ ▲ ▲ ▲ ▲ ▲ ▲ ▲ ▲ ▲ ▲ ▲ ▲ ▲ ▲ ▲ ▌ ";
710   PRINT "▣ ▣ ▣ ▣ ▣ ▣ ▣ ▣ ▣ ";RC$;S$
720   PRINT "▐ ";L$;"▌ ▐ ";L$;"▌ ";
730   FOR I=0 TO 6‡PRINT T$(I);"▲ ▲ ▲ ▲ ▲ ▲ ▲ ▲ ▲ ▌ ";T$(I)
      ;"▲ ▲ ▲ ▲ ▲ ▲ ▲ ▲ ▲ ▌ ";‡NEXT
740   PRINT "■ ▚ ";L$;"▞ ▚ ";L$;"▞ "‡PRINT "▣ ▣ ▣ "
750   GOSUB 2360‡GOSUB 840‡GOSUB 2460‡GOSUB 850
760   PRINT CV$;"▣ ▣ ▣ ▣ ▣ ■ ▲ ▲ ▲ ▲ ▲ ▲ ▲ ▲ S H I P ▲ D A
      T A ▲ F O R ▲ ";S$
770   PRINT "▣ ▣ ▲ ▲ T O N N A G E ▲ ▲ ▲ ▛ ";‡PRINT
      USING"# # # # # # # ";SS;
780   PRINT "▣ ▲ ▲ ▲ D A M A G E ▲ ▲ ▲ ▲ ▛ ";‡PRINT
      USING"# # # # # ";DM
790   PRINT "▣ ▣ ▣ ▣ ▣ ▣ ▣ ▣ ▣ ▣ ▣ ▣ ▣ ▣ ▣ ▣ ▣ ▣ ▣ ▣ ▣ ▣ ▣ ▣
      ▣ F U E L ▲ ▲ ▲ ▲ ▛ ";‡PRINT USING"# # # # # . # ";
      GD(7,1)
800   PRINT ‡PRINT "▣ ▲ ▲ L A S E R ▲ P O D S ▲ ▲ ▛ ";‡
      PRINT USING"# # # # # ";LP;
810   PRINT "▣ ▲ ▲ ▲ D E F L E C T O R S ▛ ";‡PRINT
      USING"# # # # # ";DF
820   PRINT "▣ ▲ ▲ M I S S I L E S ▲ ▲ ▛ ";‡PRINT USING"#
      # # # # # # # ";MS;
830   RETURN
840   PRINT CV$;"▛ ▲ ▲ ";PL$(L);"▲ S T A R D A T E ▲ ";‡
      PRINT USING"# # # # # . # # ";SD;‡RETURN
850   CC=SS‡FOR I=0 TO 6‡CC=CC-GD(I,1)‡NEXT‡CC=CC-INT(GD(
      7,1))-10*(LP+DF)-MS
860   PRINT CV$;"▣ ▣ ▣ ▣ ▣ ▣ ▣ ▣ ▣ ▣ ▣ ▣ C A R G O ▲ C A P
      . ▛ ";‡PRINT USING"# # # # # # # ";CC‡RETURN
870   PRINT N$‡PRINT ‡PRINT "S Y S T E M ","P O P L . ▲ ▲
      ▲ ▲ T E C H . ▲ ▲ ▲ ▲ A G R I C U L T U R E "‡
      PRINT
```

Library Information

```
880   FOR I=0 TO 9:PRINT :IF L=ITHEN PRINT "* ";
890   PRINT PL$(I),P(I,3),P(I,4),P(I,5):NEXT
900   RETURN
910   PRINT N$:L1=L
920   PRINT "■ ▌ ▲ ▲ ▲ ▲ ▲ ▲ ▲ ▲ D E S T I N A T I O N ▲ S
      Y S T E M ▲ ■ ";PL$(L1)
930   FOR I=0 TO 4:PRINT "■ ■ ";CHR$(I+48);": ■ ";:IF I
      =LTHEN PRINT "■ ";
940   PRINT PL$(I);"▀ ■ ";,P(I,6),;
950   PRINT "■ ";CHR$(I+53);": ■ ";:IF I+5=LTHEN PRINT "■
       ";
960   PRINT PL$(I+5);"▀ ■ ";,P(I+5,6):NEXTI
970   PRINT "■ ■ ■ ▲ ▲ ' 0 ' . . ' 9 ' ▲ T O ▲ S E L E C
      T ▲ D E S T I N A T I O N ":PRINT "▲ ▲ ▲ ▲ ▲ ▲ ▲ ▲ T
      H E N ▲ R E T U R N ▲ T O ▲ L A U N C H . "
980   RETURN
990   IF CC<0ORGD(7,1)<=0THEN SOUND 1,200,5:RETURN
```

Hyperjump Table and Random Interstellar Events

```
1000  GOSUB 910
1010  GETA$:IF A$=""THEN 1010
1020  IF A$="Q "THEN 530
1030  IF L1=LANDASC(A$)=13THEN GOSUB 690:GOSUB 840:
      RETURN
1040  IF ASC(A$)<>13THEN 1110
1050  K=P(L1,6):L=L1:FOR Z=1 TO K:GOSUB 1140:SD=SD+.01:
      IF CR>0THEN CR=CR+CR/500
1060  IF CR<0THEN CR=CR+CR/150
1070  NEXTZ
1080  FOR I=0 TO 9:P(I,6)=FNDS(I):NEXT:GOSUB 2200:
      SOUND 1,1000,10
1090  IF RND(0)*CR*CR/1000000>50000/SDTHEN PRINT "■ ■ ▲ ▲
       ▲ Y O U R ▲ S H I P ▲ W A S ▲ R E P O S E S S E D
      . . . ":GOTO 2860
1100  B=2*CS+500:GOSUB 2540:GOSUB 690:RETURN
1110  IF ASC(A$)<48ORASC(A$)>57THEN 1010
1120  L1=VAL(A$):PRINT "■ ■ ■ ■ ▐ ▐ ▐ ▐ ▐ ";RC$;"▲ ▲ ▲ ▲
      ▲ ▲ ▲ ▲ ▲ ▲ ▌▌ ▌▌ ▌▌ ▌▌ ▌▌ ▌▌ ▌▌ ▌▌ ▌▌ ";PL$(L1);
1130  GOTO 1010
1140  GD(7,1)=GD(7,1)-0.1
1150  IF GD(7,1)<0THEN PRINT "■ ■ ▲ ▲ ▲ Y O U ▲ R A N ▲ O
       U T ▲ O F ▲ F U E L ▲ I N ▲ M I D - F L I G H T .
      . . ":GOTO 2860
```

```
1160  IF RND(0)>.06THEN RETURN
1170  IF RND(0)>.3THEN 1220
1180  DM=DM+INT(RND(0)*5+1):SOUND 3,400,20
1190  PRINT CY$;"▣ ▣ ▣ ▣ ▣ ▣ ▲ ▲ ▲ ▲ ▌S P A C E ▲ D E B
      R I S ! ! ▀ ":FOR J=1 TO 400:NEXTJ
1200  IF DM>=SSTHEN PRINT "▙ ▣ ▣ ▣ ▪ Y O U R ▲ S H I P ▲
      W A S ▲ D E S T R O Y E D ▲ B Y ▲ A ▲ M E T E O R "
      :GOTO 2860
1210  RETURN
1220  IF RND(0)>.1THEN 1250
1230  GD(7,1)=GD(7,1)-INT(RND(0)*10)-1:SOUND 3,1000,20
1240  PRINT CY$;"▣ ▣ ▣ ▣ ▣ ▣ ▣ ▣ ▣ ▲ ▲ ▲ ▲ ▌M I S - J U M
      P ! ! ▀ ":FOR J=1 TO 400:NEXTJ:RETURN
1250  IF RND(0)>L↑2/120THEN RETURN
1260  GOSUB 1710:RETURN
```

Trading Goods and Trade Table

```
1270  PRINT N$:PRINT "▣ ▪ ▲ ▲ ▲ ▲ ▲ ▲ ▲ ▲ ▲ ▲ ▲ ▲ ▲ ▲ T R A D E
       ▲ P R I C E S ▲ F O R ▲ ";PL$(L)
1280  PRINT "▞ ═ ═ ═ ═ ═ ═ ═ ═ ═ ═ ┳ ═ ═ ═ ═ ═ ═ ═ ═ ═ ═
      ═ ┳ ═ ═ ═ ═ ═ ═ ═ ═ ═ ═ ═ ═ ═ ═ ═ ═ ▚ "
1290  PRINT "▌ ▲ I T E M ▲ ▲ ▲ ▲ ▲ ▲ ▌ ▲ ▲ ▲ ▲ P R I C E ▲
      ▲ ▌ ▲ ▲ ▲ ▲ ▲ ▲ ▲ ▲ ▲ ▲ ▲ O W N E D ▲ ▌ ";
1300  PRINT "┣ ";L1$;"┫ "
1310  FOR I=0 TO 6:PRINT LEFT$(T$(I),3);:IF IX=ITHEN
      PRINT "▣ ";
1320  PRINT RIGHT$(T$(I),8);"▀ ▌ ";:PRINT  USING"# # # #
      # # # . # # ";TP(I);
1330  PRINT "▲ ▌ ▲ ▲ ▲ ▲ ▲ ▲ ▲ ▲ ▲ ▲ ▲ ▲ ▲ ▲ ▲ ▲ ▲ ▌ ":NEXT
1340  PRINT "┣ ";L1$;"┫ "
1350  PRINT T$(7);"▌ ";:PRINT USING"# # # # # # # . # # "
      ;TP(7);:PRINT "▲ ▌ ▲ ▲ ▲ ▲ ▲ ▲ ▲ ▲ ▲ ▲ ▲ ▲ ▲ ▲ ▲ ▲ ▌
      ";
1360  PRINT "┣ ";L1$;"┫ "
1370  PRINT T$(8);"▌ ";:PRINT  USING"# # # # # # # . # #
      ";TP(8);:PRINT "▲ ▌ ▲ ▲ ▲ ▲ ▲ ▲ ▲ ▲ ▲ ▲ ▲ ▲ ▲ ▲ ▲ ▲ ▌
       ";
1380  PRINT "▚ ═ ═ ═ ═ ═ ═ ═ ═ ═ ═ ┻ ═ ═ ═ ═ ═ ═ ═ ═ ═ ═
      ═ ┻ ═ ═ ═ ═ ═ ═ ═ ═ ═ ═ ═ ═ ═ ═ ═ ═ ▞ "
1390  PRINT "' B ' - B U Y ▲ ▲ ' S ' - S E L L ▲ ▲ ' Q '
      - Q U I T ▲ ▲ ' R ' - R E P A I R ":DN$="":GOSUB 16
      50
1400  IN=-1:I$="":GD(8,1)=0
1410  PRINT CY$;CD$;NL$
1420  GETA$:IF A$=""THEN 1420
1430  IF A$="Q "THEN GOSUB 690:RETURN
1440  IF A$<>"R "THEN 1480
```

ChexSum Tables

```
10    =  4035
20    =  2726
30    =  1068
40    =  2271
50    =  6608
60    =  8724
70    =  4329
80    =  1711
90    =  2395
100   =  6929
110   =   141
120   =  7007
130   =  4197
140   =  2885
150   =  3352
160   =  2623
170   =   809
180   =  3216
190   =  3436
200   =  4969
210   =  1033
220   =  4463
230   =  3695
240   =  1382
250   =  3317
260   =  3173
270   =  3178
280   =   834
290   =  2455
300   =  3124
310   =  6440
320   =  1216
330   =   946
340   =  1678
350   =  1678
360   =  1674
370   =  2779
380   =  2869
390   =  1750
400   =  2204
410   =  2194
420   =  1189
430   =  5673
440   =  3722
450   =  1733
460   =  1507
470   =  2564
480   =  2563
490   =  2285
500   =  2184
510   =  1212
520   =   528
530   =  2406
540   =  1212
550   =  1015
560   =   919
570   =  1958
580   =  1547
590   =  2379
600   =  4649
610   =  3794
620   =  1664
630   =  1760
640   =  1338
650   =  2384
660   =  4645
670   =  3794
680   =  1664
690   =  2221
700   =  3328
710   =   922
720   =  1673
730   =  3377
740   =  2311
750   =  1548
760   =  2503
770   =  2757
780   =  2507
790   =  3349
800   =  3023
810   =  2675
820   =  2783
830   =   143
840   =  3658
850   =  5941
860   =  3364
870   =  4202
880   =  1975
890   =  2077
900   =   143
910   =   723
920   =  2927
930   =  3492
940   =  1505
950   =  2925
960   =  2162
970   =  5823
980   =   143
990   =  2539
1000  =   303
1010  =  1276
1020  =   946
1030  =  2523
1040  =  1440
1050  =  5688
1060  =  1880
1070  =   221
1080  =  3244
1090  =  7374
1100  =  2022
1110  =  2124
1120  =  4628
1130  =   579
1140  =  1339
1150  =  5499
1160  =  1133
1170  =  1171
1180  =  2455
1190  =  3551
1200  =  5688
1210  =   143
1220  =  1168
1230  =  3139
1240  =  3513
1250  =  1636
1260  =   558
1270  =  3231
1280  =  8840
1290  =  3482
1300  =   970
1310  =  2902
1320  =  3126
1330  =  1562
1340  =   970
1350  =  4031
1360  =   970
1370  =  4037
1380  =  8830
1390  =  4214
1400  =  1743
1410  =   856
1420  =  1275
1430  =  1294
1440  =  1194

TOTAL= 385287
```

2 Save the first half of Star Trader by entering SAVE "STAR TRAD FIRST" for tape or SAVE "STAR TRAD FIRST", 8 for disk.

3 Load and run the Merge program by typing LOAD "MERGE" for tape or LOAD "MERGE",8 for disk, and then entering RUN.

4 From your games tape or disk, load the first half of Star Trader: enter LOAD "STAR TRAD FIRST" for tape or "LOAD STAR TRAD FIRST",8 for disk. Do not RUN the program at this time.

5 Enter SYS16331.

6 Load ChexSum by entering LOAD "CHEXSUM" for tape or LOAD "CHEXSUM", 8 for disk.

7 Enter SYS16355 to merge the first half of Star Trader with ChexSum.

8 Enter RUN 62000 to activate ChexSum.

9 The program will respond with the prompt:

    LINE NUMBER: ?

Pressing the RETURN key at this point will cause ChexSum to start with the first line of Star Trader, first half. Entering a line number will start ChexSum at that line.

10 ChexSum next prompts with:

    PRINTER (Y/N) ?

A 'Y' will send the ChexSum table to the printer or an 'N' will send it to the screen.

11 Check your grand total for the first half with that printed above. If they differ, a line has been typed incorrectly. Compare line numbers until you locate the bad lines and then edit them.

12 Repeat steps 8 to 10 until the games program is debugged. In step 8, enter the number of the first bad line to avoid ChexSum verifying the games program from the first line.

13 Erase ChexSum from the end of the first half by entering DELETE 62000-62196.

14 Save the first half as "STAR TRAD OK1".

15 Enter the second half of Star Trader, lines 1450 to 2880 (which follow), and save it: SAVE "STAR TRAD SEC" or SAVE "STAR TRAD SEC",8.

```
1450  PRINT CY$;CD$;"■ ▲ ▲ R E P A I R S ▲ ";DM;‡INPUT N‡
      IF N>DMTHEN N=DM
1460  IF INT(N)*TP(8)>CSTHEN N=INT(CS/TP(8))
1470  DM=DM-INT(N)‡CS=CS-INT(N)*TP(8)‡GOSUB 1650‡GOTO 141
      0
1480  IF A$<>"B "THEN 1560
1490  PRINT CY$;CD$;"■ ▲ ▲ B U Y I N G ▲ ";
1500  IF IN<0THEN GOSUB 1620
1510  PRINT RIGHT$(I$,8);"( ";
1520  PRINT  USING"# # # # # # ";INT(CS/TP(IN));‡PRINT ")
       ";
1530  PRINT "▲ ▲ ▲ ▲ ▲ ▲ ▲ ▲ ▲ ▲ ▲ ▲ ▲ ▲ ▮ ▮ ▮ ▮ ▮ ▮ ▮ ▮ ▮ ▮ ▮
      ";
1540  INPUT N‡IF TP(IN)*INT(N)>CSTHEN N=INT(CS/TP(IN))
1550  CS=CS-TP(IN)*INT(N)‡GD(IN,1)=GD(IN,1)+N‡GOSUB 1650‡
      IN=-1‡GOTO 1410
1560  IF A$<>"S "THEN SOUND 1,200,5‡GOTO 1410
1570  PRINT CY$;CD$;"■ ▲ ▲ S E L L I N G ▲ ";‡IF IN>=0
      THEN PRINT "■ ■ ■ ■ ■ ■ ■ ■ ";‡GOTO 1590
1580  GOSUB 1620‡PRINT RIGHT$(I$,8);‡IF IN>7THEN SOUND 1,
      200,5‡IN=-1‡GOTO 1410
1590  PRINT "▲ ▲ ▲ ▲ ▲ ▲ ▲ ▲ ▲ ▲ ▲ ▲ ▲ ▲ ▲ ▲ ▲ ▲ ▲ ▲ ▲ ▮ ▮ ▮ ▮
      ▮ ▮ ▮ ▮ ▮ ▮ ▮ ▮ ▮ ▮ ▮ ▮ ▮ ▮ ▮ ▮ ▮ ▮ ▮ ▮ ";
1600  INPUT N‡IF INT(N)>GD(IN,1)THEN N=GD(IN,1)
1610  CS=CS+TP(IN)*INT(N)‡GD(IN,1)=GD(IN,1)-N‡GOSUB 1650‡
      IN=-1‡GOTO 1410
1620  GETA$‡IF A$=""THEN 1620
1630  IF ASC(A$)>=48ANDASC(A$)<=55THEN IN=ASC(A$)-48‡I$
      =T$(IN)‡RETURN
1640  SOUND 1,200,5‡GOTO 1620
1650  GOSUB 850‡PRINT CY$;"■ ■ ■ ■ ■ ■ ■ ■ ▲ ▲ C A S H ▲
      ▲ ▲ ▲ ▲ ▲ ▲ ▲ ▲ ▲ ▲ ▲ ▲ ▮ ▮ ▮ ▮ ▮ ▮ ▮ ▮ ▮ ▮ ▮ ▮ ▮ ▮ ▮ ";
1660  PRINT USING "$ # # # # # # # # # # # . # # ";CS
1670  DN$=""‡FOR I=0 TO 6‡PRINT "■ ■ ■ ■ ■ ■ ■ ■ ■ ■ ■ ■
      ■ ■ ■ ■ ■ ■ ■ ";DN$;RC$;
1680  PRINT  USING"# # # # # # # ";GD(I,1)‡DN$=DN$+"■ "
      ‡NEXT‡DN$=DN$+"■ ■ ■ ■ ■ ■ ■ "
1690  PRINT "■ ■ ■ ■ ■ ■ ■ ■ ■ ■ ■ ■ ■ ■ ■ ";DN$;RC$;‡
      PRINT USING"# # # # . # ";GD(7,1)‡
1700  PRINT "■ ■ ■ ■ ■ ■ ■ ■ ■ ■ ■ ■ ■ ■ ■ ■ ■ ■ ";DN$;RC$;
      ‡PRINT USING"# # # # # ";DM‡RETURN
```

Ambushed By Pirates!

```
1710  PRINT "■ "‡COLOR1,8‡COLOR0,2,4‡DR=0‡PS=480‡SK=0‡OS
      =0
1720  SN=0‡BT=500‡FOR I=1 TO INT(SS/100)‡SN=SN+INT(RND(0)
      *2)‡BT=BT+500+INT(RND(0)*600)‡NEXT
```

```
1730  PF(0,0)=SS+INT(RND(0)*SS/100+2)*100:IF SN>9THEN PF(
      0,0)=PF(0,0)+(SN-9)*100:SN=9
1740  PF(0,1)=INT(RND(0)*SS/100+2)+INT(RND(0)*L/2)
1750  FOR J=1 TO 9:PF(J,0)=INT(RND(0)*SS/10+SS/10):PF(J,1
      )=INT(RND(0)*SS/500+1)
1760  IF J>SNTHEN PF(J,0)=0
1770  NEXT
1780  FOR J=0 TO 9:PF(J,3)=30+INT(RND(0)*9):PF(J,2)=8+
      INT(RND(0)*6):NEXT:TG=0:OS=SN+1
1790  DR=DR-10*DF:IF DR<0THEN DR=0
1800  DM=DM+INT(DR):DR=DR-INT(DR)
1810  IF GD(7,1)<=0THEN PRINT "◘◘◘◘Y O U ▲ R A N ▲ O
      U T ▲ O F ▲ F U E L . . . ":DM=SS+1:FOR I=1 TO 1000
      :NEXT
1820  IF DM>=SSTHEN PRINT "◘■◘◘◘◘◘L O O T E D ▲ B
      Y ▲ P I R A T E S ! ":FOR I=0 TO 6:GD(I,1)=0:NEXT:C
      S=0:GOTO 2860
1830  PRINT N$:PRINT "◘▲ ' E ' ▲ E V A D E ▲ ' C ' ▲ C L
       O S E ▲ ' 0 ' . . ' 9 ' ▲ T A R G E T ":PRINT "▲ '
       M ' ▲ N U K E ▲ ▲ ' L ' ▲ L A S E R "
```

Get Player's Combat Instructions
Draw Combat Display and Resolve Combat

```
1840  GOSUB 760:GOSUB 2050
1850  IF SN=-1THEN 1930
1860  PRINT CV$;RC$;CD$;"◘◘▲ ▲ T A R G E T ▲ ▲ ▲ ▲ ▲ ▲
      ▲ ";:PRINT USING"# # ";TG;:GETA$:IF A$=""THEN 1860
1870  IF A$="L "ANDLP>0ANDPF(TG,0)>0THEN GOSUB 1970:
      GOTO 1790
1880  IF A$="M "ANDMS>0ANDPF(TG,0)>0THEN GOSUB 2000:
      GOTO 1790
1890  IF A$="E "ANDGD(7,1)>0THEN GOSUB 2040:GOTO 1790
1900  IF A$="C "THEN IF RND(0)<.7THEN EV=-3:GOTO 1790
1910  IF ASC(A$)>47ANDASC(A$)<58THEN TG=ASC(A$)-48:
      GOTO 1860
1920  GOTO 1860
1930  COLOR0,2:PRINT "◘ ":IF OS<>SKTHEN RETURN
1940  PRINT "◘◘◘■Y O U ▲ D E F E A T E D ▲ T H E ▲ P
      I R A T E ▲ F L E E T "
1950  CS=CS+BT:PRINT "◘A N D ▲ C O L L E C T E D ▲ ";:
      PRINT USING"# # # # # # # ";BT;:PRINT "▲ I N ▲ B
      O O T Y ! "
1960  FOR I=1 TO 2000:NEXT:PRINT "◘ ":RETURN
1970  SOUND 3,1020,8:SOUND 1,970,8:PF(TG,0)=PF(TG,0)-(150
      *LP)/PF(TG,3)
1980  IF PF(TG,0)<=0THEN SOUND 3,900,20:SN=SN-1:SK=SK+1
1990  RETURN
```

```
2000  SOUND 3,600,20:MS=MS-1:IF RND(0)*100<PF(TG,3)
      THEN RETURN
2010  SOUND 3,800,30:PF(TG,0)=PF(TG,0)-INT(RND(0)*50)-
      INT(RND(0)*50)
2020  IF PF(TG,0)<=0THEN SOUND 3,950,20:SN=SN-1:SK=SK+1
2030  RETURN
2040  GD(7,1)=GD(7,1)-.1:EV=INT(RND(0)*3+1):RETURN
2050  POKE 3072+PS,42:POKE 2048+PS,127
2060  FOR J=9 TO 0 STEP -1:IF PF(J,0)<=0THEN 2180
2070  MV=INT(RND(0)*3):IF PF(J,3)+EV-MV>=1THEN PF(J,3)=PF
      (J,3)+EV-MV
2080  IF PF(J,3)>39THEN PF(J,0)=0:SN=SN-1:GOTO 2180
2090  IF INT(PS/40)>PF(J,2)ANDRND(0)<.3THEN PF(J,2)=PF(J,
      2)+1
2100  IF INT(PS/40)<PF(J,2)ANDRND(0)<.3THEN PF(J,2)=PF(J,
      2)-1
2110  IF J=0THEN POKE 3072+PF(0,2)*40+PF(0,3),65:POKE 204
      8+PF(0,2)*40+PF(0,3),127:GOTO 2140
2120  POKE 3072+PF(J,2)*40+PF(J,3)-40,J+48:POKE 2048+PF(J
      ,2)*40+PF(J,3)-40,113
2130  POKE 3072+PF(J,2)*40+PF(J,3),87:POKE 2048+PF(J,2)
      *40+PF(J,3),127
2140  IF RND(0)<PF(J,3)/40THEN 2180
2150  SOUND 3,1020-10*J,5:DX=(PF(J,1)*400)/(PF(J,3)↑2)
2160  DR=DR+DX:IF RND(0)<DX/(SS-DM+DX)ANDDF>0THEN
      SOUND 3,1020,10:SOUND 3,990,15:DF=DF-1
2170  IF RND(0)<DX/(SS-DM+DX)ANDLP>0THEN SOUND 3,1000,10:
      SOUND 3,900,10:LP=LP-1
2180  NEXTJ
2190  EV=0:RETURN
2200  TP(0)=20/SQR(P(L,5))
2210  TP(1)=2000/(5*P(L,4)+P(L,5)/5)
2220  TP(2)=40000/(10*P(L,4)+P(L,3))
2230  TP(3)=(12000+INT(RND(0)*2000))/SQR(10*P(L,4))
2240  TP(4)=100000/SQR(4*P(L,4))
2250  TP(5)=100000/SQR(P(L,5)/2)
```

Determine Trade Value of Goods

```
2260  TP(6)=15000*P(L,3)/(5*P(L,4))
2270  TP(7)=100/SQR(2*P(L,4))
2280  TP(8)=500-P(L,4)*22
2290  FOR I=0 TO 7:IF RND(0)<.4THEN TP(I)=TP(I)-RND(0)*(T
      P(I)/(7+L/2)):GOTO 2310
2300  TP(I)=TP(I)+RND(0)*TP(I)/(10+2*L)
2310  NEXT:IX=INT(RND(0)*7):IF INT(RND(0)*10)<>LORRND(0)
      <50/(SD*10)THEN IX=-1:RETURN
2320  NS=(RND(0)*P(L,3)+8)/4:G$="S H O R T A G E ":IF
      RND(0)<.5THEN G$="G L U T ":NS=4/NS
```

```
2330 PRINT "▙ ▣ ▣ ▣ ▙ T H E R E ▲ H A S ▲ B E E N ▲ A ▲
     ";G$;"▲ O F ▲ ";RIGHT$(T$(IX),8);". "
2340 PRINT "P R I C E S ▲ A R E ▲ ▮ ";:PRINT USING"# # .
     # # ";NS;:PRINT "▬ ▲ T I M E S ▲ N O R M A L ! ! !
     "
2350 FOR I=1 TO 2500:NEXT:TP(IX)=TP(IX)*NS:RETURN
2360 DN$=""
2370 PRINT "▙ ":FOR I=0 TO 6:PRINT "▚ ▣ ▣ ▣ ▣ ▮ ▮ ▮ ▮ ▮
     ▮ ▮ ▮ ▮ ▮ ▮ ";DN$;:PRINT  USING"# # # # # # # # ";G
     D(I,0)
2380 PRINT "▚ ▣ ▣ ▣ ▣ ▮ ▮ ▮ ▮ ▮ ▮ ▮ ▮ ▮ ▮ ▮ ";RC$;DN$;:
     PRINT  USING"# # # # # # # # ";GD(I,1)
2390 DN$=DN$+"▣ ":NEXT:RETURN
2400 PRINT CY$;NL$
2410 PRINT CY$;"▞ ▲ ▲ ▲ B O R R O W I N G ▲ ";
2420 INPUT N:IF INT(N)>BTHEN N=B
2430 CS=CS+INT(N):CR=CR-INT(N):B=B-INT(N):GOSUB 2460
2440 PRINT CY$;NL$
2450 RETURN
2460 PRINT CY$;"▜ ▣ ▣ ▲ ▲ ▲ ▲ C A S H ▲ ▲ ▲ $ ▲ ";:
     PRINT  USING"# # # # # # # # # # # # # # . # # ";CS
2470 PRINT CY$;"▜ ▣ ▣ ▣ ▲ ▲ ▲ ▲ C R E D I T ▲ $ ▲ ";:
     PRINT  USING"# # # # # # # # # # # # # # . # # ";CR
     :RETURN
2480 PRINT CY$;NL$
2490 PRINT CY$;"▞ ▲ ▲ ▲ D E P O S I T I N G ▲ ";
2500 INPUT N:IF INT(N)>CSTHEN N=CS
2510 CS=CS-INT(N):CR=CR+INT(N):B=B+INT(N):GOSUB 2460
2520 PRINT CY$;NL$
2530 RETURN
2540 IF RND(0)>P(L,4)/40THEN RETURN
2550 IF RND(0)>.2THEN 2620
2560 CT=P(L,4)*100+1000*RND(0)+RND(0)*(CS/1000)+CS/1000
2570 IF CT>CSTHEN RETURN
2580 PRINT "▙ ▣ ▣ ▣ ▛ Y O U ▲ H A V E ▲ B E E N ▲ O F F
     E R E D ▲ A ▲ B I G G E R ▲ S P A C E - "
2590 PRINT "▣ S H I P ▲ F R O M ▲ A ▲ C O M P A N Y ▲ O
     N ▲ ";PL$(L)
```

Special Offers When Arriving at a New Planet

```
2600 PRINT "▣ I T ▲ C O S T S ▲ ";:PRINT USING"# # # # #
     # # # ";CT;:PRINT "▲ C R . ";
2610 PRINT "▲ W I T H ▲ A ▲ T R A D E - I N . ":GOSUB 28
     20:SS=SS+100:RETURN
2620 IF RND(0)>.25THEN 2680
2630 CT=160*(25-P(L,4))+RND(0)*(CS/1000)+CS/1000
2640 IF CT>CSTHEN RETURN
```

```
2650 PRINT "{CLR}{DOWN}{DOWN}{DOWN}{RVS}THERE IS A NEW LASER POD FOR SALE HERE."
2660 PRINT "{DOWN}IT COSTS A MERE ";:PRINT USING"########";CT;:PRINT " CR."
2670 GOSUB 2820:LP=LP+1:RETURN
2680 IF RND(0)>.15THEN 2740
2690 CT=200*(25-P(L,4))+RND(0)*(CS/800)+CS/800
2700 IF CT>CSTHEN RETURN
2710 PRINT "{CLR}{DOWN}{DOWN}{DOWN}{RVS}THERE IS A DEFLECTOR SHIELD AVAILABLE"
2720 PRINT "{DOWN}COSTING JUST ";:PRINT USING"########";CT;:PRINT " CR."
2730 GOSUB 2820:DF=DF+1:RETURN
2740 CT=70*(25-P(L,4))+RND(0)*(CS/1000)+CS/1000:N=INT(RND(0)*P(L,4)/2+P(L,4)/3+1)
2750 IF CT*N>CSTHEN N=INT(CS/CT)
2760 IF N=0THEN RETURN
2770 PRINT "{CLR}{DOWN}{DOWN}{DOWN}";N;"{RVS} NUCLEAR MISSILES ARE OFFERED."
2780 PRINT "{DOWN}TOTAL COST IS ";:PRINT USING"########";CT*N;:PRINT " CR."
2790 INPUT "{DOWN}HOW MANY DO YOU WISH TO BUY";NM:IF NM<0THEN NM=0
2800 IF NM>NTHEN NM=N
2810 MS=MS+NM:CS=CS-NM*CT:RETURN
2820 PRINT "{DOWN}ARE YOU WILLING TO MAKE THE PURCHASE ?"
2830 GETA$:IF A$<>"Y"ANDA$<>"N"THEN 2830
2840 IF A$="Y"THEN CS=CS-CT
2850 PRINT "{CLR}":RETURN
2860 PRINT "{RVS}{DOWN}{DOWN}         CASH POSESSED ";CS:PRINT "{DOWN}         BANK BALANCE ";CR;
2870 PRINT "{HOME}{DOWN}{DOWN}         GOODS POSESSED{DOWN}"
2880 FOR I=0 TO 6:PRINT "{RIGHT}         ";T$(I);":{LEFT}";GD(I,0)+GD(I,1):NEXT
```

ChexSum Tables

Line		Sum
1450	=	3658
1460	=	2807
1470	=	3822
1480	=	1180
1490	=	1643
1500	=	1076
1510	=	916
1520	=	2438
1530	=	2484
1540	=	3302
1550	=	5255
1560	=	2248
1570	=	4274
1580	=	4000
1590	=	4136
1600	=	2517
1610	=	5255
1620	=	1277
1630	=	4538
1640	=	1272
1650	=	4444
1660	=	1404
1670	=	2863
1680	=	4046
1690	=	2764
1700	=	2685
1710	=	3461
1720	=	6817
1730	=	6856
1740	=	3505
1750	=	5764
1760	=	1410
1770	=	131
1780	=	6138
1790	=	2300
1800	=	2334
1810	=	5485
1820	=	6726
1830	=	5470
1840	=	739
1850	=	1112
1860	=	4851
1870	=	3416
1880	=	3414
1890	=	2665
1900	=	3018
1910	=	3736
1920	=	589
1930	=	2110
1940	=	3022
1950	=	4983
1960	=	1711
1970	=	4502
1980	=	3710
1990	=	143
2000	=	3560
2010	=	4207
2020	=	3715
2030	=	143
2040	=	3074
2050	=	1926
2060	=	2550
2070	=	5346
2080	=	3278
2090	=	3964
2100	=	3965
2110	=	6128
2120	=	5555
2130	=	4562
2140	=	1767
2150	=	3597
2160	=	6243
2170	=	5188
2180	=	205
2190	=	591
2200	=	1433
2210	=	2520
2220	=	2398
2230	=	3319
2240	=	1953
2250	=	1956
2260	=	2318
2270	=	1786
2280	=	1504
2290	=	5425
2300	=	2910
2310	=	5699
2320	=	6025
2330	=	3796
2340	=	4387
2350	=	2804
2360	=	445
2370	=	3773
2380	=	2783
2390	=	1247
2400	=	611
2410	=	1671
2420	=	1541
2430	=	3644
2440	=	611
2450	=	143
2460	=	3028
2470	=	3369
2480	=	611
2490	=	1762
2500	=	1717
2510	=	3644
2520	=	611
2530	=	143
2540	=	1647
2550	=	1173
2560	=	4246
2570	=	941
2580	=	3700
2590	=	2570
2600	=	3003
2610	=	3151
2620	=	1234
2630	=	3663
2640	=	941
2650	=	3790
2660	=	3507
2670	=	1382
2680	=	1234
2690	=	3558
2700	=	941
2710	=	3761
2720	=	3373
2730	=	1352
2740	=	7065
2750	=	2154
2760	=	757
2770	=	3406
2780	=	3654
2790	=	3988
2800	=	1144
2810	=	2362
2820	=	3452
2830	=	2405
2840	=	1640
2850	=	577
2860	=	4582
2870	=	2001
2880	=	3675
TOTAL	=	419602

16 Load Merge if you have reset or switched off your computer — see step 3.
17 From your tape or disk, load the second half of Star Trader: LOAD "STAR TRAD SEC" or LOAD "STAR TRAD SEC",8.
18 Perform steps 5 to 13 to run ChexSum on the second half of Star Trader.
19 Save the second half as "STAR TRAD OK2".
20 Load Merge if necessary — see step 3.
21 Load the first half by entering LOAD "STAR TRAD OK1" for tape or LOAD "STAR TRAD OK1",8 for disk.
22 Enter SYS16331.
23 Load the second half by entering LOAD "STAR TRAD OK2" for tape or LOAD "STAR TRAD OK2",8 for disk.
24 Enter SYS16355 to complete the merge.
25 The program will now run!

Appendix A
Using Joysticks

All the games in the book are designed to be played from the keyboard, usually using the following scheme:

KEY	ACTION
I	Left
P	Right
Q	Up
Z	Down
Space	Fire

The Commodore 16 has an inbuilt function JOY(N) which is used to read joystick input. The variable N is set to 1 to read joystick Ø and to 2 to read joystick 1. When the fire button is not depressed, the JOY(N) function returns values from Ø to 8 to indicate the deflection of the joystick; when the joystick is deflected and the fire button is depressed, values from 128 to 136 are returned (see diagram below and overleaf).

JOYSTICK VALUES, NOT FIRING

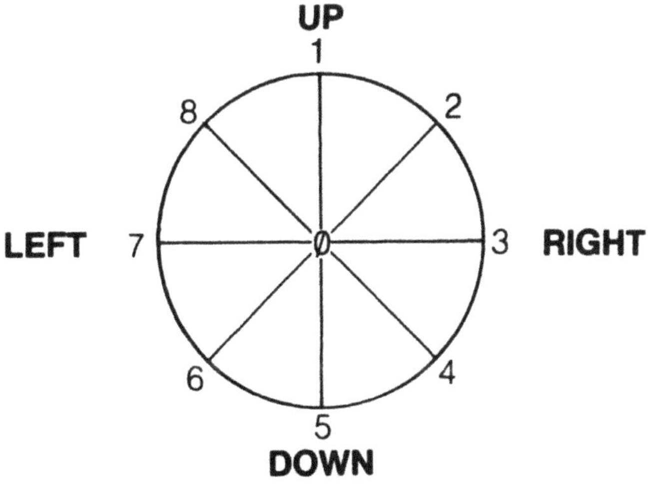

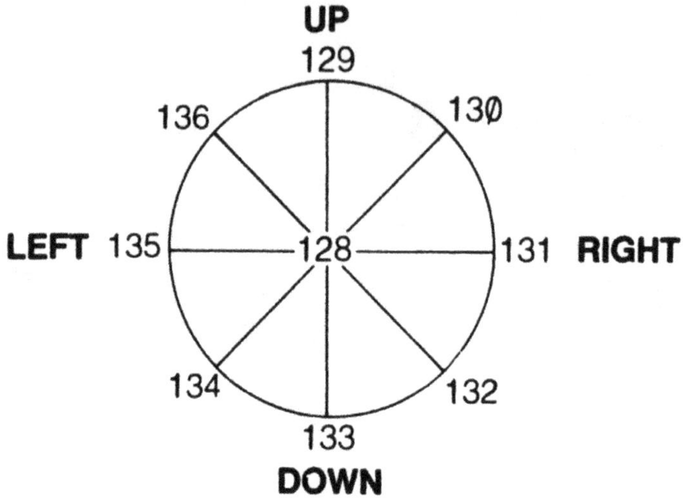

Thus, the statement

```
10 IF JOY(2) = 130 THEN (action)
```

would cause the appropriate action to take place when the joystick was moved to half-past two and the firing button depressed. Armed with this information, you should be able to alter the GET A$ statements in the programs so that they will operate with the joysticks.

Appendix B
Software Sprite Utility

WHAT IT IS AND HOW IT WORKS

This utility allows the user to move a block of characters in a 3 × 3 square around the screen. To use this program simply POKE the X and Y co-ordinates of the block into locations 16357, 16358 and then do a SYS16Ø5Ø. To move the block round the screen just change the X and Y co-ordinates and repeatedly call the SYS routine.

For this program to work correctly the screen must not scroll. Type in the program and save it to disk or tape, then run ChexSum on it.

When executed it will place a machine language program at 16Ø3Ø decimal and set the top of memory pointer to this location to prevent BASIC from overwriting it. Once executed, the program will sit there until you overwrite it, reset the top of BASIC pointers or switch off the computer. You can either tack it onto the ends of your programs and use it as a subroutine or load it in, run it and load in another program which calls it.

Sprite Utility

```
10      POKE 55,158:POKE 56,62:CLR
20      FOR I=16050 TO 16050+321:READA:POKE I,A:C=C+A:
        NEXT
30      IF C<>44960THEN  PRINT "C H E C K ▲ S U M ▲ E R R O
         R ▲ I N ▲ P R O G R A M ";C:STOP
40      STOP
50      DATA165,240,141,241,63,165,241,141,242,63
60      DATA173,232,63,201,0,208,7,173,231,63
70      DATA201,0,240,3,32,160,63,32,23,63
80      DATA32,92,63,173,230,63,141,232,63,173
90      DATA229,63,141,231,63,173,242,63,133,241
100     DATA173,241,63,133,240,96,169,0,133,240
```

```
110   DATA169,12,133,241,172,234,63,152,240,16
120   DATA24,165,240,105,40,133,240,169,0,101
130   DATA241,133,241,136,208,240,165,240,24,109
140   DATA233,63,133,240,169,0,101,241,133,241
150   DATA96,173,230,63,141,234,63,173,229,63
160   DATA141,233,63,32,234,62,160,0,140,235
170   DATA63,140,236,63,162,3,142,237,63,162
180   DATA3,142,238,63,174,235,63,172,236,63
190   DATA177,240,157,162,62,238,235,63,238,236
200   DATA63,206,238,63,208,234,173,236,63,105
210   DATA37,141,236,63,206,237,63,208,216,96
220   DATA173,229,63,141,233,63,173,230,63,141
230   DATA234,63,32,234,62,160,0,140,236,63
240   DATA169,127,141,240,63,162,3,142,237,63
250   DATA162,3,142,238,63,172,236,63,173,240
260   DATA63,145,240,238,236,63,238,240,63,206
270   DATA238,63,208,237,173,236,63,105,37,141
280   DATA236,63,206,237,63,208,219,96,173,232
290   DATA63,141,234,63,173,231,63,141,233,63
300   DATA32,234,62,160,0,140,235,63,140,236
310   DATA63,162,3,142,237,63,162,3,142,238
320   DATA63,174,235,63,189,162,62,172,236,63
330   DATA145,240,238,235,63,238,236,63,206,238
340   DATA63,208,234,173,236,63,105,37,141,236
350   DATA63,206,237,63,208,216,96,0,0,0
360   DATA0,0,0,0,0,0,0,0,0,0
370   DATA 0,130
```

ChexSum Tables

10	=	1207	130	=	2245	250	=	2090
20	=	3160	140	=	2128	260	=	2144
30	=	3991	150	=	2088	270	=	2140
40	=	145	160	=	2016	280	=	2157
50	=	2175	170	=	2010	290	=	2075
60	=	1992	180	=	2032	300	=	2014
70	=	1824	190	=	2211	310	=	1978
80	=	2025	200	=	2127	320	=	2093
90	=	2151	210	=	2079	330	=	2205
100	=	2096	220	=	2144	340	=	2157
110	=	2144	230	=	1959	350	=	1817
120	=	2086	240	=	2100	360	=	1120
						370	=	390
						TOTAL	=	74515

SPRITE DEMONSTRATOR

Type in the sprite utility and run it to place the utility in upper memory, then enter NEW to clear the BASIC loader. Now type in the following demonstration program:

```
10 PRINT CHR$(147);
20 FOR I=1 TO 20
30 POKE 16357, I   :REM SET X CO-ORDINATE
40 POKE 16358, I   :REM SET Y CO-ORDINATE
50 SYS 16050       :REM MOVE SPRITE
60 NEXT
70 GET KEY A$ : GOTO 20
```

When you run the program, the screen will clear and a block of characters will go from the top of the screen to the bottom. Hitting any key will move the block again. The characters in the block are from 127 ASCII to 135.

SHAPE DEMONSTRATION

It is possible to create differently shaped 'sprites' by redefining the characters in the 3 × 3 block. Enter this program:

```
 10 POKE 55,255: POKE 56, 47 :REM SET TOP OF
 15 B=12                     :REM MEMORY TO 12287
 20 POKE 65298, 192          :REM POINT AT NEW
 30 POKE 65299, 192+4*B      :REM CHARACTER DEFINITION
 40 P=1024*B
 50 SP=P+32*8                :REM DEFINE SPACE
 60 FOR I=SP TO SP+7:POKE I, 0 : NEXT
 70 IN=P+(127*8) :REM Define charsacters 127 - 135
 80 FOR I=IN TO IN+71=POKE I, 255 : NEXT
 90 POKE 16357, 5
100 POKE 16358, 5
110 SYS 16050
```

A solid 3 × 3 block will appear at co-ordinates 5, 5 on the screen.

In the program, lines 20 to 40 tell the computer to get its character set from memory starting at 12288. Each character is stored as eight bytes of memory and each bit in the byte represents one pixel (or dot) of the character. The first byte of the character represents the top pair of eight dots, while the second byte represents the next row of dots down and so on.

CHARACTER SHAPE VALUES

Binary	Hex	Decimal
Ø Ø 1 1 1 1 Ø Ø	3C	6Ø
Ø 1 Ø Ø Ø Ø 1 Ø	42	66
1 Ø 1 Ø Ø 1 Ø 1	A5	165
1 Ø 1 Ø Ø 1 Ø 1	A5	165
1 Ø Ø Ø Ø Ø Ø 1	81	129
1 Ø 1 1 1 1 Ø 1	BD	189
1 Ø Ø Ø Ø Ø Ø 1	81	129
Ø 1 1 1 1 1 1 Ø	7E	126

To restore the normal character set, hold down the RUN/STOP key, then press reset. This will land you in the monitor! To escape, just press the X and then the RETURN key.

To find out the order of characters in memory, check the ASCII table in your reference manual. Use the formular SP=P+(A*8) to calculate the position of a character in memory, where A is the ASCII value of the character, and P is the start of character memory.

CAUTIONS

Please note these important facts:

1. The range of movement of the sprite is Ø to 37 for the X axis and Ø to 22 for the Y axis. The routine does no range testing, so it is up to you to make sure that the X and Y co-ordinates are in range.
2. The screen must not scroll.
3. Do not let your program place a sprite in location (Ø, Ø), which is reserved.

Appendix C
Merging Programs

The Merge program can be used to join other programs besides ChexSum and games programs, overcoming the lack of a MERGE command in Commodore BASIC. An important limitation to remember is that the smallest line number in the second program must be greater than the largest in the first program.

1. Load the Merge program by entering
   LOAD "MERGE" for tape or
   LOAD "MERGE", 8 for disk.
2. Enter RUN to cause Merge to place a machine language routine in high memory and to protect it by changing the top-of-memory pointer for BASIC.
3. Load the first program by entering
   LOAD "first program" for tape or
   LOAD "first program", 8 for disk.
4. Enter SYS16331.
5. Load the second program by entering
   LOAD "second program" for tape or
   LOAD "second program", 8 for disk.
6. Enter SYS16355 to complete the merge.

Appendix D
Printout Symbols

To aid clarity, the graphic symbols of the Commodore 16 computer have been represented in this book by special symbols designed to look like the pictographs which appear on the Commodore 16 keyboard.

COLOUR AND CONTROL CHARACTERS *

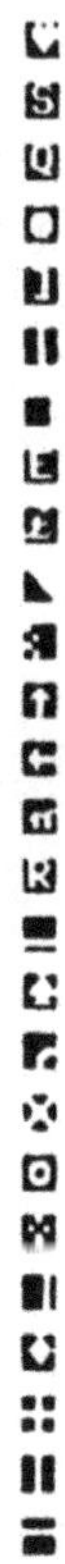

Symbol in book	Key
	CLR
	HOME
	CURSOR DOWN
	CURSOR UP
	CURSOR RIGHT
	CURSOR LEFT
	CTRL 1
	CTRL 2
	CTRL 3
	CTRL 4
	CTRL 5
	CTRL 6
	CTRL 7
	CTRL 8
	CTRL 9
	CTRL 0
	C= 1
	C= 2
	C= 3
	C= 4
	C= 5
	C= 6
	C= 7
	C= 8
	CTRL .
	CTRL .

* These characters are designed to emulate the characters which appear on the screen.

KEYBOARD CHARACTERS *

Symbol in book	Key	Symbol in book	Key
	C= E		C= ↑
	C= W		C= R
	C= D		C= Q
	C= C		C= F
	C= B		C= V
	C= T		C= +
	C= U		C= Y
	C= O		C= I
	C= @		C= P
	C= G		C= -
	C= J		C= H
	C= L		C= K
	C= M		C= N
	C= S		C= £
	C= A		C= X
	C= *		C= Z
	SHIFT L		SHIFT @
	SHIFT O		SHIFT P
	SHIFT I		SHIFT U
	SHIFT K		SHIFT J
o	SHIFT W	●	SHIFT Q
+	SHIFT +	×	SHIFT V
\	SHIFT M	/	SHIFT N
♦	SHIFT Z	♥	SHIFT S
♣	SHIFT X	♠	SHIFT A
	SHIFT E		SHIFT D
	SHIFT *		SHIFT C
	SHIFT F		SHIFT R
	SHIFT T		SHIFT G
	SHIFT B		SHIFT -
	SHIFT H		SHIFT Y
	SHIFT £	←	SHIFT =
↑	SHIFT ZERO		

* These characters are designed to emulate the pictographs which appear on the front of the keys. The C= symbol is the special shift key located to the left of the left hand shift key.

Unfortunately different keyboard characters can produce identical symbols on the screen and printout. If a program doesn't work, these symbols may have been interchanged in a string:

	CTRL ,	CURSOR LEFT
	SHIFT *	SHIFT C
	SHIFT B	SHIFT -

You may also enjoy...

CPSIA information can be obtained
at www.ICGtesting.com
Printed in the USA
BVHW080823160721
612048BV00001B/68

9 781789 825879